Migration and Mobility in Europe

Trends, Patterns and Control

Edited by

Heinz Fassmann

Professor of Applied Geography, Regional Research and Spatial Planning, University of Vienna, Austria

Max Haller

Professor of Sociology, University of Graz, Austria

David Lane

Fellow of Emmanuel College, Cambridge, UK

Edward Elgar
Cheltenham, UK • Northampton, MA, USA

Published by
Edward Elgar Publishing Limited
The Lypiatts
15 Lansdown Road
Cheltenham
Glos GL50 2JA
UK

Edward Elgar Publishing, Inc.
William Pratt House
9 Dewey Court
Northampton
Massachusetts 01060
USA

A catalogue record for this book
is available from the British Library

Library of Congress Control Number: 2009936228

ISBN 978 1 84844 371 6

Printed and bound by MPG Books Group, UK

Contents

Migration and mobility in Europe

Contributors

Canan Balkır, Professor at the Institute of Social Studies, Dokuz Eylul University, Turkey.

Bente Puntervold Bø, Professor, Oslo University College, Norway.

Michael Braun, Project Manager at ZUMA and Professor at the University of Mannheim, Germany.

Dennis Broeders, PhD Student at the University of Rotterdam, Researcher in the Dutch Scientific Council for Government Policy (WRR), Netherlands.

Raquel Martinez Buján, Assistant Professor, Faculty of Sociology, University of La Coruña, Spain.

David Cairns, Postdoctoral Researcher at Centre for Research and Studies in Sociology (CIES-ISCTE) Lisbon, Portugal.

Peter Ester, Director of OSA (Institute for Labour Studies), Professor of Sociology at Tilburg University, the Netherlands.

Heinz Fassmann, Professor of Applied Geography, Regional Research and Spatial Planning, University of Vienna, and Head of the Commission of Migration and Integration Research, Austrian Academy of Sciences, Austria.

Fjalar Finnäs, Professor of Demographics at the Åbo Akademi University, Finland.

Didier Fouarge, Professor at the Research Centre for Education and the Labour Market (ROA) of the Maastricht University, the Netherlands.

Max Haller, Professor of Sociology, Karl-Franzens-University in Graz, Austria.

James Hampshire, Lecturer in Politics at the Sussex Centre for Migration Research, University of Sussex, UK.

Franz Heschl, Researcher, Chamber of Labour, Styria, Austria.

Berna Kırkulak, Assistant Professor, Dokuz Eylül University, Izmir, Turkey.

Olga Kutsenko, Professor, National T. Shevchenko University of Kyiv, Ukraine.

David Lane, Principal Investigator in Sociology and a Fellow of Emmanuel College, Cambridge, UK.

Guglielmo Meardi, Associate Professor of Industrial Relations, Warwick Business School, University of Warwick, UK.

Ettore Recchi, Professor, Universita degli studi di Firenze, Italy.

Robert Rowthorn, Emeritus Professor and Fellow of King's College, Cambridge, UK.

Jan Saarela, Adjunct Professor in Economics, Åbo Akademi University, Finland.

Kathryn Vincent, Research Assistant, University of Aberdeen, UK.

Claire Wallace, Professor of Sociology, University of Aberdeen, UK.

Preface

This book has grown out of an international conference on 'Migration in Europe: threat or Benefit', held in Vienna on 28–29 September 2007. It was the fifth conference of the Network 'Strategic Elites and EU Enlargement', sponsored by the British Council and organized by David Lane. The call for papers resulted in 80 proposals of which 22 were presented at the conference. The conference, locally organized by Max Haller, Professor of Sociology at the University of Graz, took place in the 'Theatersaal' of the Austrian Academy of Sciences in Vienna. In addition to the paper givers, it was also attended by many interested persons from Austria.

After the conference the organizers decided to publish a sample of the papers. They invited Heinz Fassmann, Professor of Geography at the University of Vienna and Head of the Commission for Migration and Integration Research in the Austrian Academy of Sciences to be one of the editors. After a critical reflection in the present volume, 13 papers have been included with one additional paper by James Hampshire.

We would like to thank all those who have contributed in financial terms to the conference: the British Academy, the Commission for Migration and Integration Research of the Austrian Academy of Science, the Austrian Chamber of Labour and the Austrian Economic Chamber. Furthermore, we would like to thank those who helped to finalize this volume: Angelika Horvath who standardized the references, Walter Lang who drew the figures and Carolyn Slaughter who improved the language of some papers. Finally we would like to thank Edward Elgar for accepting this volume.

Heinz Fassmann, Vienna

Max Haller, Graz

David Lane, Cambridge

1. Migration and mobility in Europe: an introduction

Heinz Fassmann and David Lane

This collection contains an overview of different aspects of mobility and migration in the development of the enlarged European Union. The chapters address the forms which these phenomena are taking and the social, political and economic problems involved. The book has an introductory chapter followed by sections on the costs and benefits of migration, patterns of migration and mobility, problems of migration, and state control and citizen rights.

1.1 OVERVIEW

Migration out of, to, and within Europe is nothing new. Politically and religiously motivated displacement, the migration of the highly qualified, the seasonal migration of farm labourers, and the migration of trades people and students, had already existed before the nineteenth century in various forms. What changed with the industrialization of the eighteenth and nineteenth centuries was the quantitative degree of intra-European and intercontinental migration, as well as the average distance of migration. Geographical mobility exploded in the nineteenth century and the amount of long distance migration reached previously unseen numbers leading to this phase being labelled as the 'century of the great drift'.

Europe is currently experiencing a new period of the great drift. The aggregation of national statistics (even with all their ambiguities and omissions) shows that in the EU27 the foreign born population constitutes about 40.5 million people, representing about 8.8 per cent of its total population. Less than half of them have adopted the citizenship of their respective country of destination. Around 22.9 million are still foreigners by citizenship. The highest absolute number of foreign citizens was reported by Germany, France, the United Kingdom, Italy, Spain, Belgium, Austria, Greece and the Netherlands. Living in those nine member states are 89 per cent of all of the foreign citizens in the whole EU27. When looking at the foreign born, a slight change in the rank list of the member states can be observed. The first five positions remain the same followed by the Netherlands, Austria, Belgium and Sweden. However, the highest proportions of foreigners in the total population of the country are found in the smaller countries of Europe like Andorra, San Marino, Liechtenstein and Switzerland where the foreigners represent one-fifth of the total population. In Luxembourg, which is part of the EU15, the proportion rises to a remarkable 34 per cent.

Many of the chapters in this collection demonstrate the constant demand for cheap labour in many economic sectors in most of the countries of the EU27. The demand itself is dependent on overall economic development. A growing economy entails a rising demand for labour if the factors 'productivity' and 'work time' are kept constant. External events may play a special role that leads towards an above-average increase in the demand for labour. Such developments may be large investments within short periods of time (such as world championships or Olympic games). They result in an especially strong demand in low wage sectors such as tourism, agriculture and building, as well as in industry and the service sector, which makes immigration an attractive option. Native employees leave low wage sectors if there are other job options in a growing economy and their jobs are subsequently taken by foreign workers.

The relative shortages in some branches are related to the dramatic demographic changes in Europe. Decreasing numbers of births lead – after a time delay – towards falling numbers of entrants into the labour market. The expansion of life expectancy accelerates the ageing process and is one the main drivers for a growing demand for labour in health, care and other personalized service sectors.

Finally, the ability of the EU and the member states to control immigration flows (i.e. entries and stays) is to some extent an illusion. The ability to control flows greatly varies between countries on account of a number of factors. In some countries it is considerable, in others very limited. This clearly affects the degree of consistency between policies and outcomes, which in turn may influence the public mood towards immigration. It also affects the relative weight of types of flows (regular or irregular, more or less asylum demand). However, migration persists despite the efforts to control or to stop it.

The countries of western Europe are undergoing a rapid and sustained change in their ethnical and cultural composition. The European Union is characterized by freedom of movement for capital, services and labour. Freedom of labour entails migration. The expansion of the EU to include eight former state socialist countries in 2004 and another two in 2007 opened up (at least in theory) the possibility of over 100 million east Europeans being able to move to the western parts of the Union. As noted by many of the contributors below, the possibility of immigrants from low-income countries gives rise to concerns in the old member states. If existing trends continue they will have a dramatic impact and may have serious implications for social cohesion and national identity. There is growing public anxiety in western Europe about what is happening and opposition to immigration is increasing. Some of this opposition is based on cultural or racial grounds and some on economic considerations. Those who support a liberal immigration policy either play down the scale of the transformation that is now occurring, or else praise it on the grounds that greater racial or cultural diversity is to the benefit of the indigenous populations of western Europe. They also claim that large-scale immigration will be of great economic benefit to the existing inhabitants of western Europe.

1.2   COST AND BENEFITS OF MIGRATION

The book begins with a discussion of the costs and benefits of migration, which is of crucial importance. Do European societies need more migration, what are the societal and economic effects and who can benefit from further migration? The answers to these questions are influenced by normative ideologies and are often answered very controversially.

In the first part of the book, Robert Rowthorn discusses the winners and losers of migration in the European context (Chapter 2). The potential winners and losers – in general, people who are affected by migration – can be divided into three groups: the migrants themselves, the existing inhabitants of the receiving country, and those who remain in the sending country. As a general rule, those who migrate normally benefit from their decision. The impact of migration on the other parties involved is not so clear-cut. Some types of migration are beneficial to the existing inhabitants of the receiving country and others are harmful, and the same is true for those who remain in the sending country. For the migrants themselves, the financial consequences of migration are often large. This is mostly not the case for the other parties involved, although there are certain exceptions.

After discussing the economic impact of migration Rowthorn presents an economic overview of the demographic situation and migration within an enlarged EU and he examines the impact of outward migration from Eastern Europe on the labour market, age structure and government finance within the receiving countries of western Europe. He argues that large-scale migration from eastern Europe to the west will have only a minor economic impact on the average citizen in the receiving countries. Some will benefit from the inflow of migrants while others will lose. He contends that the often cited argument that large-scale migration can halt or reverse the ageing process of society is false. Rowthorn shows how little difference immigration makes in terms of the dependency ratio compared with improvements in the operation of the labour market. If the present underemployment of the European population continues, the dependency ratio will rise strongly, irrespective of the rate of immigration. Finding jobs for the existing labour force is far more effective than immigration to reduce this ratio. The chapter concludes by considering the implications of further EU expansion embracing Turkey, the Ukraine and eventually North Africa.

The question of the costs and benefits of international migration for the receiving countries is always answered based on collective interest. The costs and benefits are seen by unions and representatives from employees in a different way to employers. Franz Heschl, in Chapter 3, shows this debate with the Austrian example. In the first parts of his chapter he tries to describe the objective facts and figures linked to international migration. He shows that labour migration to Austria in the context of the European integration process is closely associated with the distribution of income and wealth. The increase in immigration has led to increases in unemployment, and a shift of income from labour to capital. However, he also concedes that labour immigration had positive effects on employment rates and economic growth in certain time periods. The rise in productivity is not passed on to labour, as the growth in supply weakens its bargaining position.

In Chapter 3, Heschl thematizes the often cited demand for more skilled migration and he emphasizes that such demands are part of a myth building process. With constant repetition, the myth of a shortage of skilled workers is believed as reality by wide sections of the public. What Heschl shows is that there is always a shortage of workers who will work more efficiently for lower wages than the existing workforce. The decade of membership of the EU, he concludes, coincides with a slower rise in real wages than was previously the case.

The discussion of the costs and benefits of migration is picked up by Didier Fouarge and Peter Ester in a different way. They focus on the migration intentions of Europeans and investigate the main determinants of such intentions. The authors use the special module on mobility of the Eurobarometer Survey (EB 64.1) carried out in September 2005. Data were collected in all 25 EU member states. The survey is the most comprehensive recent Europe-wide survey on mobility intentions. Their findings indicate that most Europeans have no intentions to move to another country: only 5.4 per cent of the working-age population intends to move to another country within the next five years. Although intentional cross-border migration – percentage-wise – is not a widespread phenomenon in Europe, migration intentions in new member states (more specifically in the Baltics and Poland) are at a significantly higher level compared with the old member states. Furthermore, highly educated and single young Europeans – especially students – are the most mobile. Mobility intentions appear to be strongly linked to past migration: people who have migrated in the past are likely to migrate again in the future. Movers tend to stay movers. The reason for past mobility, however, plays an important role in future migration intentions. People who crossed borders for labour-market related reasons are likely to do so again in the future, and particularly, 'study migration' appears to be strongly significant. To the extent that this reflects a cohort effect, we could expect that Europe's investment towards the mobility of students is likely to result in larger migration streams in the future.

Perceived labour market opportunities – better employment opportunities and wage prospects – are decisive motives for migration. People holding positive views about migration – in the sense that it is good for individuals and their families – apparently perceive larger returns to migration and are therefore more likely to express an intention to migrate. However, the findings of Fouarge and Ester do not imply that all people with an intention to migrate will actually do so: existing social ties and sociocultural differences, as well as language, represent important costs to cross-border migration.

David Cairns, in Chapter 5, researches the opposite question: why are the migration intentions of the young Portuguese population so low? Despite the occasional media panic regarding a potential youth exodus from Portugal, demographic analysis reveals that recent overall net migration from Portugal is at a lower level than the European average. Likewise, Eurobarometer statistics indicate that a very small number of people in Portugal, perhaps as few as 0.02 per cent of the population, have intentions to be transnationally mobile in the future. Other recent research at a comparative European level, and incorporating a qualitative dimension, has also revealed that Portuguese youth are among the least likely to migrate in Europe. The reasons seem to be low household income to finance student mobility, and a complex web of family, peer and communal attachments which effectively negate migration intentions. The strength of these influences is enough to keep these young people sedentary despite negative assessments of both their countries and their own economic prospects.

1.3   PATTERNS OF MIGRATION AND MOBILITY

Europe experiences not only a new period of inflows but also changing forms of intra-European migration patterns. As the internal borders of the European Union are removed, migration patterns within the continent take a different shape. Complementing free movement policies, cross-country transportation has expanded in scope, speed and cost; the price of travel has fallen significantly. Europeans conceive of international mobility on a continental scale offering more flexibility and diverse purposes. Yet, considerable increases in living standards and welfare entitlements in the traditional sending countries of southern Europe have at the same time reduced incentives for migration. The traditional migrant strategy of labour-led resettlement is being supplemented, if not entirely replaced, by multifaceted life-plans and strategies of mobility. Perhaps the lifting of the Iron Curtain and the inclusion of eastern European countries into the EU have recently led to a revival of the traditional guest-worker migration, given the extreme wage differences between some new member states and western Europe. But it is also plausible that such movements will weaken progressively due to economic convergence between east and west and a decline of fertility in the sending countries.

While there is a widespread awareness that this is the overall picture of the changing migration landscape within the EU borders, we know surprisingly little about the objective and subjective profile of the emerging population of free-moving Europeans. Official statistics, indeed, have great difficulty in tracking down mobility flows within the EU – be it for the inherent difficulties of mapping immigrants of all sorts, for the inconsistencies of national statistical systems, or for citizens' reluctance to residence registration which is further boosted by the philosophy of free movement. Michael Braun and Ettore Recchi in Chapter 6 offer an overview on the 6.3 million EU non-nationals living in the EU15 in 2004 and they present the results of the 'European Internal Movers' Social Survey' (EIMSS) including 4919 interviews with nationals who migrated there between 1974 and 2003.

Braun and Recchi's chapter seeks to map out the objective and subjective differences within the rather loose category of intra-EU migrants in the five largest EU15 countries (Germany, the UK, France, Italy and Spain). By using multiple correspondence analysis, they draw a parsimonious portrait of western-European mobile citizens. This analysis leads them to single out two key dimensions that seem to extract two basic inputs and outputs of individual migration choices – namely, social status and integration. Migrants who originally came to study show the highest values on both dimensions. Those who came for love/family reasons are lower on the status dimension than those who came for work reasons, but both groups share an above average integration into the target country. The least well integrated are those who moved exclusively to improve their quality of life – such as retirement migrants.

An example of the new pattern of migration and mobility within Europe are Polish citizens in the UK, often referred to as the 'Polish plumber' phenomenon. The influx of Polish workers into the UK requires a revision of migration theories and presents important empirical puzzles. Both problems stem from the specificity of this migration wave, which does not correspond to classical models. The inadequacy of classic migration theories is demonstrated by the inaccuracy of forecasts from before 2004. The 'optimistic' forecasts foresaw an influx many times smaller than the actual one. But the 'pessimistic' forecasts were wrong when expecting a large movement induced by a need to receive social benefits.

The chapter 'A suspended status: the puzzle of Polish workers in the West Midlands' by Guglielmo Meardi shows how the influx of Polish workers is different from previous migration waves. It is, at least in intention, short term, and includes a high proportion of young women. In addition, these workers maintain strong contacts and networks with their home country (through frequent travel, new communication technologies, etc.), they often compare living conditions between different European countries, and show an unforeseen willingness to join local trade unions. They live in two different societies (in that of the target country and of the country of origin), they interact in a transnational space and they develop, to some extent, something like a hybrid identity. The issue is whether these people qualify for the definition of (classic) 'migrants', or of 'transnational migrants' or even of 'cosmopolitans'.

A further example of new patterns of mobility and migration are the citizens of western Europe in Turkey. For many decades, Turkey was an emigration country for guestworkers who were moving to Germany, Switzerland or Austria. However, Turkey has been a receiving country as more and more pensioners from Western Europe choose Turkey as a country of residence where they can spend their active years of retirement. International retirement migration (IRM) is a new form of international human mobility which entails the movement of people in their later lives to new places with different challenges and opportunities in pursuit of a better way of life. It can be considered as a combination of permanent and temporal/seasonal migration. It is more than long stay tourism in that there is a degree of permanence and long-term commitment.

The major immigration flows to Turkey have tended to consist of Muslim or Turkish expatriates. But Turkey has increasingly become a popular European retiree destination, particularly for British, German,

Nordic and Dutch citizens. There are several cities in Turkey where significant elderly-immigrant communities have established themselves. Canan Balkır and Berna Kırkulak, in Chapter 8, present the results of their survey of retired migrants in one of the main destinations, namely Antalya and its districts. The research project involves intensive fieldwork including questionnaire-based surveys and in-depth interviews both conducted with the retired migrants and with the local community. The key questions asked included the motivations of retired migrants for coming to Antalya, the income and expenditure patterns, the problems encountered, housing patterns, their impact on the social and economic structure of the host community as well as the sensitivity of the local community concerning the international retirement migration.

The enlargement of the European Union to the east in 2004/2007 gave the EU some new neighbours. Countries that were formerly part of the Soviet Union (Belarus, Moldova, Ukraine, Armenia and Georgia) were now found on the 'eastern frontiers'. Part of the accession negotiations involved strengthening the borders with those countries, yet migration from them has increased. Based on an ethnosurvey funded by the International Association for Cooperation with Scientists from the former Soviet Union (INTAS), Claire Wallace and Kathryn Vincent explore the migration of people between 2005 and 2007, into the EU and elsewhere using a survey of their homelands combining quantitative and qualitative methods. The chapter challenges conventional notions of migration based upon a one-way passage to a new land. It argues that recent migrations (at least post-1989) are characterized rather by temporary circulation of people and hence would not be classically called 'migration'. They include both temporary employment and various kinds of studentship. The project focuses upon people who had already migrated and returned by 2004. It was found that the main destination country for migrants was Russia, reflecting the more welcoming migration policies there to fulfil labour needs. For the European Union, migrants went to northern European countries mainly by using schemes and agencies, while they went to the south and the new member states using more informal means.

Immigration to the EU is based in most cases on structural features in the receiving societies. One of the demand factors is derived from the ageing process. Immigrants are, in many European countries, the main care providers for the elderly. Raquel Martínez Buján, in Chapter 10, uses Spain as a unit to explore how care for the elderly becomes a new employment area for immigrants. The inclusion of women into the labour market, the peculiarities of the hidden economy and the lack of institutional provision where geriatric care is concerned, help to explain this process.

1.4   PROBLEMS OF MIGRANT INTEGRATION

The integration of different immigration groups in a given country are studied by some of our contributors. Research where this relation is considered is very rare: that is, one specific immigration group living within different country specific contexts. In a comparative study, Olga Kutsenko researches Turkish minorities or Turkish migrants living in five different national contexts: Bulgaria (Turkish minority), Germany (Turkish-speaking minority in Berlin), Moldova (Gagauz minority), Russia (Tatars in Tatarstan) and Ukraine (Crimean Tatars in the Crimea). Kutsenko analyses the interethnic integration between an ethnic community and a dominant society within certain national borders and under different economic, cultural and political conditions. Findings include mechanisms of societal ethnic-based integration as well as the types of integration strategies used by different ethnic communities under varying social conditions. The study of the roots of interethnic conflicts and their impact on societal integration, national security and stability makes evident that such processes are under the strong influence of economic and political interests.

Return migration is a highly important topic as the European Commission tries to implement new forms of circular migration. However, a comprehensive picture of return migrants' employment situation is still lacking. The fundamental reason is that, in most countries, there are no population registers allowing researchers to distinguish people who have lived abroad. Jan Saarela and Fjalar Finnäs attempt to fill this gap in our knowledge by using longitudinal population register data from Finland, and they provide some interesting results. Finnish return migrants, both men and women, have odds of employment that are only about half those of non-migrants, even when factors such as age, education, mother tongue and place of residence are accounted for. Within the group of higher educated people, return migrants are in a worse employment position than observably similar non-migrants. Employment opportunities tend to deteriorate with migration duration and improve with time subsequent to return migration. This suggests that there could be an effect of lost contact with the home country labour market while abroad, which may override any premium that accrues through human capital of foreign work experience or other practices gained. Also, return migrants with short stays abroad and long periods at home are in a poor relative position. The findings of Saarela and Finnäs illustrate that the return migrants are highly selected with regard to some latent personal characteristics with severe negative effects on job finding probability, and that this non-negligible group in the labour market should be given more policy attention.

1.5   STATE CONTROL AND CITIZEN RIGHTS

The fourth part of the book deals with control as one of the major dilemmas of migration. Control has not emerged as an isolated issue. It is a consequence of the growing levels of migration.

James Hampshire uses the concept of a 'migration state' to describe the fundamental dilemma with which every migration state is confronted. Migration states seek competitive advantage by opening their economies and societies to international migration, but at the same time they must also accommodate powerful political forces that drive them towards closure. Wealth creation, generally facilitated by immigration, has to be balanced with the provision of security – the increased risk of terrorism, and organized crime. Faced with these conflicting dynamics, migration states seek to manage migration in their interests by encouraging or 'soliciting' some flows, while preventing or 'stemming' others. Techniques of risk management are harnessed in the control of migration. Hampshire illustrates this development with the example of the UK where the reconceptualization of migration in terms of risk, and the reorganization of migration management as a form of risk management can be observed. These processes, he contends, have to be studied in the context of a conflict between expert knowledge (or risk assessment) and public and media opinion. The management of migration is as much about the public perception of migration risks as about the actual risk.

Dennis Broeders shifts the emphasis from migration within the EU to the issue of illegal migration and how nation states may control it. Such migration and asylum seekers have become prominent and controversial political topics. In a unified Europe, internal migration control means that national states also have to turn to the European level to construct the tools necessary for these types of exclusion. Broeders points to the ways in which border control is being tightened through different forms of electronic surveillance and he describes the Schengen Information System (II), the Eurodac database and the Visa Information System. These systems are able to 're-identify' parts of the population of irregular migrants on the basis of digital traces of their migration history and are therefore a major, and growing, contribution to the efforts of those member states developing surveillance systems. However, the emphasis is changing and policies of migration control have shifted responsibility to employers and to the exclusion of (illegal) migrants from public services. The objective here is to eliminate illegal migrants from the labour and housing market. He also draws attention to the tendencies of 'survillance creep', by which systems originally intended to meet specific problems are applied to new ones when required by changed political circumstances. In such cases, legal and other requirements are often disregarded.

Bente Puntervold Bø describes the recent tendencies in immigration control policies in Europe with particular reference to Norway. She emphasizes the threat of undermining legal safeguards and refugee protection. Countries, in seeking to control immigration, are often guilty, she contends, of breaking international law and conventions. She describes and discusses the limitations of people's rights consequent on the war against terrorism. These difficulties are compounded by the de-professionalization of control regimes, the criminalization of asylum seekers, the regionalization of protection and the limitation of the scope of refugee protection.

Perhaps paradoxically, our book ends with policies which are at variance with those of the European Union with respect to migration. Those who live in the EU have the right to free movement within it – this is their human right and concurrently contributes to the wealth of the EU; whereas those whose birthplace is outside are increasingly excluded.

PART I

Costs and benefits of migration

2. Winners and losers of migration in the European context: economic aspects

Robert Rowthorn

2.1 INTRODUCTION

The countries of western Europe are undergoing a rapid and sustained change in their racial and cultural composition. The driving forces are migration for reasons of economic gain, asylum, and family reunification, together with differential birth rates reflecting the high fertility of certain ethnic minorities and a sharp decline in the fertility of the indigenous populations. If these trends continue they will have a dramatic impact on the countries of western Europe and may have serious implications for social cohesion and national identity. There is growing public concern in western Europe about what is happening and opposition to immigration is increasing. Some of this opposition is based on cultural or racial grounds and some on economic grounds. Those who support a liberal immigration policy either play down the scale of the transformation that is now occurring, or else praise it on the grounds that greater racial or cultural diversity is to the benefit of the indigenous populations of western Europe. They also claim that large-scale immigration will be of great economic benefit to the existing inhabitants of western Europe.

2.2 THE ECONOMIC IMPACT OF MIGRATION[1]

The people who are affected by migration can be divided into three groups: the migrants themselves, the existing inhabitants of the receiving country, and those who remain in the sending country. As a general rule, those who migrate normally benefit from their decision. The impact of migration on the other parties involved is not so clear-cut. Some types of migration are beneficial to the existing inhabitants of the receiving country and others are harmful, and the same is true for those who remain in the sending country. For the migrants themselves, the financial consequences of migration are often large. This is mostly not the case for the other parties involved, although there are certain exceptions.

Empirical investigation into the effects of modern immigration into Europe and the United States suggests that in aggregate its economic impact on the local inhabitants has been small. George Borjas estimates that the total annual benefit to existing Americans of all the immigration that has taken place since 1960 is equivalent to at most US$20 billion, which is 0.2 per cent of GDP (Borjas 2001).[2] In the case of Britain, Walmsley and Winters estimate that an influx of 1.1 million temporary workers would confer an annual benefit of around GBP550 million on the local population.[3] This figure is the same as the extra output that would be generated if the average worker in Britain were to work one hour more per year.[4] These estimated benefits of immigration take no account of the public expenditures involved in administering the immigration programme or in catering for immigrants, nor the costs arising from the resulting population growth. Moreover, the British estimate makes the questionable assumption that all temporary workers find employment and that no local workers are thereby displaced.

It is often claimed that immigrants benefit the local population because they pay more in tax than they receive in the form of public expenditure. This is certainly true for those immigrants who find a well-paid job or set up a successful business. It is also true for many temporary workers who pay indirect and other taxes, but make little claim on the welfare state because they are young and without dependants in the host country. However, there are also immigrants who remain in the lower income bracket indefinitely and rely heavily on the welfare state, especially if they have families or when they grow old. The overall impact of immigration on government finances depends on the balance between these various types of immigrants. In the case of large-scale immigration, there will normally be a broad spectrum of immigrants, some of whom make a positive fiscal contribution and others a negative contribution. Most of these individual effects cancel out, which explains why most empirical studies find that the aggregate impact of large-scale immigration on public finances is relatively small and is rarely greater than ± 0.5 per cent of GDP (Coleman and Rowthorn 2004; Rowthorn 2005).

In addition to its overall impact on the receiving country, immigration may also affect the internal distribution of income. For example, a recent international study by the IMF finds that immigration into the high-income economies has increased the share of profits at the expense of wages (IMF 2007). It may also impoverish some people by creating unemployment. In their comprehensive econometric study of EU countries,

Angrist and Kugler (2003) conclude that the addition of 100 immigrants to the labour force leads eventually to the loss of 83 jobs for native workers. The effect is greatest in countries where native workers enjoy the most job protection. In such countries, employers cannot easily fire existing workers, but when filling new jobs they will choose immigrants, who are easier to fire than native workers. The authors conclude that more labour market 'flexibility' would facilitate the absorption of immigrants and eventually reduce unemployment amongst native workers. If employers could easily dismiss native workers they would have no reason to prefer immigrants.

The impact of immigration on the local workforce depends on the type of immigrant concerned. Provided their talents are fully utilized, the immigration of skilled workers or entrepreneurs will raise the demand for unskilled labour in the recipient country and will thereby benefit existing unskilled workers. The immigration of unskilled workers may have the opposite effect. If the immigrants are able to compete freely with unskilled local workers, the economic position of the latter may get worse. The competition from cheap immigrant labour may push down the wages of unskilled locals to the benefit of more privileged locals who utilize their services. Alternatively, competition from immigrant labour may deprive some locals of employment.

One influential study by George Borjas, Richard Freeman and Lawrence Katz (1997) found that immigration explained 27 to 55 per cent of the decline in the relative wages of high school dropouts in the United States over the period 1980–95. This is many times larger than the effect of competition from low wage imports from developing countries. The authors conclude that, 'Immigration has had a marked adverse impact on the economic status of the least skilled US workers (high school dropouts and those in the bottom 20 per cent of the wage distribution)' (Borjas *et al.* 1997, p.3). This conclusion has been confirmed in a number of subsequent papers by Borjas (Borjas 2003, Borjas 2006, Borjas *et al.* 2006; for an opposing view see Smith and Edmonston 1997). Using a different methodology, David Card finds that in some of America's gateway cities, such as Los Angeles, large-scale immigration during the period 1985–90 'significantly reduced employment rates for younger and less educated native workers'(Card 2001, p. 58).

These results are confirmed in a recent study by Dustmann *et al.* (2007) of the impact of immigration on the British labour market. The following are some extracts from the press release summarizing this report:

> The research looks at the period from 1997 to 2005 and finds evidence of an overall positive impact on immigration on the wages of native born workers,

although the magnitude of the effect is modest. Immigration during these years contributed about one twentieth of the average 3 per cent annual growth in real wages . . . The report goes on to say that although the arrival of economic migrants has benefited workers in the middle and upper part of the wage distribution, immigration has placed downward pressure on the wages in receipt of lower levels of pay. Over the period considered, wages at all points of the wages distribution increased in real terms, but wages in the lowest quarter would have increased quicker and wages further up the distribution would have risen more slowly if it were not for the effect of immigration. (Dustmann *et al.* 2007).

One way of protecting local workers against competition from immigrants is to give them a privileged position through some form of job reservation or job creation. For example, supervisory or public sector jobs may be reserved for local workers. This was done under apartheid in South Africa and is still the practice in the Gulf States and certain other countries that rely heavily on temporary migrant labour.

As far as the sending countries are concerned, the most valuable kind of emigrant is normally the temporary, unskilled worker (Faini 2006). Remittances from such workers can be of great benefit to their families and are an important source of overseas income for some individual countries such as Egypt or Morocco. The worst kind of emigrant is normally the skilled worker or entrepreneur who emigrates permanently. Remittances from such emigrants are relatively small and the loss of their talents may be damaging to their country of origin. The trend in rich OECD countries is to encourage permanent immigration of skilled workers and entrepreneurs from poor countries. This 'brain drain' represents a redistribution of human talent from the poor to the rich. Despite their importance for certain families and certain countries, remittances are rather small in relation to the world economy as a whole. The World Bank estimates that the total value of remittances received by low and middle income countries from migrants in 2005 was between US$133 billion and US$154 billion (Ratha and Shaw 2007). This is around 1.4 per cent of the total income of these countries and around 0.2 per cent of world income. Against these financial benefits must be set the loss from the brain drain to high income countries. Nevertheless, it remains true that remittances are of value to many families in the sending countries and in some cases make a useful contribution to economic development. Remittances can also act as an obstacle to growth because of the perverse incentives they create in the sending country. Indeed, a recent econometric study for the IMF on this issue found that on average migrants' remittances are harmful to economic development (Chami *et al.* 2003).

2.3 AGEING AND DEPENDENCY

Throughout Europe, both east and west, birth rates have fallen in recent decades and are now well below the level required to reproduce the existing population. UN demographers predict that without immigration the population of almost every European country would decline over the next fifty years: in the EU15 from 372 millon to 311 millon and in all European countries (excluding Russia) from 351 million to 289 million by 2050.

At the same time life expectancy is increasing and the proportion of older people in society is rising (from 16.5 per cent in 2000 to 30 per cent in 2050). The latter development is often used to argue for more immigration as a way to rejuvenate the countries of the European Union. More immigration, it is said, is the only way to provide the young workforce that is needed to support an ageing population. This argument is misleading for several reasons. It ignores the fact that, just like the rest of us, immigrants grow old and if they remain in the country they must be supported in old age just like the existing inhabitants. It also ignores the fact that there is currently a large surplus of under-utilized labour that could be used to support the aged and infirm. Only 64 per cent of the EU population between 15 and 64 years of age is now in gainful employment. In Iceland, by contrast, the figure is 84 per cent. If the EU were to emulate the Icelandic example, this would generate more than 50 million jobs and increase the number of employed workers by around a third. These additional workers would be easily enough to meet the needs of an ageing population.

What may happen to the 'dependency ratio' in the EU during the next fifty years under various assumptions about employment and migration? The dependency ratio indicates how many non-employed persons the average person in gainful employment must support. As defined here, the dependency ratio ignores the useful work that is performed as unpaid work by such persons as housewives, volunteers and the like. This point should be borne in mind when interpreting variations in the dependency ratio. Since children are, on average, less costly to support than adults the ratio is expressed in adult equivalents. Four different scenarios are illustrated in Figure 2.1 which is based on UN (2001).

These are characterized by the amount of immigration they assume and the number of people in paid employment. Under the 'zero migration', 'high migration' and 'very high migration' scenarios, respectively, there is a net inflow of zero, 47 million and 79 million migrants into the present EU countries during the period 2000–2050. Under these scenarios, the proportion of the working age population (15–64 years old) in employment remains constant at around 64 per cent. Under the 'high employment' scenario, there is no immigration, but the employment rate increases

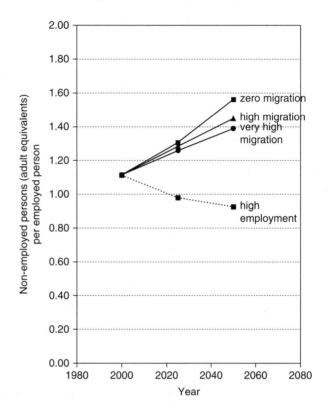

Notes:
According to the *OECD Employment Outlook* (June 2001, p. 209), the employment rate (=
employment/population age 16–64) in 2000 was 63.6 per cent in the EU and 84.6 per cent
in Iceland. The continuous lines assume that the employment rate is equal to 61 per cent
over the whole period. The broken line assumes that the employment rate rises linearly
from 63.6 per cent in 2000 to 83.6 per cent in 2050. The high immigration scenario assumes
net immigration of 47 million into the EU15 over the period 2000–50. To calculate the
dependency ratio it is assumed that each child under 15 is equivalent to 0.4 adults.

Source: own calculation.

Figure 2.1   Dependency Ratios in the EU15

from 64 per cent in 2000 to 84 per cent by 2050. By the end of the period
the proportion of the working age population with a job is the same under
this scenario as it is in Iceland today.

The zero-migration scenario shows what would happen to economic
dependency in the EU in the absence of immigration and with no improvement in the operation of the labour market. The other scenarios show

how immigration and job creation affect the dependency ratio. The most striking feature is how little difference immigration makes compared to improvements in the operation of the labour market. If the present under-employment of the European population continues, the dependency ratio will rise strongly, almost irrespective of the rate of immigration. Finding jobs for the existing labour force is far more effective than immigration at reducing this ratio. Without any immigration at all, the high employment scenario shown in the lower part of the chart would result in a large fall in the dependency ratio.

Current fears about the consequences of population ageing are exaggerated. The idea that Europe is on the verge of running out of labour is absurd. Moreover, dire warnings about collapsing birth rates should be treated with caution. Long-term demographic projections are notoriously unreliable. For example, demographers in the 1930s were convinced that the population of the UK was going to fall rapidly, and they totally failed to predict the growth resulting from the 1950s baby boom. As far as ageing is concerned, there is no immediate case for large-scale migration into Europe. The problem that Europe faces at the moment is not a looming scarcity of labour, but how to employ its presently underutilized population.

2.4 EU ENLARGEMENT

In 2004, eight former communist countries together with Malta and Cyprus joined the European Union. They were followed in 2007 by Bulgaria and Romania. The combined population of these countries is around 100 million and their entry increased the population of the EU by about a third. The per capita income of these countries is on average about 40 per cent of the existing EU countries, and in the case of Bulgaria and Romania the gap is much wider. The entry of such a large group of relatively poor countries has given rise to fears that workers from the east will flood into western Europe, disrupting labour markets and damaging the interests of the existing workforce. These fears are especially serious in Austria and Germany, which share a common border with the newcomers. Such fears prompted some of the existing EU countries to insist on a transition period during which restrictions on inward migration from the new member states would be retained. When the first wave of enlargement took place in 2004, Britain and Ireland imposed no restrictions and the result was a massive, and unexpected, flow of migrants from the first wave of new member states. In the light of this experience, there has been a shift of policy and migration from the next wave of new countries, Bulgaria and Romania, is now restricted.

Sustained migration from the east following enlargement will have a number of implications. The outflow of skilled labour may continue, thereby damaging the sending countries; and unskilled labour may come west on a large-scale thereby damaging the position of unskilled workers in the receiving countries. There could also be a collapse of agricultural employment in the new member states leading to a large outflow of peasants from the countryside. In the absence of strong economic growth to absorb these people locally, many of them would come to seek unskilled work in the west. The effect of migration on the age structure of the west will depend on whether the migrants are temporary or permanent. If, as seems likely, many of them are permanent then migration will have only a marginal long-term impact on the age structure of the west, since the migrants themselves will eventually age and require support. Only temporary migration can make a major difference in this regard, since temporary migrants go home before they get old. In both east and west populations are ageing because of low birth rates and longer life expectancy. To the extent that the west rejuvenates itself by importing labour from the east, it will exacerbate the ageing problem in the east.

The impact of migration following enlargement depends on how many people move from east to west. There will probably be a surge in migration immediately after restrictions on labour mobility are removed, but what happens thereafter is uncertain. Over the longer term, the number of migrants depends on economic conditions in the two regions and the generosity of welfare benefits in the west. If the new entrants to the EU experience strong economic growth, then incomes and job opportunities in the east will rapidly converge towards those in the west, and the incentive for migration will decline accordingly. The incentive for migration will be further reduced if fiscal reform in the west reduces the generosity of welfare benefits. Conversely, migration may continue on a large scale for many years if the economic performance of the new member states is poor and if the existing regulations regarding equal treatment mean that the host countries of western Europe provide generous welfare benefits for migrants from the east.

The official view of the European Commission at the time was that EU enlargement would lead to an eventual migration of around 3 million people from the ten countries due to enter the EU in 2004 plus Bulgaria and Romania who joined later (European Commission 2001). This is equivalent to about 1 per cent of the population of the present EU countries (the EU15) and about 3 per cent of the population of the sending countries. This forecast was based on a study by Boeri and Bruecker (2000). However, another prominent research team led by Hans-Werner Sinn from the IFO Institute in Munich arrived at a much higher figure for potential migration (Sinn 2001). In the absence of transitional restrictions on the movement of workers, they estimated that in the first 15 years of EU membership net migration from the new members from eastern Europe (including Bulgaria and Romania) *into Germany alone* would be in the range 4 to 5 million. Although Germany is the preferred destination for most migrants from these countries, Austria is also popular and many would go to Britain and elsewhere in the Union. Allowing for such additional destinations, Sinn's estimates implied that migration from the candidate countries into the existing EU15 countries would be in the range 5 to 7 million, which is around 5 to 7 per cent of the population of the sending countries.

There has been a surge of migration from eastern Europe into Britain and Ireland, but this may be temporary. It is also unclear how far it is a guide to what will happen when restrictions are lifted in other rich EU countries such as Germany. Some would argue that a better guide is what happened when Greece, Portugal and Spain joined the EU in the 1980s. When these countries joined there were transition periods during which the movement of labour was restricted. When such restrictions were lifted it was expected that there would be large-scale migration to the richer EU countries. This did not happen. Thus, the experience of past EU enlargement suggests that the scale of migration when the existing restrictions are lifted will be modest. Other experience, however, suggests just the opposite. Over the period 1940–90 roughly 20 per cent of the population of Ireland migrated to Britain, and over a similar period about 25 per cent of the population of Puerto Rico migrated to the United States. It seems unlikely that the eventual migration from east to west within the EU will be on this scale, but such figures should alert us to the possibility that migration may turn out to be on a larger scale than any of the above estimates imply (Blanchard 2001).

2.5   TOWARDS A GREATER EU

Bulgaria and Romania have recently joined the EU. What happens now will be the subject of a political struggle whose outcome is by no means clear. Turkey is pressing for admission to the EU, but other influential forces are opposed to this application. Giscard D'Estaing, who was in charge of drafting the new EU constitution, has said that Turkey should never be allowed to join the Union because the vast bulk of the country lies outside of Europe and its culture is alien. Many Europeans share this view, including the governments of France and Germany, although few politicians would be quite so overt as Giscard. This dispute points to a basic weakness in the European project as presently conceived. There has never been an official statement as to where the ultimate boundaries of the European Union should lie. Some people, such as the historian Tony Judt (1996), have argued that the natural boundary of the EU is what used to be known as Western Christendom. This would include Hungary, Poland and the Czech Republic, but exclude Bulgaria and Romania. Others would argue that the EU should only include countries that are geographically within Europe. Apart from minor exceptions like Albania, this geographical criterion would confine the EU to Christian and post-Christian countries. Whatever one thinks of these cultural or geographical arguments, none of them is reflected in the official criteria for EU membership. These criteria, which were laid down at a meeting of the European Council in Copenhagen in June 1993, are as follows:

- *Political Criterion:* An applicant must have stable institutions, guaranteeing democracy, the rule of law, human rights, and the protection of minorities.
- *Economic Criterion:* An applicant must have a functioning market economy and the capacity to cope with competitive pressures within the single market of the EU.
- *The Acquis Communautaire:* An applicant must be able to take on the obligations of membership, including adherence to the aims of political, economic and monetary union.

Within the not too distant future many countries on the periphery of the EU may able to satisfy these criteria. Turkey almost certainly will, as indeed may a number of east European countries such as the Ukraine or Belarus, or even Russia. So too may the countries of North Africa. Ultimately, the whole world may eventually satisfy the Copenhagen criteria. Long before that stage is reached, the EU must either collapse or specify some additional criteria to limit its expansion.

2.6   MIGRATION AND POPULATION IN A GREATER EU

What implications for migration and population might further waves of EU enlargement have? To answer this, I consider what I call the 'Greater European Union'. This union consists of all the countries of Europe (excluding Russia), plus Turkey and the countries of North Africa. Most of these countries have annual per capita incomes that are well below the present EU average (23 600 per capita income in USD and purchasing

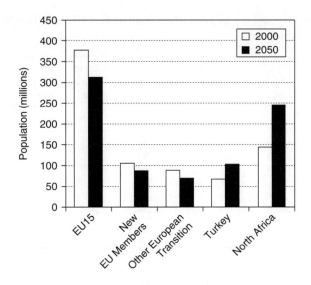

Source: UN-Population prognosis; own calculation.

Figure 2.2   Population projection, 2000–2050

power parities in 2000; the equivalent income in Turkey was 7000 and in the North African Countries 4200). There is also a sharp demographic contrast between the European and non-European members of the Greater EU. In the absence of migration, the population of almost every European country, both east and west, would fall. The opposite is the case in Turkey and North Africa, where the population is predicted to rise by around 60 per cent over the next 50 years in the absence of migration.

Figure 2.2 presents some crude projections of migration and population in the regions that belong to the Greater EU. These projections are designed merely to illustrate the orders of magnitude involved and they make no claim to scientific accuracy. The figures for migration shown in this table refer to net flows of migrants into the existing EU countries. All other migration flows are assumed to be zero. Net migration from the new members of the EU into western Europe (EU15) is assumed to average 100 000 a year over the period 2000–2050. This gives a cumulative total of 5 million, which is around 5 per cent of the population of the sending countries. This figure is a compromise between the estimates of Boeri and Sinn described above. A similar percentage is assumed for migration into western Europe from other regions of the Greater EU. Immigration from outside the Greater EU is assumed to average 500 000 a year.

Table 2.1   Migration and population in a Greater EU: 2000–2050
(millions)

	Actual population 2000	Natural change	Effects of migration direct	Effects of migration indirect	Projected population 2050
EU15	377	−66	48	15	373
New EU members	105	−18	−5	−1	81
Other European transition	88	−19	−4	−1	64
Turkey	67	35	−4	−1	96
North Africa	143	102	−10	−3	232
Sub-total: New and potential EU members	403	100	−23	−7	473
Sub-total: Greater EU	780	34	25	8	847
Rest of the World	5277	3226	−25	−8	8470
Total: World	6057	3260	0	0	9317

Notes: Greater EU = New and Potential EU Members + EU15; New EU Members =
Bulgaria, Cyprus, Czech Republic, Estonia, Hungary, Latvia, Lithuania, Malta, Poland,
Romania, Slovakia, Slovenia; Other European Transition = Albania, Belarus, Bosnia,
Croatia, Macedonia, Moldova, Ukraine, Yugoslavia; North Africa = Algeria, Egypt,
Libya, Morocco, Tunisia, Western Sahara.
   Projected population in 2050 = actual population in 2000 + natural population growth
2000–2050 + effects of migration (Total migration from new and potential EU members =
5 per cent of their natural population in 2050; Net migration from the rest of the world to
EU15 = 0.5 million annually; Ratio of indirect to direct effect of migration = 0.3).

Source: Actual population in 2000 and natural population growth are taken from the UN
Population Report 2000 (2002 update).

The overall change in the population of each region is divided into natural
change plus the direct and indirect effects of migration. The term 'natural
change' refers to the UN projection of what population growth in the
region would be in the absence of migration. The direct effect of migration
consists of the transfer of people from one region to another. There is also
an indirect effect due to the fact that migration alters birth and death rates.
Migrants are mostly rather young and many of them come from cultures
where fertility rates are still relatively high. As a result, migration causes
birth rates to rise in receiving countries and fall in sending countries. It has
the opposite effect on death rates. Following the example of UN demographers, the indirect effect of migration on population is assumed to
equal 30 per cent of its direct effect.
   The main points to note about Table 2.1 are as follows. Over the period
shown, the EU15 countries receive a net inflow of 23 million immigrants
from elsewhere in the Greater EU plus another 25 million from the rest of
the world, giving a total of 48 million. This is equivalent to around 3 per

1000 annually, which is similar to the rate of legal immigration observed in recent years in the United States. Taking into account its impact on the birth rate, immigration is almost enough to maintain the population of the existing EU countries at its present level. In the former communist countries of central and eastern Europe, population decline is exacerbated by outflow to the west, and their population falls by an average of 25 per cent. In Turkey and Africa, population growth is massive despite substantial emigration.

Despite its prominence in recent discussion, the inflow of migrants from the new members of the EU is only about a tenth of total immigration into western Europe that is envisaged in Table 2.1. Immigration resulting from the present enlargement may be important for certain countries, but in the overall scheme of things it is quite small. With the expansion of the EU envisaged in Table 2.1 the scale of migration into western Europe would be many times larger and its impact much greater.

The impact on government finances of the migration shown in Table 2.1 would probably be negative. Most of the migrants would occupy low-paid jobs and would pay less tax than they and their families would eventually receive in the form of welfare benefits and public services. Their inflow would depress the wages of local unskilled workers (including those of immigrant descent) and increase the unemployment rate amongst the unskilled, thereby reducing government revenue and creating new demands on the public purse. There would, of course, be a plentiful supply of cheap servants and services for the more privileged members of society.

Table 2.1 also throws an interesting light on the likely social and political nature of a Greater EU. Taking account of the fact that some immigrants who arrived prior to 2000 would still be alive at the end of the period, the stock of first generation immigrants would be around 15 per cent of the population of western Europe by 2050. This is higher than in the USA today. Given their geographical origin many of these immigrants would be Muslims. In the Greater EU as a whole perhaps 40 per cent of the population would be nominally Muslim. Most of these would, of course, be located in North Africa and Turkey, whose combined share of the Greater EU population would be around a third. The share of individual European countries, such as France, Germany or the UK, in the Greater EU population would be in the region of 10 per cent or less.

Given this arithmetic, it is clear that extending the EU to include Turkey and eventually North Africa would have profound social and political implications. The figures shown in Table 2.1 are merely informed guesswork, but they are accurate enough to indicate the consequences of pursuing the present logic of EU enlargement without limit. Unless some clear boundaries are placed on enlargement, the balance of power in the EU will shift dramatically, and the countries that presently dominate the Union will no longer do so, either individually or collectively. With an expansion of the kind envisaged in Table 2.1, Muslims would become a large and growing minority in western Europe and Islam would become the dominant religion in the Greater EU as a whole. Some might welcome these developments, while others would view them with alarm. Either way, the result would be a profound transformation in the nature of the European Union, which should be openly debated before embarking on further waves of enlargement.

For those worried about the consequences of the scale of migration indicated in Table 2.1, a possible solution would be to make full admission to the EU conditional upon the level of development of a candidate country. For example, the movement of labour could be restricted until the per capita income of a country had reached some given percentage, say 70 per cent, of the EU average. With an income gap of this magnitude, the likely scale of migration into the present EU countries would be quite small. For those worried about the political consequences of future enlargement, a possible solution would be to reverse the current process of centralization in the EU and turn it into a much looser confederation confined mainly to trade and related matters. For the centralizers like Giscard, who seek a close federal union, it is important that the EU be a relatively compact and culturally homogeneous area. For those who would prefer a looser and more decentralized EU, the preservation of cultural homogeneity across the union as a whole is not a crucial objective.

2.7   CONCLUDING REMARKS

Migration is normally beneficial to the migrants themselves. Its impact on sending and receiving countries depends on the type of migration and the country concerned. Large-scale immigration would bring little collective benefit to the existing inhabitants of the advanced economies. It would benefit some of these inhabitants and hurt others. Its effect on income distribution would be retrogressive. It would benefit highly skilled workers and the owners of capital, and harm the unskilled. Large-scale immigration is not an effective way of dealing with the problems of ageing in Europe. A more effective solution would be to find work for the tens of millions of Europeans whose energies and talents are currently under-utilized. The impact of migration on the sending countries is positive in some cases and negative in others.

The eventual scale of migration following EU enlargement is uncertain.

A figure of 5 million for the total migration from the new members (including Bulgaria and Romania) seems reasonable. Compared to total immigration into the existing EU countries, this figure is quite small if spread over a number of years and over a number of countries. However, as current British experience indicates, migration on this scale may pose serious local problems if it occurs within a short space of time and is focused on a small number of geographical areas. Moreover, it is notoriously difficult to predict the scale of migration flows, and the figure of 5 million for east to west migration within the existing EU may turn out to be a gross underestimate.

The present logic of EU enlargement is towards indefinite expansion. In the relatively near future, such logic could lead to the formation of a Greater EU incorporating Turkey, North Africa and the remaining transition economies of eastern Europe. The result would be large-scale migration into the existing EU countries and a radical shift in the balance of power in the Union. It would have profound economic, social and political implications for the existing EU countries.

NOTES

1. For an extensive survey of the issues discussed in this section see Coleman and Rowthorn (2004).
2. Borjas estimates that immigration has caused an efficiency gain in the USA of between US$5 billion and $10 billion. This is in addition to earlier estimates of the gains from immigration (which are typically below US$10 billion).
3. The exact figures are as follows: unskilled immigrants 575.1 thousand, skilled immigrants 558.9 thousand, gain to British population US$851.03 million (as given in Tables 1 and 3 of their paper).
4. In the year 2000 the average employed person in Britain worked 1708 hours (OECD 2001) and total GDP was equal to GBP 950 415 (*Monthly Digest of Statistics*, April 2003, p. 3). Assuming constant returns to scale, this implies that one hour's extra work by the average worker would increase GDP by GBP556 million.

REFERENCES

Angrist, J.D. and A.D. Kugler (2003), 'Protective or Counter-Productive? Labour market institutions and the effect of immigration on EU natives', *Economic Journal*, **113** (488), 332.

Blanchard, Olivier (2001), 'The EU enlargement and immigration from eastern Europe', mimeo.

Boeri, T. and H. Buecker (2000), *The Impact of Eastern Enlargement on Employment and Labour Markets in the EU Member States*, Berlin and Milan: DIW, CEPR, FIEF, IGIER, HIS.

Borjas, G.J. (2001), 'Does immigration grease the wheels of the labor Market?', *Brookings Papers on Economic Activity*, I, 70.

Borjas, G.J. (2003), 'The labour demand curve is downward sloping: reexamining the Impact of Immigration on the labor market', *Quarterly Journal of Economics*, **11**, 1335–74.

Borjas, G.J. (2006), 'Native internal migration and the labor market impact of immigration', *Journal of Human Resources*, **41** (2), 221–258.

Borjas, G.J., R. Freeman and L.F. Katz (1997), 'How much do immigration and trade affect labour market outcomes', *Brookings Papers on Economic Activity*, I, 62.

Borjas, G.J., J. Grogger and G.H. Hanson (2006), 'Immigration and African-American employment opportunities: the response of wages, employment, and incarceration to labor supply shocks', NBER working paper 12518.

Card, D. (2001), 'Immigrant inflows, native outflow, and the local labor market impacts of higher migration', *Journal of Labor Economics*, **19** (1), 22–64.

Chami, R., C. Fullenkamp and S. Jahjah (2003), 'Are immigrant remittance flows a source of capital for development?', IMF working paper 03, 189.

Coleman, D. and R. Rowthorn (2004), 'The economic effects of immigration into the United Kingdom', *Population and Development Review*, **30** (4), 579–624.

Dustmann, C., I. Preston and T. Frattini (2007), *A Study of Migrant Workers and the National Minimum Wage and Enforcement Issues that Arise*, London: University College Centre for Research and Analysis of Migration.

European Commission (2001), 'The free movement of workers in the context of enlargement', European Commission information note 3.

Faini, R. (2006), 'Remittances and the brain drain', IZA discussion paper 2155.

IMF (eds) (2007), *World Economic Outlook*, Chapter 5.

Judt, T. (1996), *A Grand Illusion?*, London: Penguin Books.

Monthly Digest of Statistics (2003), April, Newport: Office for National Statistics.

OECD Employment Outlook (2001), *OECD Employment Outlook*, 209, Paris: OECD.

Ratha, D. and W. Shaw (2007), *South-South Migration and Remittances*, Washington, DC: World Bank, Table 4.

Rowthorn, R. (2005), 'A simulation model of the fiscal effects of immigration, fertility and employment', Oxford Centre for Population Research working paper 27.

Sinn, H.W. (2001), *EU–Erweiterung und Arbeitskraeftemigration*, Munich: IFI Institute, p. xvii.

Smith, J.P. and B. Edmonston (eds) (1997), *The New Americans: Economic, Demographic and Fiscal Effects of Immigration*, Washington, DC: National Academy Press.

United Nations (2000), *UN Population Report*, New York: United Nations.

United Nations (eds) (2001), *Replacement Migration: Is it a Solution to Declining and Ageing Populations?*, New York: United Nations, Table IV.22.

Walmsley, T.L. and A. Winters (2003), 'Relaxing the restrictions on the temporary movement of natural persons: a simulation analysis', CEPR discussion paper 3719.

3. Shortage of skilled workers: myths and realities

Franz Heschl

3.1 INTRODUCTION

In the last twenty years the impact of migration on the labour market has become a subject of research. The methods and concepts used to study migration differ in various aspects, with the results being strongly influenced by the underlying assumptions. Trying to sum up the results of the approaches – if only cursorily and thus fragmentarily – one could note some key points:[1] The macroeconomic impacts of migration or the cumulated effects of immigration on labour markets are relatively small; such a general view, however, obscures the distribution effects. These effects depend on the current wage system: if this system is very flexible, wages are more likely to change; if the system is more rigid, it is rather the unemployment rates which will change. In many cases, migration leads to the redistribution of income from employees to the owners of capital. Among a group of employees, the level of qualification determines the direction and extent of how an individual is affected. Immigration also brings with it a redistribution of wealth from employees who compete with immigrants for persons who use or consume the services of immigrants.

The social foundations and the societal impact of these redistribution processes are of great importance. It would be beneficial to know how different groups in society bring up migration issues against the backdrop of various interests in the public media debate and which instruments they use for doing so. This chapter proposes an answer to the public debate about immigration to Austria caused by the European integration process. The aim is complicated as both public and scientific debates about the consequences of immigration on the labour market show nuances – obviously because of the interests behind them and the consequences for distribution. The debates show strong polarization: they are dominated by accusations and reproaches from 'xenophobia' to 'disproportionate political correctness'.

3.2   LABOUR MIGRATION TO AUSTRIA

The basic developments in the Austrian labour market over the past two decades are characterized by a steady growth in the number of employees throughout the entire period. The different forms of illegal employment – even if they influence one of the other developments which are analysed – are not discussed here. The growth in the number of employees was mainly the result of a significant increase in part-time employment. During the same period, the number of employees not holding Austrian nationality also rose steadily. The increase in employees without Austrian nationality grew moderately between 1985 and 1989, before the fall of the Iron Curtain, and skyrocketed between 1990 and 1991. The reason for this significant rise stemmed mainly from developments in the former Yugoslavia, and also from the fall of the Iron Curtain. However, while the employment rate rose, there was a significant increase in the unemployment rate during this period.

After tightening the regulations for the admission of foreign workers into the Austrian labour market from 1993 onward, the change in the number of foreign employees again showed a moderate yet steady growth. In 1985, 140 205 people not holding Austrian nationality worked in the Austrian labour market; in 2006 there were 389 894 people. During the same period the share of foreigners doubled from 5.1 per cent in 1985 to 11.9 per cent in 2006. From 1996 to 2006, 287 160 people were naturalized, many of these naturalizations not being relevant for the labour market (cf. Statistik Austria, Statistisches Jahrbuch Österreichs 2007, 86). The OECD, in its 'International Migration Outlook 2007' holds that, in 2005, 15.5 per cent of all working people in Austria were not born in the country. This percentage places Austria as one of the countries with the highest proportion of foreigners within the EU.

Regarding the composition of the migrant workforce in Austria by countries of origin, immigration from former Yugoslavia and Turkey prevailed in the period before the fall of the Iron Curtain. In 1980, 82.1 per cent of all labour migrants in the Austrian labour market came from Yugoslavia and Turkey, in 1989 the proportion was still 77.7 per cent (cf. Bundesministerium für Arbeit und Soziales, Ausländerbeschäftigung 1989, 34). In the course of the fall of the Iron Curtain, Austria's accession and the eastern enlargement of the EU, the composition of the foreign workforce changed considerably, as will be explained later.

Furthermore, foreign born individuals in the Austrian labour market are predominantly male. The proportion of male employed foreigners was 63 per cent in 1995 and 60 per cent in 2006.[2] Initially, immigration met the need for unskilled labour. For instance, in 1995, 83 per cent of all employed labour migrants were unskilled wage earners. However, the level of qualifications and skills has risen in the last 10 years; the proportion of clerical workers has risen from 17 to 29 per cent in the years 1995 to 2006. Most immigrants traditionally worked in the production, building, trade and hotel industries, with a recent increase occurring in those working in corporate services.[3]

Experiences from the Early 1990s

Since the mid-1990s, there has been a heightened interest by both the public and academia in the impact of migration on the Austrian labour market. The increased interest can be attributed to the permanent rise of salaried employment, the increased employment of foreigners in Austria in the last twenty years and the jump in employment of foreigners in the years 1990 and 1991. Interest has also been generated by a desire to understand the manner in which the employment of foreign workers impacts on unemployment and wages. From the mid-1990s onward, a number of economic studies have been published, showing the different effects of employment of foreigners.

Rudolf Winter-Ebmer and Josef Zweimüller have produced a detailed study of the effects of the increasing employment of foreigners on the Austrian labour market in the years 1988–91. In their work, they refer to the fact that 'the enormous increase of labour potential within a rather short period' (Winter-Ebmer and Zweimüller 1996, 55) should help in analysing the labour market's reaction to immigration. They also state that the rise in labour migration to Austria occurred at a time of economic growth. Data of employment rates and income trends from the Austrian social security funds form the basis of their empirical research.

With regard to the risk of unemployment, they conclude that there has been no significant effect on native women due to competition with foreign employees. Men, on the other hand, do suffer from the increasing employment of foreigners in their unemployment rates. In the timeframe investigated, there had been a general effect on the income level of nationals at the time of a growing presence of foreigners in the Austrian labour market. This result is especially interesting as concerns income subgroups. Winter-Ebmer and Zweimüller divided the people investigated, according to their median income, into recipients of low income and high income. As regards women, there is no significant negative effect of the concentration of foreigners on the income in any subgroup. With men the picture was different:

> if the income is below median, most of the results are negative. The most negative effect is on men above 50. An increase of 1 per cent in the proportion of

Table 3.1 Developments in the Austrian labour market of the last two decades

Year	Salaried employees	Annual percentage change %	Development of part-time employment	Recorded unemployed	Annual percentage change %	Unemployment rate in %	Development in the number of foreign employees	Annual percentage change %	Proportion of foreigners in % of employees
1985	2 759.432			139 447		4.8	140 205		5.1
1986	2 779.865	+0.7		151 973	+8.2	5.2	145 963	+3.9	5.3
1987	2 785.442	+0.2		164 468	+7.6	5.6	147 382	+1.0	5.3
1988	2 808.334	+0.8		158 631	−3.7	5.3	150 915	+2.3	5.4
1989	2 859.932	+1.8		149 177	−6.3	5.0	167 381	+9.8	5.9
1990	2 925.396	+2.2		165 795	+10.0	5.4	217 611	+23.1	7.4
1991	2 995.361	+2.3		185 029	+10.4	5.8	266 461	+18.3	8.9
1992	3 054.065	+1.9		193 098	+4.2	5.9	273 884	+2.7	9.0
1993	3 055.271	+0.0		222 265	+13.1	6.8	277 511	+1.3	9.1
1994	3 069.424	+0.5		214 941	−3.4	6.5	291 018	+4.6	9.5
1995	3 069.536	+0.0	382 039	215 716	+0.4	6.6	300 328	+3.1	9.8
1996	3 046.904	−0.7	381 670	230 507	+6.4	7.0	300 271	−0.0	9.9
1997	3 055.305	+0.3	415 694	233 348	+1.2	7.1	298 797	−0.5	9.8
1998	3 075.850	+0.7	454 867	237 794	+1.9	7.2	298 566	−0.1	9.7
1999	3 106.120	+1.0	481 598	221 743	−7.2	6.7	305 783	+2.4	9.8
2000	3 133.173	+0.9	494 060	194 314	−14.1	5.8	319 394	+4.3	10.2

2001	3 148.177	+0.5	535 805	203 883	+4.7	6.1	329 261	+3.0	10.5
2002	3 154.512	+0.2	573 314	232 418	+12.3	6.9	334 132	+1.5	10.6
2003	3 184.117	+0.9	595 718	240 079	+3.2	7.0	349 559	+4.4	11.0
2004	3 197.250	+0.4	731 000	243 880	+1.6	7.1	361 767	+3.4	11.3
2005	3 228.777	+1.0	750 900	252 654	+3.5	7.3	373 692	+3.2	11.6
2006	3 280.878	+1.6	791 100	239 174	-5.6	6.8	389 894	+4.2	11.9

Notes: Data from 2004 are not directly comparable to the years before.

Source: Bundesarbeitskammer, Wirtschafts- und Sozialstatistisches Taschenbuch, various years, own calculation; Statistik Austria, Mikrozensus Jahresergebnisse und Mikrozensus-Arbeitskräfteerhebung, various years, respectively.

foreigners reduces the monthly income by 0.3 per cent . . . With the high income group, a high proportion of foreigners results in significantly higher incomes . . . An exception being the group over 50 and foreigners themselves (Winter-Ebmer and Zweimüller 1996, 93–4).

The authors then divided their test groups into those people who have changed sectors in the timeframe investigated ('movers') and those people who have not ('stayers').

With men, an increase in employment of foreigners results in a significant negative effect on the income level of the movers . . . . If the proportion of foreigners increases by one percentage point, increase in income is reduced by two-thirds. On the stayers, the effect is also negative, though insignificantly. This outcome rather argues for moving that is not conducted out of free will in connection with a change in foreign employment. With women there are no significant negative effects. (Winter-Ebmer and Zweimüller 1996, 96)

Fritz Breuss and Fritz Schebeck have used an econometric model to determine the labour market relevant consequences of the high immigration rates during these years. Their central result is:

We can see from the reaction of the labour market that income flexibility has risen considerably. The heavy temporary inflow of foreign workforce in the years 1989 to 1992 quickly curbed pay increases. Compared to the basic scenario (without immigration), gross pay decreased by 2.25 per cent between 1989 and 1992. As a consequence, oversupply in the labour market could be absorbed and unemployment rise could be alleviated. Pressure on pay increase abated price increase, which led to a slight actual growth in national demand. So, due to immigration, real GDP additionally grew by 0.2 per cent until 1994. The sharp rise in unemployment (especially until 1992) burdened the public budget in the form of unemployment benefits (Breuss and Schebeck 1996, 145).

On the basis of a random sample of 1521 enterprises which had at least one employee per year between December 1988 and December 1991, Brandel *et al.* (1994) found out that the heavy inflow of immigrants at the end of the 1980s and beginning of the 1990s considerably squeezed out of the labour market both Austrian workers and those foreigners working in Austria. So, 60 per cent of all businesses in the random sample, whose employment rates jumped during this period, increased employment of the immigrant workforce (cf. Brandel *et al.* 1994, Pollan 2000). Summarizing the main result of their study, their final remarks are a good example for the 'disproportionate political correctness' which was referred to earlier as one pole in the debates on immigration:

the study produces some evidence for partial replacement processes in the employment system triggered by the shock of workforce supply in the years

1989 to 1991. According to the results presented, it was especially foreign labourers who had been in the country longer that suffered the most from competition with the new arrivals; some national labourers, however, also saw themselves confronted with unfavourable income prospects. The study also makes very clear how such restructuring measures in the employment system are embedded in a general high dynamics of fluctuation of work places and workforce (Brandel *et al.* 1994).

In another study based on data from social security funds, Gudrun Biffl elaborated that heavy labour migration at the beginning of the 1990s led to cut-throat competition among the foreign workforce:

> The quick extension of the foreign workforce in the early 1990s led to a temporary oversupply in some work sectors. In these sectors, competition among the employed toughened in such a way that not only wage pressure (as documented by the widening of wage differences of national and foreign workforce) but also the unemployment rate of foreigners increased. Foreigners' unemployment rate is . . . always higher than that of nationals, and this gap widened remarkably in the early 1990s. (Biffl 2002, 548)

The author concludes that an increase in the proportion of the foreign workforce in employment by one percentage point would raise the unemployment rate of foreigners by 0.6 percentage points. She points out that the effects of an increase in supply of foreign workers in the Austrian labour market always depends on the role various groups of foreigners play in a certain business or sector:

> If national and foreign employees perform the same activities, they are potentially interchangeable; in the case of demand fluctuations, members of core staff or people with workplace protection will stay employed and temporary staff will be dismissed. In the case of re-employment, wage adjustment downwards is possible. In certain sectors, the foreign workforce complements the national workforce, for example in very specialised activities in high income groups (banks and insurance) and in low income groups (night shifts in the textile sector). Under the terms of complementarity, the foreign workforce adds to job stability, and can even increase the employment of nationals. (Biffl 2002, 548)

Even if it is very difficult to summarize the sophisticated outcomes of these studies concisely, it cannot be disputed that the jump in labour migration to Austria at the beginning of the 1990s had positive effects on employment rates and economic growth, but problematic effects regarding the risk of unemployment and the income level for some subgroups in the labour market.

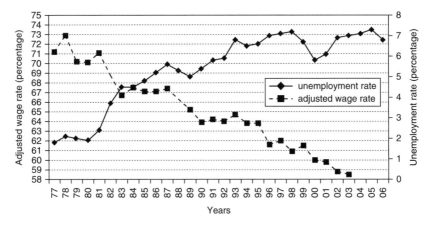

Source: Guger and Marterbauer (2004), 7, 43.

Figure 3.1   Development of unemployment rate and wage rate in Austria

Developments in the Decade After

Due to the experiences in the years 1990 and 1991, regulations for the foreign workforce in the Austrian labour market – the central instrument being the Foreign People Employment Act – were formulated more restrictively from 1993 onward. By passing these measures, further jumps in the employment of foreign workers were prevented, though the foreign workforce increased steadily in the following one-and-a-half decades. There were also investigations carried out regarding labour market relevant effects due to the rise of foreign people employed in Austria. These studies all point to the positive effects on growth and employment which were quoted before. Many of these investigations, however, point out that thereby – in combination with other factors, such as the growing employment of women or reforms in retirement and old age pension insurance which delay the starting of retirement – *the workforce supply in Austria has increased to such an extent that the labour market could not fully absorb it.*

In the 1990s and at the beginning of the twenty-first century, unemployment in Austria was therefore on the rise. This rise and the constantly high level of unemployment – again in connection with other factors, such as the increasing internationalization of the Austrian economy due to the European integration process – had significant effects on the change in functional income distribution. Figure 3.1 correlates the unemployment rate to the wage rate. It shows a significant decrease of the wage rate and at the same time an increasing and high unemployment rate in Austria

Table 3.2   Growth of real wages and productivity (average annual growth rate in %)

	1960/ 1970	1970/ 1980	1980/ 1990	1990/ 2000	2000/ 2003	1960/ 2003
Productivity (real GDP per labour force)	+5.0	+2.9	+2.2	+2.0	+0.8	+2.9
Growth of real wages per capita	+4.9	+3.6	+1.3	+1.0	+0.3	+2.5

Source: Guger and Marterbauer 2004, 6.

over the past 30 years. Alois Guger and Markus Marterbauer described this correlation as follows:

> Like in most of the other industrial nations, inequality in functional and personal distribution of income has increased in Austria. After a rise of wage rate in the 1970s, the wage share in national income has decreased notably, mainly due to rising unemployment and a sharp increase in capital income . . . For a long-term development of functional distribution, the labour market situation is of vital importance. On the one hand, recipients of unemployment benefits drop out as income recipients, and on the other hand, an increase in unemployment changes the economic balance of power and forces the trade union's wage policy onto the defensive. In the 1980s and 1990s, the wage policy was not able to make use of the scope in real wages given by the development of productivity, and so the adjusted wage rate was continuously on the decline. (Guger and Marterbauer 2004, 38–9)

The growth of per capita real wages corresponded with the growth of productivity or rather exceeded it during the decades of low unemployment in Austria, that is, the years 1960–80. The growth of real wages however stayed noticeably behind the growth of productivity in the 1980s when unemployment was markedly on the rise in Austria.

It is also important to note that the increasing internationalization of the Austrian economy and intensified west-eastern integration in Europe contributed to the slow growth in wages as well. Some studies have elaborated on this connection. Guger and Marterbauer (2004) state, for example:

> Globalisation in the course of east-western integration and increased initial public offerings of businesses form the structural basis for changes in functional distribution. Restructuring measures and dismissals of co-workers to form lean businesses tighten the labour market situation and weaken the position of the employees, and, facing integrationally determined adjustment problems, wage policy had to comply with international competitiveness rather than with the goal of stable distribution. (Guger and Marterbauer 2004, 39)

Alfred Stiglbauer arrives at a similar conclusion:

> As measured by the negotiated wages, real wages increased on average by 1.8 per cent in the reference decade and since the accession to the EU by 0.7 per cent. The median annual increase of wages and salaries . . . per capita amounted to 2 per cent from 1985 to 1994 and 0.3 per cent in the EU-decade . . . Though the growth in work productivity has decreased, the change of real wages has noticeably stayed behind the growth of work productivity since the EU accession. (Stiglbauer 2005, 171)

Arguing along the same lines, Fritz Breuss (2007) sees a close connection between the eastern enlargement of the EU and the decrease of wage rates in Austria. He states that the strong commitment of Austrian businesses in the European East has led to the sharp rise of their profits. This sharp rise of profits in relation to the wages, due to new market prospects in eastern Europe, has – according to Breuss – also contributed to the sinking of the wage rate in Austria.

Against this background, with high unemployment rates having a disciplinary effect on the employees, and with the Austrian labour market facing increased global competition, the EU-integration process has considerably increased the pressure to perform for employees. Therefore, many of them see European integration process as a 'giant machine to enforce efficiency'; they experience European integration as a process putting increased pressure to perform on them while at the same time real wages stagnate or sink (see Heschl 2004, Heschl and Kirisits 2000).

3.3   THE AUSTRIAN DEBATE ON THE EASTERN ENLARGEMENT OF THE EU

The debate on the potential effects of the eastern enlargement of the EU on the Austrian labour market must be considered in light of the country's earlier experiences with labour migration as described in the previous section. A number of scientific papers were published at that time – not only in Austria, but also in other EU states. Many of these papers tried to calculate the possible migration potential of the new member states into the 'old' EU member states.[4] In one important study, Ewald Walterskirchen and Raimund Dietz concluded in 1998:

> In the course of the eastern enlargement of the EU, there will be – after granting mobility – an inflow of foreign workforce, amounting to the same level as the one at the beginning of the 1990s. The calculations of WIFO (Austrian Institute for Economic Research) show that – because of the high differences in

income and due to held-back supply – there would be an additional workforce supply of about 47 000 people in the Austrian labour market as a result of an immediate eastern enlargement of the EU without transitional arrangements. Of these 47 000, 26 000 would be commuting from their residence and 21 000 would immigrate. It is highly improbable, though, that we will see an immediate accession of the eastern states without transitional arrangements. It is more realistic to assume that accession of the central and eastern European countries will occur around the year 2005. If there are no transitional arrangements on the labour market, then we still have to anticipate about 42 000 immigrants and commuters annually because of the considerable difference in living standards. (Walterskirchen and Dietz 1998, 1–2)

Although these conclusions have been criticized in the scientific community and by the public – other studies in this context arrived at (slightly) different migration potentials (cf. Huber and Brücker 2003) – the hardly disputed core of the debate concluded that an enlargement of the European Union without the introduction of transitional arrangements for labour mobility would put Austria in the same situation it experienced in the years 1990 and 1991. In fact, Austrian employee representatives had already demanded these transitional arrangements from the Austrian federal government in the late 1990s. Within the European Union and due to a similar geographical position, only the Federal Republic of Germany faced the same situation. Therefore, debates about the introduction of transitional arrangements originated in both countries; in each case the debates were dominated by the competing interests of employers' and employees' lobbies.

The situation in Austria regarding lobbyists was unique in that Austria has two different organizations that represent employers' interests. The *Wirtschaftskammer Österreich* (Austrian Federal Economic Chamber, based on legal and obligatory membership) and the *Industriellenvereinigung* (Federation of Austrian Industry, based on association statutes and voluntary membership) differ regarding their members and thus also regarding the interests they represent. The Austrian Federal Economic Chamber is formed by many small and medium-sized businesses; big companies are a minority in the Chamber. Members of the Federation of Austrian Industry are mostly big, export-oriented Austrian industrial enterprises. Due to this difference the Federation of Austrian Industry pleaded predominantly against transitional arrangements. From the employers' point of view, this makes sense; the expected migration flows without transitional arrangements would have held workforce supply constant and high, thus further strengthening the employers' bargaining power in framing work relationships.

The Austrian Federal Economic Chamber, on the other hand, had to balance a number of different interests. In general, the small and medium-sized businesses that dominate the Austrian Federal Economic Chamber are also interested in a large and increasing workforce supply. This supply strengthens their position and widens their scope in bargaining collective contracts, which traditionally happens between organizational units of the Austrian Federal Economic Chamber and trade unions in Austria. On the other hand, representatives of the Austrian Federal Economic Chamber were aware that the adoption of the four fundamental freedoms by the new member states and their full integration into the Single European Market would bring their members new competitors in the Austrian merchandise and service markets. The big, export-oriented businesses represented by the Federation of Austrian Industry were better prepared to cope with this new pressure of competition, due to their experience of highly competitive markets. However, the smaller businesses that they represented, which normally operated on a regional basis, viewed this scenario more as a threat. Positioning the Austrian Federal Economic Chamber and weighing different interests concerning transitional arrangements was therefore difficult from the outset.

When it became clear in the course of the EU accession negotiations with central and eastern European states that transitional arrangements in labour mobility would also mean transitional arrangements in services (mainly because of Germany's pressure), the Austrian Federal Economic Chamber committed itself to accepting this package of transitional arrangements for labour mobility and services mobility. A balance of interests of the majority of employers' and employees' lobbies in Austria was thus achieved at that time and a stable political majority concerning this issue was obtained. As a consequence of this majority, the Austrian federal government decided to make use of this package of transitional arrangements from the beginning of the enlargement on 1 May 2004. For labour mobility, this meant that Austria could – temporarily, for two years – retain the regulations of the Foreign People Employment Act in a modified form, and then after providing notice to the EU, it could retain it for three more years. The labour market transitional arrangements will end on 30 April 2009. If Austria can provide evidence for current or future disruptions to the labour market, the transitional arrangements can be called upon for two more years.

After the enlargement the use of transitional arrangements remained a central point of discussion among employers' and employees' lobbies, the media, and in scientific and sociopolitical debates. One could often hear the wrong argument that transitional arrangements would bring with them a complete sealing-off of the Austrian labour market for citizens of the new member states. Statements like 'immigrants of the new EU member states now have the right of residence but no access to the legal labour market' (Münz 2007, 113) or 'the ban of the workforce from the new EU states in the Austrian labour market is being loosened. In principle, the labour market is completely closed until 2011' ('Zeit im Bild'– the most popular news programme on Austrian TV, February 2007) exemplify these arguments. Every now and then they were supplemented with reproaches by the employees' lobby for defending the transitional arrangements out of sheer populism, 'backward thinking', 'global resentment' or because of their latent xenophobia. It should have become clear in the course of the earlier analyses of labour market and income growth in Austria that the employee lobby possesses different motives for retaining transitional arrangements, namely that the use of these transitional arrangements has not led to a 'complete sealing-off' of the labour market, but to a controlled access.

Labour Migration to Austria since 2004

From 2004 to 2006, the employment of people from the new EU member states, especially Poland, Hungary, the Czech Republic and Slovakia, increased by about 6000 people (calculated as full-year employments). This number does not, however, include other employment forms where statistical data is not available, such as self-employment, freelance contracts or employees in limited part-time employment. At the same time, the number of labour migrants from the traditional immigration countries, Turkey and the former Yugoslavia stagnated. Moreover, due to high immigration numbers from Germany, the proportion of people from Turkey and the former Yugoslavia of all employed foreigners in 2007 was only 53.9 per cent. It is clear that the use of transitional arrangements has not led to a complete sealing-off of the Austrian labour market for people from the new EU member states. If – as laid down in the accession treaties – the goal of the transitional arrangements is a slow and balanced integration into the labour market, then this goal has been partially achieved. The first trend changes which were aimed at are discernible; labour migration from the traditional immigration countries stagnates and labour migration from the new EU member states is on the rise.

Other evidence strongly countering the rhetoric about 'sealing-off' the country is the growth in the number of labour migrants from the new member states and the development of various forms of legal status for these people in the Austrian labour market. The Foreign People Employment Act provides different forms of authorization, such as short-term temporary authorizations ('Saisonniers', 'Erntehelfer'), those linked to a certain company ('Beschäftigungsbewilligung') or to a certain federal country

Table 3.3   Employed foreigners according to nationality from 1995–2006

Nationality	1995	2000	2004	2005	2006	Change 1995–2006 in %
All foreigners	300328	319394	361767	373692	389894	+29.8
EEA-countries	21476	32456	53103	61997	71226	+231.7
EU15	21101	32237	52848	61743	70950	+ 236.2
EFTA	375	219	255	254	276	-26.4
Former Yugoslavia	147030	158276	159756	156886	156000	+5.6
(Slovenia)	(5802)				(4951)	
Turkey	54733	57098	54655	53483	54071	1.2
Germany	13438	20822	38593	46726	55006	+ 309.3
Poland	11186	11154	11968	12591	13384	+19.7
Hungary	9423	10378	13567	14657	15732	+67.0
Romania	9575	9642	11016	11305	11675	+21.9
former Czechoslovakia	10455	9968	12346	13682	14698	+40.6
Bulgaria	1478				2118	+43.3
Italy	2627	3856	4796	5101	5429	+106.7
Switzerland	872	1154	1387	1498	1631	+87.0
Others	31959	37046	5 683	57763	62268	+94.8

Source: Hauptverband der österreichischen Sozialversicherungsträger, Statistische Daten aus der Sozialversicherung. Beschäftigte Ausländer in Österreich, Jahresdurchschnitte 1995–2006 [statistical data from social insurance funds. Employed foreigners in Austria. Annual average 1995–2006].

('Arbeitserlaubnis') and two different authorizations which guarantee full mobility in the Austrian labour market: the so-called 'Befreiungsschein', and since the eastern enlargement of the European Union for citizens from the new EU member states the so-called 'Freizügigkeitsbestätigung'. The number of *Freizügigkeitsbestätigungen* for new EU citizens and their relatives has reached almost 28000 between 2004 and 2006. The beneficiaries can take up salaried employment in any sector and at any time anywhere in Austria (cf. Arbeitsmarktservice Österreich, Geschäftsbericht 2006, 43).

The regulatory function of the transitional arrangements for the Austrian labour market concerning the still existing bigger migration potential from the new member states shows itself by the obvious violation of these regulations in the field of 'Scheinselbstständigkeit' [pseudo-self-employment]. The transitional arrangements in labour mobility only concern salaried employment; self-employment is not restricted. By registering a trade, employees from the new member states formally appear as entrepreneurs. In reality, however, they perform the same work as employees. In some subtrades in the construction industry, the number of trade registrations by citizens of the new member states has skyrocketed since 1 May 2004.

Restricting access to the labour market by using the transitional arrangements for a maximum of seven years was also undertaken to guarantee that the immense differences in wages between the new and old EU member states could be lessened and that the high level of unemployment in the new member states at the time of accession could be reduced. The basis of these considerations was the favourable growth prospects for the new EU member states. Even if such wage differences are rather rigid and will not level off in the foreseeable future, the developments over the last few years show a noticeably higher wage rise in the new EU member states than in Austria (cf. OECD Economic Outlook 2/2006).

The retention of the transitional arrangements in Austria is currently a much discussed politico-economic matter. The Federation of Austrian Industry vehemently demands that the arrangements be eased or abolished. If this occurs, an increase in the supply of the workforce and thereby the bargaining power of the employers is likely. To this end, the myth of 'shortage of skilled workers' is revived – again.

Myths as Instruments in Distribution Matters

Corroborating statements, arguments, positions and demands with concrete numbers or at least rough quantitative calculations play an important role in the public discourse surrounding the labour market. Behind these numbers and the calculations there are generally tangible interests, the production and dissemination of myths which rely on numbers is a crucial feature in public debate about labour market matters. It is only through simplification by the mass media that complex, labour market relevant political contexts become understandable; it is only through the reduction of complexity by the mass media that political policy formation is basically made possible. This is considerably facilitated by a system of politics which knows about the dependences, conditions and requirements of the other system and can therefore deliver suitable input for the mass media.

It is not the coarse isolated simplifications which are more likely to be 'believed' by the public, but the simple correlations, comprehensible, easily disseminated and capable of gaining the character of truth mainly through constant repetition – in the media, but also in one's own social peer group. These simplification techniques are outstandingly well used for the building of myths. According to Roland Barthes a myth is a statement, a specific system of information, a message, and a way of meaning (Barthes 1964, 85–133). The myth is a specific projection giving a specific meaning to a specific statement. The meaning of the myth postulates knowledge. However, the knowledge incorporated in the myth is clouded, made from indeterminate, infinite associations.

It is exactly this diffuse meaning, this openness for associations that turns a myth into an apt instrument to push certain interests in labour market matters. Barthes also pointed at this instrumentalization of myths, which is based on interests. Myths never exist out of themselves; they always serve a specific purpose or are useful for specific interests. The intentions, which lie behind a myth, are not hidden as a matter of principle, yet they seem natural. A myth also has a challenging, interpellative character. These features of expression of expectations and insinuation of how to act are characteristic of the revival of the myth of the 'shortage of skilled workers' in the public debate in Austria about the enlargement of the European Union and about retention versus abolition of transitional arrangements in labour mobility.

The myth of the 'shortage of skilled workers' has been part of the standard repertoire of public and media debates in Austria for the past twenty years. As early as 1989, Zilian noted that 'the media lament about the shortage of skilled workers . . . has become chronic, the topic having mutated to a classic' (Zilian 1989, 18). In this paper, Zilian makes a detailed analysis of the problem of entrepreneurs or businesses in filling vacancies according to their wishes and desires and how they could contrive the social and economic problem as a 'shortage of skilled workers'.

We do not want to deny the real problems entrepreneurs or businesses have in filling certain vacancies. These problems are based on a wide range of factors. These include specific insecurities of economic life, which make long-term planning almost impossible for entrepreneurs, as well as specific human resource policy adjustment strategies of entrepreneurs as a reaction to fluctuations in capacity utilization. They want to keep staff numbers small because of competition, which of course quickly leads to a sudden demand in workforce with peak capacity. Poor or below average working and payment conditions in an enterprise may also contribute to this problem.

It is, however, only the convergence of entrepreneurs' wishes and a media spotlight supportive of this position which turns individual employment problems into a 'general shortage of skilled workers'. It is obvious that employers are generally interested in such a public myth. If the public image of the 'shortage of skilled workers' prevails, politics will tend to take action to extend workforce supply. Regulations may be introduced defining jobs which an unemployed person must accept, as well as with regard to matters concerning the employment of foreign people. These measures to extend workforce supply are, in principle, beneficial for the employers. On the one hand, they expand the options of the employers; on the other, they have a controlling effect on the employees because the risk that they will be exchanged out of the now bigger workforce supply increases. Employers do indeed always look for someone who performs the same work with the same quality but cheaper, faster, more flexibly,and so forth. In this sense – and only in this sense – employers do indeed have a 'shortage of skilled workers'.

The myth of the shortage of skilled workers was reactivated and reinforced again and again in the course of the EU enlargement debate and then in the debate about retaining transitional arrangements. When the two central Austrian employees' lobbies – *Arbeiterkammer* (Chamber of Labour) and *Österreichischer Gewerkschaftsbund* (Federation of Austrian Trade Unions) – warned against a quick opening of the labour market after the enlargement and advocated transitional arrangements, the employers' organizations used the shortage of skilled workers argument and the manner such a state can threaten the welfare system.

In 2001, a study compiled by the Austrian Institute for Economic Research (Walterskichen 2001) and commissioned by the Austrian Federal Economic Chamber projected a shortage of 165 000 workers until 2005. In the following years, 2002 and 2003, the revived myth of 'shortage of skilled workers' was again cultivated. The following is an example of the use of the myth in 2002:

> The president of the Federation of Austrian Industry . . . advocates selective immigration of the qualified workforce from the EU accession countries to Austria. He says, it is only then that the imminent shortage of skilled workers can be met. The negotiated transitional arrangements for the labour market should be shortened in the course of the EU enlargement . . . As Austria anticipates a large-scale shortage of skilled workers from 2004, the qualified workforce from the EU accession countries should be allowed to work in Austria before the transitional arrangements have expired. He says, enhanced training and re-training in the next years will not be enough to cover the immense shortage of tens of thousands of skilled workers. (Der Standard, 8/9 June 2002)

Another example comes from a newspaper article in 'Die Presse' in 2003 (20 September 2003). The article reports a general shortage of skilled workers based on the study by WIFO, according to which 'in the year 2008 we will see a shortage of 165 000 wage earners in the Austrian labour market due to demographic changes.' The 'shortage' of 165 000 taken from the media coverage of the year 2001 emerges here again, but in 2001 it was a 'shortage' in 2005, and in 2003 the shortage was postponed to 2008.

In the years 2006 and 2007, the revival of the myth of the shortage of skilled workers reached its peak. By the end of April 2006, Austria had to decide whether to retain the transitional arrangements; part of the employers' lobby (Federation of Austrian Industry) led the public debate about it almost exclusively by employing the myth of the shortage of skilled workers. The Austrian Federal Government decided to prolong the transitional arrangements, but this decision continues to be fought to this day. Headlines such as: 'Shortage of skilled workers. Even retirees are being called back' (Kronen Zeitung, 19 July 2007), 'Survey: Shortage of qualified workforce is biggest impediment to growth' (Die Presse, 11 July 2007), 'Shortage of qualified workforce is spreading' (Die Presse, 11 July 2007), 'Qualified workforce already scarce' (Kronen Zeitung, 13 June 2007), 'Shortage without borders' (Kleine Zeitung, 23 April 2007), 'Shortage of thousands of skilled workers' (Der Standard, 24/25 February 2007) replaced other economic issues in the media.

The 'calculations' of the quantitative dimension of the alleged problem reveal the mythical character of the statements in these articles. At the end of February 2007, the secretary general of the Federation of Austrian Industry was cited: 'there is an annual shortage of 5000 to 7000 skilled workers' (Der Standard, 24/25 February 2007). Three weeks earlier the Austrian Federal Economic Chamber claimed that there will be a shortage of 15000 to 16000 skilled workers in the years 2007 and 2008 respectively (NZZ, 27/28 January 2007). In May 2007, the president of the Austrian Federal Economic Chamber said that there will be a demand for 50000 new skilled workers in the next seven years (Kleine Zeitung, 19 May 2007). Weeks earlier a commentary in a newspaper reported that according to the Ministry of Economics there would be a shortage of 50000 skilled workers by 2009 (Die Presse, 25 April 2007). Some months before that, there was a quotation from the president of the Austrian Federal Economic Chamber saying, 'in Austria there is a shortage of 150000 skilled workers' (Der Standard, 22 January 2007).

3.4 CONCLUSION

This chapter shows that the issue of how to steer labour migration in Austria in the context of the European integration process is closely associated with income distribution issues. Political positions are legitimated by myth building and myth utilization; an example of which is the creation of the myth of the shortage of skilled workers. Zilian (1989) described the permanent existence of this myth and its tight interrelation with the media and some sectors of entrepreneurial activity. This interrelation can spur a dynamic which suddenly turns vague announcements of expansion, or rather diffuse, non-concrete, far-future estimations of entrepreneurs into the 'shortage of skilled workers', of which large parts of the public – including the entrepreneurs themselves – are then virtually convinced that it represents an objective economic problem.

This chapter supplements this argument with the notion that entrepreneurs do, in fact, always have a shortage of skilled workers, but only in the sense that they are generally looking for employees who would perform the job at the same quality but cheaper, faster and more flexibly than the ones who are already employed. Furthermore, the permanent retention of the media construct 'shortage of skilled workers' meets the employees' lobby halfway in many respects and facilitates the political implementation of employees' interests. This was made clear with the example of the revival of the myth of the 'shortage of skilled workers' in the course of the EU enlargement debate and the debate about the extension of transitional arrangements concerning labour mobility.

Apart from these distributional and mythical aspects, the chapter also demonstrated that the use of the transitional arrangements has not led to a complete sealing-off of the Austrian labour market for citizens of the new EU member states; quantitatively, their number has risen, qualitatively, their legal status has improved by the so-called *Freizügigkeitsbestätigung*. The transitional arrangements could thus be regarded as an instrument of balance between employers' and employees' interests concerning the issue of labour migration. Their usage has not hindered a rise in workforce supply, though this rise was organized moderately in the interest of the employees; the consequence has been not the complete sealing-off of the country, but immigration which is partly regulated.

NOTES

1. These key points have been developed from Brandel *et al.* (1994), Winter-Ebmer and Zweimüller (1996) and Pollan (2000).
2. In the group of Austrians with salaried employment, this number was 52.94 per cent for men in 2006.
3. For the sectors of employment of foreign people cf. Hauptverband der österreichischen Sozialversicherungsträger, Statistische Daten aus der Sozialversicherung. Beschäftigte Ausländer in Österreich, Jahrgänge 1995–2006 (employed foreigners in Austria, years 1995–2006).
4. Fassmann and Münz (2003) offer an excellent overview of the results and the research methods of these investigations.

REFERENCES

Arbeitsmarktservice Österreich (1994–1999), Bewilligungspflichtig beschäftigte AusländerInnen.
Barthes, R. (1964), *Mythen des Alltags*, Frankfurt am Main: Suhrkamp-Verlag.
Biffl, G. (2002), 'Ausländische Arbeitskräfte auf dem österreichischen Arbeitsmarkt', *WIFO-Monatsberichte*, 8, 537–50.
Brandel, F., H. Hofer and K. Pichelmann (1994), *Verdrängungsprozesse am Arbeitsmarkt*, IHS-Forschungsbericht 345, Wien: IHS.

Breuss, F. (2007), *Globalization, Eu Enlargement and Income Distribution*, WIFO working paper 296, Wien:WIFO.

Breuss, F. and F. Schebeck (1996), 'Ostöffnung und Osterweiterung der EU. Ökonomische Auswirkungen auf Österreich', *WIFO–Monatsberichte*, 2, 139–51.

Bundesarbeitskammer (2003), Fünf Forderungen für eine faire EU-Erweiterung, ein Memorandum der AK an die Regierung.

Bundesarbeitskammer (various years), Wirtschafts- und Sozialstatistisches Taschenbuch.

Bundesministerium für Arbeit und Soziales (1989–1993), Ausländerbeschäftigung.

Fassmann, H. and R. Münz (2003), 'Auswirkungen der EU-Erweiterung auf die Ost-West-Wanderung', *WSI–Mitteilungen*, 1, 25–32.

Guger, A. and M. Marterbauer (2004), *Die langfristige Entwicklung der Einkommensverteilung in Österreich*, Wien: WIFO.

Hauptverband der österreichischen Sozialversicherungsträger (1995–2006), Statistische Daten aus der Sozialversicherung, Beschäftigte Ausländer in Österreich.

Heschl, F. (2004), '. . . mehr können wir eh nicht mehr arbeiten . . .', EU-Erweiterungsperspektiven von Arbeitnehmerinnen und Arbeitnehmern im Kontrast zu arbeitsweltbezogenen Mythen in der öffentlichen EU-Erweiterungsdebatte, Graz: Arbeiterkammer.

Heschl, F. and M. Kirisits (2000), *Es weht ein rauerer Wind! Aspekte eines Stimmungsbildes zu den Auswirkungen von EU–Mitgliedschaft, Ostöffnung und Globalisierung in steirischen Industrieunternehmen*, Graz: Arbeiterkammer.

Huber, P. and H. Brücker (2003), *Auswirkungen und Ausnutzung von Übergangsfristen für die Freizügigkeit der Arbeitskräfte nach der EU–Erweiterung*, Wien: WIFO.

Münz, R. (2007), 'Migration in Europa, migration in der Welt', *Europäische Rundschau*, 2, 105–122.

OECD (2006), *OECD Economic Outlook 2006, Issue 2*, Paris: OECD.

OECD (2007), *International Migration Outlook 2007*, Paris: OECD.

Pollan, W. (2000), 'Die volkswirtschaftlichen Auswirkungen der Zuwanderung von Arbeitskräften. Ein Literaturüberblick', *WIFO–Monatsberichte*, 2, 95–112.

Statistik Austria (various years), Mikrozensus Arbeitskräfteerhebung.

Statistik Austria (various years), Mikrozensus Jahresergebnisse.

Statistik Austria (various years), Statistisches Jahrbuch Österreichs.

Stiglbauer, A. (2005), 'Hat der EU- und WWU-Beitritt den österreichischen Arbeitsmarkt verändert? Bestandsaufnahme und Handlungsagenda', *Geldpolitik & Wirtschaft*, 2, 164–81.

Walterskirchen, E. (2001), 'Knappheit an Arbeitskräften', *WIFO-Monatsberichte*, 6, 391–5.

Walterskirchen, E. and R. Dietz (1998), *Auswirkungen der EU-Osterweiterung auf den österreichischen Arbeitsmarkt*, Wien: WIFO.

Winter-Ebmer, R. and J. Zweimüller (1996), 'Die Auswirkungen der Ausländerbeschäftigung auf den österreichischen Arbeitsmarkt 1988 bis 1991', in R. Holzmann and R. Neck (eds), *Ostöffnung: Wirtschaftliche Folgen für Österreich*, Wien: Manz Verlag, pp. 55–104.

Zilian, H.G. (1989), *Wo ein Wille ist, ist auch ein Werk: Arbeitsbedingungen und Arbeitslosigkeit im Wohlfahrtsstaat*, unter Mitarbeit von Hanna Begusch, Josef Hödl, Johannes Moser, Graz.

4. Understanding migration decisions in Eastern and Western Europe: perceived costs and benefits of mobility

Didier Fouarge and Peter Ester

4.1 INTRODUCTION

With the accession of ten new member states to the European Union in May 2004, the issue of geographic and labour market mobility within Europe has taken a very prominent position on the EU policy agenda. The fact that the year 2006 was officially chosen as the 'European Year of Workers' Mobility' reflects the policy saliency of the mobility issue. It is evident that the mobility question is here to stay in Europe. The idea in economics – but also in the broader social sciences – is that there are potential gains to both geographic and job mobility. Such gains are derived, in the first place, from the relocation of labour from regions with a surplus of workers to regions with labour shortages. In the second place, such gains result from a more efficient allocation of labour to activities and regions where they are (likely to be) more productive.

However, despite large differences in economic performance across regions of Europe, geographic mobility has remained at a relatively low level. According to a recent study by the European Commission, the share of non-nationals in the EU amounts to 5.5 per cent of the total population in 2004 (European Commission 2006, 210). The large majority is from outside the EU, followed by nationals from other EU15 countries. Only 0.2 per cent is from one of the new member states, but relatively larger shares are observed in Ireland, Austria and Germany (European Commission 2006). The non-national Dutch population, according to these data, amounts to 4.3 per cent. Overall in Europe, the yearly rate of cross-border mobility is estimated to be 0.4 per cent. The numbers recently published by the European Foundation suggest a similar picture: only 4 per cent of the EU population lived in another EU country in the past, and 3 per cent lived in another country outside the EU (Vandenbrande *et al.*

2006, 14). Although the rates of regional mobility are larger – 18 per cent lived in another region than the current region of residence – these figures are low compared with mobility data in the US. Europe seems to lack a 'culture of mobility'. The US Census Bureau indeed shows that 32 per cent of the US citizens live outside the state in which they were born. However, it must be noted that interstate mobility movement within the US is still mobility within the same country, language area and culture, which is not the case for intra-EU movement.[1]

Despite these actual low mobility percentages, the fear for mass migration from east to west has led most EU countries to close their borders at the time of the enlargement to labour migrants from central and eastern European countries. In fact, at the time of the 2004 enlargement, only the UK, Ireland and Sweden opened their borders to migrants from the new member states, a decision that has had no negative impact on the economic performance of these three countries (Zimmerman 2007). While more countries opened their borders to labour migrants in 2006 (Finland, and the Southern member states Greece, Italy, Spain and Portugal), other labour markets remained closed (Germany and Austria) or only accessible under specific circumstances.

The research reported in this chapter focuses on the migration intentions of Europeans and investigates the main determinants of these intentions: in particular, we shed light on the cost-benefit analysis aspects of the migration decision in different parts of Europe. The main advantage of studying mobility intentions – rather than study migrants in their destination country – is that this approach is not biased by selectivity issues. There is indeed a large body of literature showing that migrants self-select in labour markets where their return-to-skills is expected to be larger. Moreover, literature suggests that it is not mobility per se that is of interest in socio-economic models, but the potential for mobility (see also Liebig and Sousa-Poza 2004, Hadler 2006). More specifically, this chapter investigates three main issues:

- the impact of past experience with mobility – and mobility – on intended migration in the near future;
- differences and changes in migration intentions of people in the new and old members states; and
- the effect of perceived costs and benefits on migration intentions in Europe.

In doing so, this chapter aims at providing the current societal and policy debate on understanding motives of and preferences for migration. Such an input will hopefully generate a more accurate assessment of the migration intention potential in Europe through a better understanding of how people personally weigh the pros and cons of migration. We make use of the 2005 Eurobarometer Mobility Survey (EB64.1), the most recent Europe-wide survey on mobility intentions, including samples from all – both old and new – Member states (see Vandenbrande *et al.* 2006).

4.2 THEORETICAL BACKGROUND, PREVIOUS RESEARCH AND EXPECTATIONS

Costs and Benefits of Migration

There is an impressive body of theoretical and empirical socio-economic literature on migration. Generally speaking, in its most simple form the migration decision can be stated as follows: an individual will migrate from the current location A to region or country B if the expected utility of moving to B is higher that the expected utility from staying in A, net of migration costs. This means that an individual will migrate to B if:

$$U_{iA}(E_{iA}, D_{iA}, S_{iA}, M_A) < U_{iB}(E_{iB}, D_{iB}, S_{iB}, M_B) - C_{iA \to B}(f, d_i, c_i)$$
(4.1)

where U_i represents utility of individual i in A or B, that depends on socio-economic attributes (E_i; such as the labour market status, the level of human capital), demographic attributes (D_i; such as the household composition), social and cultural attributes (S_i; such as social ties or language) and how they are valued in the home country (A) and the host country (B), respectively. In addition to this, utility from migration can also depend on macroeconomic and societal characteristics that are valued by the individual (M; such as the general labour market and economic situation). C represents the costs to migration for individual i. These expenditures consist of out of pocket costs equal to all (f), costs related to the distance of the move (d), and psycho-cultural costs (c) that are specific for each individual.

Holding everything else constant, individual i will migrate if he or she expects a higher utility elsewhere, net of cost for relocation. Henceforth, the migration decision is a positive function of expected utility in the destination country (say, the benefits from migration), and a negative function of migration costs. The available migration literature specifies several factors that are likely to affect the decision to move. These factors can be classified into micro (individual level) and macro (aggregate) determinants of migration. Although in this research we only deal with micro determinants of migration, macro determinants will be briefly discussed in this section.

According to the literature, economic self-improvement is probably the most influential determinant of the migration choice. Both the immediate employment and wage opportunities in the host country (Harris and Todaro 1970), and the future expected wage and employment prospects seem to matter (Sjaastad 1962). In fact, the decision of whether or not to migrate has been shown to crucially depend on the perceived earnings growth in the host country (Chiswick 1978). In this respect, human capital is expected to be a strong determinant of migration (Sjaastad 1962).

Another major determinant of migration is related to demographics such as age and household formation or dissolution events. Also, the presence of children has been shown to affect international migration in a negative manner. Literature indicates that the migration decision is not just an individual decision, but that it is primarily a household choice. First, a household will only decide to migrate when the utility gains form migration of some of the household members compensate for the utility losses of other household members (Mincer 1978). Second, it has been argued that migration can be seen as risk-sharing behaviour (Stark 1991). Furthermore, the homeownership status of the individual and their household constitutes a major cost factor for migration (OECD 2005)

The stock social capital is important and works in two ways. Social ties in the home country appear to operate as a major cost factor to migration (Belot and Ermisch 2006a). This is because migration is expected to result in lesser social interactions with (and hence erosion of) existing social ties. However, the availability of social networks in the destination country clearly stimulates migration (Massey *et al.* 1993, Massey *et al.* 1994, Zavodny 1997, Hatton and Williamson 2002). This is because destination country social capital contributes to better information.

A further interesting finding is that future mobility is also affected by past mobility: movers tend to stay movers (Vandenbrande *et al.* 2006, Liebig and Sousa-Poza 2004). Past mobility is likely to reduce the total cost of future mobility because it lowers the psychological cost of mobility as well as its actual cost due to the availability of better information. An interesting hypothesis to be tested is whether the reason (labour-related or socio-demographic reason) people moved in the past matters.

At the macro-level the literature has investigated the effect of the overall level of unemployment and economic wealth on migration (Hatton and Williamson 2002, Pedersen *et al.* 2004). The tax and social security systems have been pointed at as triggers for migration (Borjas 1987, 1999). Finally, despite economic incentives to migration, non-economic macro determinants such as cultural and linguistic proximity, have been shown to be important determinants of the costs of migration (Belot and Ederveen 2006b).[2]

Expectations: Past Mobility and Perceived Costs and Benefits

As outlined above, the migration literature suggests a variety of factors likely to affect the decision to migrate. In this section we formulate and motivate a number of expectations with regard to the migration decision and explain in what way they relate to the parameters in Equation 4.1 specified above. There is, to date, already ample evidence suggesting that human capital is a strong determinant of migration: those who expect higher returns from migration (the highly educated) have been shown to be more likely to migrate, as well as those for whom the pay-back period for incurred costs is long (youth). The effects of demographic character-istics are well-documented too: for singles and childless people, the costs to migration are lower. What has received less attention – due to lack of data – is the effect of past mobility experience, and of perceived costs and benefits of migration.

Past migration is expected to influence the intention to move (DaVanzo 1983). People who made (frequent) moves have developed social networks in several geographical locations (parameters S_{iA} and S_{iB} in Equation 4.1), they know how to build and maintain social networks. For those who migrated in the past, the psycho-social costs of mobility are likely to be lower (parameter c_i in Equation 4.1). Besides, they have better information – based on personal experience – concerning the various cost-aspects of migration, and are consequently better able to evaluate the costs and benefits of mobility.

However, it is likely that the reason for past mobility is an important factor too. People who moved for demographic reasons (for example marriage) have invested in long-lasting relationships. They have increased their stock of social capital in the current place of residence, which makes them less likely to move again in the future (parameter S_{iA} in Equation 4.1). On the contrary, people who moved for job-related reasons are not primarily investing in long-lasting relationships. They are more aware of their employment opportunities and how to optimize work and income conditions. If better opportunities arise, they may change employers again. Therefore, we expect that people who moved for work-related reasons are more likely to express the intention to move again, while people who moved for demographic or family reasons are less likely to express such intentions.

The way people perceive the potential costs and benefits of migration is expected to codetermine the propensity to move. If people expect negative effects for their employment or income position, they will have a lower intention to move (parameter E_{iB} in Equation 4.1). By the same token, if people expect negative effects from migration for their social networks, they will be less inclined to migrate because moving would entail a reduction of their social ties (parameter S_{iB} in Equation 4.1), and because of the high psycho-social costs of mobility (parameter c_i in Equation 4.1). Finally, the lack of language skills is expected to impede people in their migration decision because it increases the costs of mobility (parameter c_i in Equation 4.1). On the contrary, perceived gains from migration – especially labour market related gains – are expected to boost migration intentions (parameter E_{iB} in Equation 4.1).

Personal views with respect to mobility and expectations with respect to the potential effects of mobility are likely to be important determinants too. People holding positive views on mobility are expected to have a higher inclination to migrate than people who hold negative views on mobility. This is because positive views about migration reflect lower psycho-social costs of migration (parameter c_i in Equation 4.1).

4.3   DATA

The findings presented in this study are based on analyses on a special module of the Eurobarometer: the Eurobarometer Mobility Survey (EB 64.1). The survey was financed by the European Commission and data were collected in all 25 EU countries in September 2005; the study was conducted in close cooperation with the European Foundation (Vandenbrande *et al.* 2006, Karpinnen *et al.* 2006, Krieger 2006).[3] The Mobility Survey is the most recent and most comprehensive survey on mobility intentions and attitudes among samples from *all* EU countries, both old and new member states, including about 24 500 respondents – aged 15 years and over – in total.[4] The basic sample design applied in all states is a multi-stage, random (probability) one. In each country, a number of sampling points was drawn with probability proportional to population size (for a total coverage of the country) and to population density. Use was made of face-to-face interviews and in the appropriate national language. As far as the data capture is concerned, CAPI (Computer Assisted Personal Interview) was used in those countries where this technique was available.

Some 1000 respondents were interviewed per country. In small countries such as Luxembourg and Malta only 500 people were interviewed. The samples for West and East Germany were merged so that we have some 1500 cases in Germany. The samples for Great Britain and Northern

Ireland were also merged, resulting in some 1300 cases for the UK. When weighted, the data are representative for the national population. The analyses presented in this chapter pertain to the population aged 18 to 64.

The Eurobarometer Mobility Survey covers a number of issues related to both geographical and labour market mobility in Europe, including short and long distance past and future mobility, motives for and effects of past and future mobility, mobility intentions (within and between . countries), and encouraging and discouraging factors to move within and outside of the EU.

Our main (dependent) variable of interest pertains to mobility intentions for the next five years. The question was phrased as follows: 'Do you think that in the next five years you are likely to move: in the same city/town/ village; to another city/town/village but in the same region; to another region but in the same country; to another country in the European Union; to another country outside the European Union; you don't think you will move.' More than one answer could be given to the question. The total number of respondents (aged 18–64) that expressed their mobility intention amounts to 17 493 persons.[5]

The Eurobarometer Mobility Survey dataset includes relevant background information of the respondent (gender, age, educational level), his or her household (marital status, children), labour market status (whether working or unemployed, occupational status), and labour market experience (age at first job, number of jobs in the past). The data also contain relevant information on respondents' past geographic mobility. The main disadvantage of this special mobility module of the 2005 Eurobarometer study, it has to be stressed, is that it neither carries information concerning the location or country people intend to move to, nor on the intended duration of the stay in the destination country.

Just how reliable are migration intentions data? The decision to move is a complex, multi-faceted choice. This is, of course, particularly true when long distances and/or cross-border moves are involved that generate a complete change of social environment that deeply impacts one's life-course. 'This often involves a loss of established social networks of family and friends and the challenge of integration into a new job, a different social security system and a new social environment, often with the need to learn a new language' (Krieger 2006, 2). Merely measuring the intention to move as a sole indicator of the act to move ignores the complexity of the move decision process. Many desiderata, possibilities, constraints, and consequences have to be taken into consideration and are very likely to mediate the relationships between the intention to move and the act to move. We know from psychological decision theory and attitude theory that behavioural intentions – as general predispositions – only under certain conditions predict actual behaviour. Moreover, the intention to act itself is a function of many factors. One of the most classic approaches is the well-known theory of reasoned action by Fishbein and Ajzen (1975) which assumes that the behaviour to act depends on the intention to perform that behaviour which in turn is a function of two factors: the attitude towards that behaviour, and the subjective norm with respect to performing that behaviour. In turn, attitude is a function of beliefs about the consequences of performing that behaviour, and one's evaluations of those consequences, whereas the subjective norm is a function of beliefs about normative consequences with respect to the behaviour, and one's motivation to comply with those expectations.

Applied to our subject of mobility: the intention to move is a function of the attitude towards moving and existing subjective norms towards moving; the attitude towards moving is a function of beliefs about the (positive and negative) consequences of moving and the evaluations of these consequences; the subjective norm towards moving is a function of the normative (positive and negative) beliefs about moving and one's motivation to comply with those beliefs. But between the intention to move and the actual move may be a world of intervening factors: individual skills, alternative behaviours available, situational constraints, institutional barriers, and so forth.

Two lessons for the subject of geographic mobility have to be learned from this short contemplation of determinants of behavioural intentions and the relationship between intention and overt behaviour: the intention to move is a complex decision, and a pro-move intention is not a perfect predictor of actual moving. The implication of all this is that we have to be cautious in interpreting direct answers to direct survey questions on the intention to move, particularly as a straightforward assessment of the actual moving potential, and particularly when cross-bordering long distance moves are concerned. But fortunately, in the Eurobarometer Mobility Survey we do have quite a variety of measurements of possible determinants of the intention to move which enables a (more) balanced interpretation of mobility intentions.

As Manski (1990) shows, the intentions do, under certain circumstances, have a predictive value for future behaviour. Many migration studies make use of (balanced) mobility intention measures: Tidrick (1971), Finifter (1976) and Chiquiar and Hanson (2002) for the US; Burda *et al.* (1998) for Germany; Faini *et al.* (1997) for Italy; Ahn *et al.* (1999) for Spain; Liebig and Sousa-Poza (2004) in an international comparative survey; and Krieger (2004) for accessing and candidate EU countries. Here, we assume that intentions are a monotonic function of the true (unobserved) future behaviour. This assumption is supported by findings of Böheim and Taylor (2002) and Gordon and Molho (1995). Using panel data for Britain, Böheim and Taylor (2002) show that the actual probability to move within Britain is three times higher for people who expressed a preference for moving than for people who did not express such a preference. Gordon and Molho (1995) report on available evidence from a 1980 British survey on actual and potential migration that suggests that at least 90 per cent of the people with a migration intention indeed moved within five years.

There are also three specific advantages to the use of balanced migration intention data. First, in migration models it is not migration itself that is the issue, but often particular migration incentives. It is typically the sheer potential for mobility that explains why countries throw barriers to migration and not mobility itself. Second, migration intentions are gathered in the sending country. This is an advantage compared with host-country migration data because intention data are not plagued by bias due to self-selection effects (see also Liebig and Sousa-Poza 2004). Third, the policy relevance of tapping (determinants of) migration intentions is undisputed and self-evident. Future migration flow is currently probably the hottest topic on the EU policy agenda, both at the level of the EC and of the individual member states.

4.4   DESCRIPTIVE FINDINGS

Migration Intentions in Europe

The following figure reports on the migration intentions in Europe in 2005. Overall 5.4 per cent of the EU citizens intend to move to another country within the next five years, but Figure 4.1 shows that the magnitude of intended migration in Europe in 2005 is very diverse: Europe is far from homogeneous in terms of national migration readiness. Migration intentions are clearly country-specific. Intentions to migrate within the next five years are particularly high in the Baltic States (Lithuania, Latvia and Estonia), Poland and Ireland. Relatively low percentages are found in countries such as the Czech Republic, Spain, Germany, Austria, Italy and Hungary. The difference in mobility intentions in the Baltic States and Poland compared with the other new member states is striking. It is beyond the scope of this chapter to make predictions on expected migration streams in Europe and previous research indeed suggests that the percentage of people with a 'firm intention' to migrate is only about a third of the percentage of the people expressing a general inclination to migrate (Krieger 2004). However, such intentions data is still very valuable when

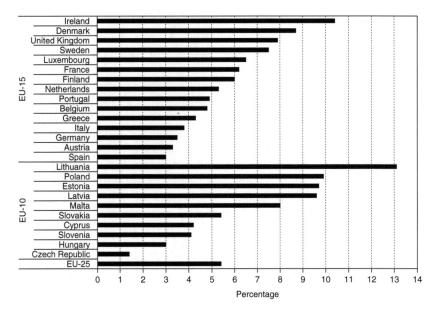

Source: EB 64.1, 2005; base: respondents aged 18–64.

Figure 4.1   Migration intentions in Europe, percentage of people intending to move to another country within or outside the EU within the next five years

it comes to monitor changes over time and to better understand what is shaping such migration preferences.

Changing Migration Patterns in Europe

The enlargement of the EU has led to major changes in actual migratory streams within Europe, especially from the new member states to the old member states. But to what extent does this reflect changes in migration intentions in Europe? Have migration intentions of residents from the new member states indeed increased in the recent past? Using a previous wave of the Eurobarometer (fielded in 2001/2002) we are able to monitor changes in migration in Europe.[6] However, because the questionnaire used in both surveys is not exactly the same, we apply the difference-in-differences method to control for such differences in questionnaires: we compare the change in migration intentions in the old member states in the period 2001–05 to the change in migration intentions in the new member states in the same period.[7]

Table 4.1   *Migration intentions in Europe by educational level,*
            difference-in-differences for the comparison of two EB waves
            (percentages)

	EU15			New member states			Difference-in-differences
	EB 2001	EB 2005	Difference	EB 2002	EB 2005	Difference	
Low or no	1.1	2.1	1.0	0.6	2.1	1.5	0.5
Average	2.4	3.9	1.5	1.5	4.4	2.9	1.4
High	4.4	6.1	1.7	3.4	9.8	6.4	4.7
Still studying	11.6	14.7	3.1	7.3	23.8	16.4	13.3
Total	3.2	5.0	1.8	2.3	7.4	5.1	3.3

Notes: respondents aged 18–64.

Source: EB 54.2, 2001; CC EB 2002.1, 2002; EB 64.1, 2005.

Table 4.1 shows that the increase in migration intentions has been three times larger among new member states compared with EU15. The removal of institutional barriers to free movement following the EU enlargement has apparently resulted in a fast adaptation of migration intentions. Moreover, the table shows that this increase has been larger for students (13 times larger) and for the higher educated (almost five times larger). For students, this is likely to reflect the increased awareness – possibly influenced by the EU's Erasmus and Socrates programmes – to 'go international'. For the higher educated, this is likely to reflect the better perception and opportunities on the labour market elsewhere. The observed relative rise in migration intentions among the new member states is illustrative for the policy relevance of systematically tapping migration intentions in Europe: it reveals a possible brain drain *within* Europe, and more specifically from new member states – particularly from the Baltic countries and Poland, to the old member states. It is not yet clear whether such intended new-to-old-member state moves are maybe the first part of a mobility stepping-stone effect with other nations (for example the United States of America) as the final destination.

4.5   MODEL ESTIMATES

In order to control for the effect of observed individual characteristics on the migration intentions, we have applied multivariate analyses techniques. Because migration intentions can take several values (migration to another country, migration to another region within the country, or mobility within the region of residence), we have applied multinomial logit regression techniques. We report three versions of the model: one for all 25 EU countries, one for each group of countries (EU15; new member states with on average low migration intentions – Czech Republic, Slovenia, Hungary, Slovakia, Cyprus, Malta; – and new member states with on average high migration intentions – Latvia, Poland, Lithuania, Estonia).

For our purpose, we have recoded the answers so that they reflect the longest geographical move (y) an individual i is willing to make: $y_i = 0$ no migration (if respondent reports he/she is not willing to move within the next five years); $y_i = 1$ local mobility (if the respondent reports he/she thinks he will move within the current region as the longest move); $y_i = 2$ regional mobility (if the respondent reports he/she thinks he will move to another region, but not outside the country); $y_i = 3$ international migration (if the respondent reports he/she will move to another country either within or outside the EU).

We estimate the probability of the longest intended move with the multinomial logistic model (Greene 2000). This implies that we take account of the fact that intentions to migrate do not stand on their own but are framed within a framework that includes other options, such as relocation within the region of residence or to other regions. No migration intention ($y_i = 0$) being the reference, the probability that individual i reports moving intention j (1, 2 or 3) equals:

$$\Pr(y_i = j|x_i) = \frac{\exp(x_i\beta_j)}{1 + \sum_{k=1}^{J-1}\exp(x_i\beta_k)} \tag{4.2}$$

with x being a vector of covariates, and β parameters to be estimated. This means that three equations are estimated, one for each destination j. We only report the results from the cross-country migration equation ($j = 3$). The full results can be obtained from the first author. As discussed above (see Equation 4.1), x includes characteristics measured at the individual level that are expected to reflect preferences for migration. The individual level variables include socio-demographic variables (gender, age and household type), economic characteristics (educational level, status in employment and homeownership status), past experience with mobility, perceived costs and benefits of migration, personal opinion on migration and country dummies.

Past migration experience is measured by a dummy for foreign born individuals, and whether mobility – within the regions, across regions or across borders – has been experienced in the past. Furthermore, we include information on the reason for the last migratory move: whether there was a demographic reason, whether the move was job related, or whether it was housing related. The migration history also includes information on whether or not the respondent has followed any schooling or training abroad in the past for more than two months.

The perceived costs and benefits of migration are assessed though a battery of questions. Perceived costs include whether the respondent fears for the loss of social contacts with family or friends when migrating, for the job or income position or for lack of language knowledge. Perceived benefits pertain to whether or not the respondent expects an improvement of the employment or income position, an improvement of social contacts, or whether the opportunity to meet with new people or discover new environments would motivate them to move abroad.

The respondent's personal opinion with respect to migration is assessed with five questions in the Eurobarometer survey. Respondents are asked whether they think that generally speaking it is good or bad (or neither of the two) to migrate for individuals, for families, for the economy, for the labour market, and for European integration. These five general views actually relate to two underlying dimensions: (1) whether one thinks that migration is good for individuals or their families, and (2) whether one thinks that migration is good or bad for the economy in general. Finally, a variable is included to reflect the extent to which respondents agree with the statement that 'It is difficult to find a good job' in their country of residence.

The model reveals a strong effect of age and education on migration intentions: young people are much more likely to migrate than older people, and so are the higher educated and students compared with people with an average or low educational level. Although not new, this is an important finding for it shows that young people are a very mobile cohort: they are quite aware that moving abroad may very well increase their human capital. It is likely that EU policies aimed at encouraging the mobility of the higher skilled and of students are contributing to the high level of mobility intentions among these groups. Interestingly, however, the effect of the educational level does not seem to hold for the new member states with low migration intentions. Furthermore, differences regarding the effect of age across countries are also striking. In all countries, potential migrants are more likely to be young, but older respondents are only less likely to report pro-migration intentions in the Baltic States and in Poland. A possible explanation could be that older individuals in the Baltics and Poland do not associate labour market opportunities with migration. For older individuals in the EU15, the migration decision is likely to be based upon different – leisure-related – arguments (see Balkır and Kırkulak in this volume)

The model also reveals some important life-course effects. For example, the presence of children in a household reduces the likelihood of mobility. This is probably because there are additional costs (financial and psycho-social) to migrating for parents of (young) children. Single people, however, are more prone to migrate, which confirms one of our expectations. This is because family bonds are weaker for them, which reduces the psychological and social costs of moving.

Stronger intentions to cross-border migration are observed for unemployed, compared with employed people in the EU25 model and the model for new member states with low mobility intentions. A possible explanation is that for the employed, the need to migrate is relatively lower, for they already have a secured economic situation. In fact, to the question whether people would consider moving to another region or country if they were unemployed and had difficulties to find a job in their home country, many report that they would indeed consider moving to another region (31 per cent) or to another country (41 per cent). However, this does not necessarily imply that more unemployed than employed people will actually migrate in the (near) future: the employed people – although they less often express an intention to migrate – have more chances to actually migrate, simply because they hold a job (migration is selective).

In addition to the standard control variables just discussed, the model includes additional variables pertaining to long distance mobility in the past and the expected effects of future migration. Past mobility turns out to be a strong predictor of future intended mobility (see also DaVanzo 1983). This confirms earlier findings according to which long distance mobility is not a phenomenon on its own, but part of other geographic transitions people make throughout their life (Vandenbrande *et al.* 2006). This conclusion is also illustrated by the effect of past labour market mobility on migration intentions: people who report more changes of employer in the past are more likely to report an intention to move abroad. The effect of past mobility suggests that past experiences reduce possible reservations (due to actual practice, better information) one might have to migrate (again) in the future. Although nationality does not determine preferences for migration, past study migration does result in stronger migration intentions for respondents in all countries. A similar result is found by King and Ruiz-Gelices (2006) upon the study of migration behaviour of students in Europe.

The outcomes concerning the main motive for the last long distance move are interesting.[8] It shows that – in EU25 at least – people who moved in the past because of job-related motives are more likely to move again in the future. This is presumably because they are less bound to the place they currently live than people who moved for non-job related (for example family-related) reasons. This effect, however, is only significant at the 10 per cent level in the country models.

Table 4.2 Estimates from multinomial logit model for intended migration (coefficients from the migration equation)

	EU25	Groups of EU member states		
		EU15	New members low mobility[1]	New members high mobility[2]
Socio-demographic attributes				
Female	−0.426**	−0.414**	−0.529*	−0.509**
Age (ref: 35–44)				
18-24	1.546**	1.763**	0.967*	1.350**
25-34	0.965**	0.974**	1.099**	0.869**
45-54	−0.459**	−0.222	−0.517	−1.088**
55–64	−0.548**	−0.352	−0.518	−1.376**
Household type (ref: couple, no child)				
Couple (with child)	−0.679**	−0.688**	−0.385	−0.828**
Single	0.479**	0.473**	1.008**	0.187
Single parent	0.065	−0.334	1.017	0.568
Divorced/separated	0.328*	−0.003	0.654	0.722**
Widowed	0.513*	0.617	0.585	0.600
Economic attributes				
Employment status (ref: employed)				
Unemployed	0.484**	0.307	1.507**	0.295
Retired	−0.026	−0.024	0.510	0.183
Housewife/man	0.334*	0.117	0.272	0.813**
Educational level (ref: average)				
Low or no	−0.113	0.163	−0.650	−1.021*
High	0.336**	0.277*	0.235	0.518**
Still studying	1.121**	1.121**	1.319**	1.226**
Homeowner	−0.615**	−0.720**	−0.395	−0.595**
Past Experience				
Non-nationals	0.257	0.310	−0.675	1.492
Past mobility (ref: never moved)				
Within region	0.230*	0.120	0.767*	0.303
Across regions	0.585**	0.724**	1.446*	−0.772
Across borders	1.243**	1.254**	2.018**	0.941
Reason for last long distance move				

Table 4.2 (continued)

	EU25	Groups of EU member states		
		EU15	New members low mobility[1]	New members high mobility[2]
Family related	−0.006	−0.118	0.188	0.925
Job related	0.295*	0.238	0.445	0.503
Housing related	−0.212	−0.044	−1.252	−0.723
Schooling abroad	0.672**	0.652**	0.726*	0.619*
Perceived benefits of future long distance mobility				
Better social contacts	0.322**	0.201	0.399	0.589**
Better employment/income	0.731**	0.574**	0.684*	1.217**
Meet new people environments	0.762**	0.875**	0.416	0.816**
Perceived costs of future long distance mobility				
Fear for social contacts	−0.493**	−0.585**	−0.677**	−0.298
Fear for employment/ income	−0.173*	−0.204	−0.077	−0.188
Language	−0.404**	−0.672**	−0.626	0.082
Personal views on mobility (factor scores)				
Good for individuals/ households	0.794**	0.680**	0.940**	0.813**
Good for economy/labour market	0.028	0.181*	0.050	−0.236*
Difficult to find good job in home country	−0.012	−0.019	0.103	−0.046
Country dummies included	yes	yes	yes	Yes
Constant	−3.469**	−3.330**	−4.801**	−3.043**
Pseudo R^2	0.178	0.172	0.206	0.193
Chi-square	5184.161	3245.393	1004.363	990.093
N	16732	10479	3592	2661

Notes:
(1) New members low mobility: Czech Republic, Slovenia, Hungary, Slovakia, Cyprus, Malta.
(2) New members high mobility: Latvia, Poland, Lithuania, Estonia.

Income and employment perspectives in the host country have been shown to be important determinants of migration (Hunt and Mueller 2004). This is largely confirmed in our data, but our results suggest that this is a more important for employed people in the new member states – especially in the Baltic States and Poland – than in the rest of Europe. Other perceived benefits such as the opportunity to meet with new people and discover new environments are also important, but perceived gains in terms of improved social contact also determine preferences for migration, albeit to a lesser extent.

On the costs side, the Table 4.2 shows that the expected loss of social contacts due to migration fundamentally inhibits the likelihood to migrate. Furthermore, a perspective of worse employment or income position when crossing borders surely affects the migration intention in a negative manner. Finally, respondents do perceive sufficient knowledge of other languages as a major difficulty for migrating in the future. Interestingly, however, none of these costs aspects enter the migration preference of potential migrants from the Baltics or Poland. This either means that people in these countries value social networks less or that they do not fear the assumed loss of social networks following migration, maybe because they do not intend to migrate permanently. While these two competing explanations need further investigation, the evidence suggests that migrants from the new member states expect to stay for at least a few years (TNS Opinion and Social 2007) and the past flows of permanent migration from new member states have increased significantly in the past few years (OECD 2007). That the fear for language barriers does not apply to potential migrants from new member states is suggestive of their readiness to invest in acquiring new language skills because their perceived gains from cross-border migration are greater too. Explaining this difference is also in need of further empirical exploration.

How people think about mobility influences their preference for migration. People expressing positive views on cross-border migration for the individual or the family are more prone to report a readiness to migrate themselves. The views on the 'macroeconomic' benefits of migration (economy, labour market, EU integration), however, affect people's migration intentions in EU15 in a positive way, but migration intentions in a negative way in the Baltics and Poland.

4.6 CONCLUSIONS

The enlargement of the EU by ten new member states has stimulated the societal and policy debate in many EU countries on whether or not the borders should be opened to allow the free movement of workers and on the effects of the free movement of workers. Will there be a massive migration of people all over Europe, particularly from new member states to old member states, from eastern to western Europe? Or will the current institutional and cultural arrangements of push and pull factors restrict an uncontrolled stream of migrants? The current EU labour market policy agenda prompts more mobility of the European workforce, specifically across borders. Setting and implementing this agenda is facilitated by a clear picture of how willing the European workforce is to be more geographically mobile, and of the main micro- and macroeconomic, social, and cultural determinants of the willingness to migrate.

This study focuses on migration intentions of Europeans and investigates the main determinants of such intentions. Although we reckon that such intentions cannot be taken on their face value as perfect predictors of real future migration flows, the aim of this chapter is primarily to assess which factors structure the cost-benefit analysis Europeans make when deciding on whether or not to migrate. For this purpose, we used the special module on mobility of the Eurobarometer Survey (EB 64.1) fielded in September 2005. Data were collected in all 25 EU member states. The survey is the most comprehensive recent Europe-wide survey on mobility intentions. In particular, the data allowed us to investigate to compare the factors that determine migration preferences of people in the old and new member states.

Findings indicate that most Europeans have no intentions to move to another country: only 5.4 per cent of the working-age population intends to move to another country within the next five years. Although intentional cross-border migration – percentage-wise – is not a widespread phenomenon in Europe, migration intentions in new member states (more exactly in the Baltics and Poland) are at a significantly higher level compared with the old member states. And as we showed, the accession of the new member states to the EU coincides with a relatively sharp increase in migration intentions in those countries. However, the magnitude of future migration from the eastern European member states will depend on the labour market and demographic development in those countries (Fassmann and Münz 2002). Because the population size is on the decrease in those countries (decline in fertility and increase in mortality), the younger cohorts are expected to benefit from better labour market opportunities in the future. This could reduce incentives to migration. On the labour market side, rising foreign investments and the availability of regional and structural funds are also likely to improve the living and working conditions.

The conclusions in this chapter confirm the main results from previous studies. Higher educated and single young Europeans – especially students – are the most mobile. Mobility intentions, furthermore, appear to be strongly linked to past migration: people who have migrated in the past are likely to migrate again in the future. Movers tend to stays movers, so it seems. The reason for past mobility, however, plays an important role in future migration intentions: people who crossed borders for labour market related reasons are likely to do that again in the future, but especially study migration appears to be strongly significant. To the extent that this reflects a cohort effect, we could expect that Europe's investment in the mobility of students is likely to result in larger migration streams in the future.

Perceived labour market opportunities – better employment opportunities and wage prospects – are decisive motives for migration. People holding positive views about migration – in the sense that it is good for individuals and their families – apparently perceive larger returns to migration and are therefore more likely to express an intention to migrate. However, our findings do not imply that all people with an intention to migrate will actually do so: existing social ties and sociocultural differences, as well as language represent important costs to cross-border migration. Interestingly, this is less the case in the Baltic States and Poland. This goes to show that there are clear boundaries to migration, but that the balance strikes differently in different regions of Europe, they have to be balanced with very diverse and diverging psychological, social and economic costs. Migration intentions are embedded in a decision-making hierarchy that involves a plurality of competing considerations.

NOTES

1. Interestingly, there is no such thing as an explicit and official federal US policy on stimulating mobility. This absence of policy intervention does not imply that mobility is seen as an unimportant issue. On the contrary, being mobile and moving to where the work is, is at the heart of American history and culture. But, mobility is seen as the outcome of free market choices of workers and employers. There is no unique or decisive role of the federal government (Bird 2007).
2. In Fouarge and Ester (2007), we investigate the effect of macroeconomic factors on the migration decision.
3. See for further information on recent migration trend studies by the European Foundation www.eurofound.eu.int/areas/populationandsociety/migration.htm, 5 June 2006.
4. Data were collected by TNS Opinion and Social, interviews were conducted between 2 September 2005 and 6 October 2005. In the 25 EU countries, the survey covers the national population of citizens of the respective nationalities and the population of citizens of all the EU member states that are residents in those countries and have a sufficient command of one of the respective national language(s) to answer the questionnaire.
5. In this chapter, we make no distinctions between people reporting the expectation to

move 'to another country in the European Union' or 'to another country outside the European Union'. Only a very limited number expressed an intention to migrate outside the EU. Henceforth, for ease of exposition, we interpret all migration intentions as intentions to move within the EU.
6. The 2001 Eurobarometer Survey (EB 54.2) collected information on migration intentions in EU15. The 2002 Eurobarometer Survey (CC EB 2002.1) collected this information for the candidate countries.
7. In the Eurobarometer, the educational attainment is measured by the age at which one finished full-time education. For ease of exposition, we have recoded this measure into three levels: those who stopped before the age of 16 qualify as lower educated; those who stopped between the age of 16 and 19 are said to have an average educational level; people who left full time education at age 20 or above are higher educated.
8. The reason for the last move is constructed from the answer to the following question: 'The last time you moved to another region or European Union country, what were the main reasons you had for moving?'

REFERENCES

Ahn, N., S. De la Rica and A. Ugidos (1999), 'Willingness to move for work and unemployment duration in Spain', *Economica*, 66, 335–57.
Balkır Canan and Berna Kırkulak (2009), *Turkey, the New Destination for Retirement Migration*, the Netherlands: Institute of Social Studies.
Belot, M. and J. Ermisch (2006a), 'Friendship ties and geographical mobility: evidence from the BHPS', IZA discussion paper 2209.
Belot, M. and S. Ederveen (2006b), 'Cultural and institutional barriers in migration between OECD countries', CPB document.
Böheim, R. and M. Taylor (2002), 'Tied down or room to move? Investigating the relationships between housing tenure, employment status and residential mobility in Britain', *Scottish Journal of Political Economy*, 49, 369–92.
Borjas, G. (1987), 'Self-selection and the earnings of immigrants', *American Economic Review*, 77 (4), 531–53.
Borjas, G. (1999), 'Immigration and welfare magnets', *Journal of Labor Economics*, 17 (4), 607–37.
Burda, M., W. Härdle, M. Müller and A. Werwatz (1998), 'Semiparametric analysis of German East-West migration intentions: facts and theory', *Journal of Applied Econometrics*, 13 (5), 525–42.
Chiquiar, D. and G. Hanson (2002), 'International migration, self-selection, and the distribution of wages: evidence from Mexico and the United States', NBER working paper 9242.
Chiswick, B. (1978), 'The effect of Americanization on the earnings of foreign-born men', *Journal of Political Economy*, 86 (5), 897–921.
DaVanzo, J. (1983), 'Repeat migration in the United States: who moves back and who moves on?', *Review of Economics and Statistics*, 65, 552–9.
European Commission (2006), 'Report on the Functioning of the Transitional Arrangements set out in the 2003 Accession Treaty' (period 1 May 2004–30 April 2006), COM 2006.
Faini, R., G. Galli, P. Gennari and F. Rossi (1997), 'An empirical puzzle: falling migration and growing unemployment differentials among Italian regions', *European Economic Review*, 41, 571–79.

Fassmann, H. and R. Münz (2002), 'EU enlargement and future east-west migration', in IOM (eds), *New Challenges for Migration Policy in Central and Eastern Europe*, Geneva: International Organisation for Migration, pp. 59–86.

Finifter, A. (1976), 'American emigration', *Society*, 13, 30–36.

Fishbein, M. and I. Ajzen (1975), *Belief, Attitudes, Intention and Behavior. An Introduction to Theory and Research*, Reading, MA: Addison-Wesley Publishing Company.

Fouarge, D. and P. Ester (2007), *Factors Determining International and Regional Migration in Europe*, Dublin: European Foundation for the Improvement of Living and Working Conditions.

Gordon, I. and I. Molho (1995), 'Duration dependence in migration behaviour: cumulative inertia versus stochastic change', Environment and Planning, A 27, 1961–75.

Greene, W. (2000), *Econometric Analysis*, Upper Saddle River, NJ: Prentice-Hall.

Hadler, M. (2006), 'Intentions to migrate within the European Union: a challenge for simple economic macro-level explanations', *European Societies*, **8** (1), 111–40.

Harris, J. and M. Todaro (1970), 'Migration, unemployment and development: a two-sector analysis', *American Economic Review*, **60** (5), 126–42.

Hatton, T. and J. Williamson (2002), 'What fundamentals drive world migration?', NBER working paper 9159.

Hunt, G. and R. Mueller (2004), 'North American migration: returns to skills, border effects and mobility costs', *Review of Economics and Statistics*, **86** (4): 988–1007.

Karppinen, J., E. Fernandez and H. Krieger (2006), 'Geographical mobility: challenges and opportunities', presented at the conference to launch the European Year of Workers' Mobility 2006: 'Workers' mobility: a right, an option, an opportunity?', Brussels, 20-21 February.

King, R. and E. Ruiz-Gelices (2003), 'International student migration and the European "Year Abroad". Effects on European identity and subsequent migration behavior', *International Journal of Population Geography*, 9, 229–52.

Krieger, H. (2004), *Migration Trends in an Enlarged Europe*, Luxembourg: Office for Official Publications of the European Communities.

Krieger, H. (2006), 'Long distance mobility within the EU: considering the Lisbon Agenda and Transitional Arrangements', discussion paper presented at a foundation seminar with stakeholders of the governing board, Luxembourg, 8 March.

Liebig, T. and A. Sousa-Poza (2004), 'Migration, self-selection and income inequality: an international analysis', *Kyklos*, 57, 125–46.

Manski, C. (1990), 'The use of intentions data to predict behavior: a best-case analysis', *Journal of the American Statistical Association*, 85, 934–40.

Massey, D., J. Arango, G. Hugo, A. Kouaouci, A. Pellegrino, and J. Taylor (1993), 'Theories of international migration: a review and appraisal', *Population and Development Review*, **19** (3), 431–66.

Massey, D., L. Goldring and J. Durand (1994), 'Communities in transnational migration: an analysis of nineteen Mexican communities', *American Journal of Sociology*, **99** (6), 1492–533.

Mincer, J. (1978), 'Family migration decisions', *Journal of Political Economy*, 86, 749–73.

OECD (2005), *Employment Outlook*, Paris: OECD.

OECD (2007), *International Mobility of Highly-skilled Workers*, Paris: OECD.

Pedersen, P., M. Pytlikova and N. Smith (2004), 'Selection or network effects? Migration flows into 27 OECD countries, 1990–2000', IZA discussion paper 1104.

Sjaastad, L. (1962), 'The costs and returns of human migration', *Journal of Political Economy*, 70, 80–93.

Stark, O. (1991), *The Migration of Labour*, Oxford: Blackwell.

Tidrick, K. (1971), 'Need for achievement, social class and intention to emigrate in Jamaican students', *Social and Economic Studies*, 20, 52–60.

TNS Opinion and Social (2007), 'Geographical mobility of citizens', report on Special Eurobarometer 67.1 to the European Commission.

Vandenbrande, T., L. Coppin, P. van der Hallen, P. Ester, D. Fouarge, A. Fasang, S. Geerdes and K. Schömann (2006), *Mobility in Europe*, Luxembourg: Office for Official Publications of the European Communities.

Zavodny, M. (1997), 'Welfare and the locational choices of new immigrants', *Economic and Financial Policy Review*, Federal Reserve Bank of Dallas, 2, 2–10.

Zimmerman, K. (1995), 'Tackling the European migration problem', *Journal of Economic Perspective*, **9** (2), 45–62.

5. The wrong Portuguese? Youth and geographical mobility intentions in Portugal

David Cairns

5.1 RESEARCH CONTEXT

In respect to the research context of this chapter, while historically a 'migration country,' in recent years Portugal has become more a receiving than a sending society. In parallel, there has been a concentration of research attention within Portugal upon seeking to explore the experiences of these recent arrivals, in particular from Lusophone Africa and South America, rather than attempting to appreciate the migration situations of the broader youth population in Portugal. While there is considerable value in much of this work, we are left with something of a deficit in respect to studying Portuguese migrants as opposed to immigrants in Portugal. As such, we presently know more about young migrants from Cape Verde, Angola or Brazil than we do about migrants or potential migrants from Lisbon or Porto.[1]

There are, however, indications that present levels of youth migration from Portugal are at an extremely low level. Despite the occasional small scale media panic regarding a potential youth exodus from Portugal, demographic analysis reveals that recent overall net migration from Portugal is at a lower level that the European average (Huber 2004, 620). Likewise, Eurobarometer statistics (2001) indicate that a very small number of people in Portugal, perhaps as few as 0.02 per cent of the population, have intentions to be trans-nationally mobile in the future (Hadler 2006, 124). Other recent research at a comparative European level and incorporating a qualitative dimension has also revealed that Portuguese youth are among the least likely to migrate young people in Europe (see Biggart and Cairns 2004).

This apparent lack of movement should be a concern for the European Union, as at European policy level, encouraging youth mobility is a priority, for example, to help encourage movement amongst tertiary-educated young people the EU funds programmes such as Erasmus and Socrates and attempts to harmonize the recognition of educational qualifications (see Peixoto 2001). The European Commission's White Paper, *A New Impetus for Youth*, is particularly clear in respect to encouraging mobility – 'the main asset of European integration' – in education: '[Mobility] has to make this transition from the exception to the general rule: mobility must become an integral part of learning from a very early age. Programmes must therefore be accessible to all young people regardless of their socioeconomic or geographical origin' (European Commission 2001, 55).

In respect to academic perspectives, the value of youth mobility is also increasingly recognized as a subject for study in its own right. For instance, pioneering work by Jones (2000) and Jamieson (2000) has explored mobility among young people in Britain while Thomson and Taylor (2005) have discussed the theme of mobility as a resource in the transition to adulthood, illustrating how young people experience a tension between the fixity of home and the escape and transformative potential of mobility, a distinction reflected in the use of Merton's 'cosmopolitans' and 'locals' categories (2005, 331).

5.2   METHODOLOGY AND DATA

The original research upon which this chapter is based is taken from a project entitled 'Culture, Youth and Future Life Orientations' (CYFLO), funded by a post-doctoral fellowship provided by the Foundation for Science and Technology (FCT) in Lisbon. The aim of this project, conducted during 2005–07, was to examine the future life orientations of highly skilled young people in Portugal, particularly in respect to geographical mobility and immobility. This entailed both quantitative and qualitative investigation. The specific geographical focus of this investigation is the city of Lisbon and its surrounding environs, not only the capital city of Portugal but along with Porto one of the country's two main metropolitan centres, a fact which should be considered in interpreting results; it may well be the case that young people in other Portuguese regions have very different mobility orientations and experiences.

In the quantitative research phase, a questionnaire was administered to a total of 200 young people in Lisbon, spread across four different academic disciplines, namely arts and humanities, social sciences, science and engineering, to provide both diversity and balance within the sample. This sample was also balanced in terms of gender and inclusion from ethnic minorities. A deliberate decision was, however, taken not to include students from courses wherein geographical mobility is mandatory as opposed to being a voluntary choice, such as languages. While not repre-sentative of Lisbon youth, this sample can be regarded as a 'mainstream' selection from the broader youth population rather than exclusively focus-ing upon those at the sub-cultural fringes in line with the awareness within European Youth Studies of the need to explore the experiences of young people at a broad level (see Shildrick and MacDonald 2006). The ques-tions themselves covered a range of topics, from family and peer relation-ships to community attachments and future life plans. For the qualitative part of this study a total of 15 follow-up interviews were conducted with respondents sourced from the initial quantitative sample. These interviews were essentially semi-structured in consisting of initial questions regard-ing mobility orientations and experiences, followed by more in-depth biographical discussion of individual-specific life events and plans, for example, time spent working or studying abroad and future life mobility intentions.

5.3 QUANTITATIVE ANALYSIS

The quantitative analysis which follows is derived from data gathered in the course of the CYFLO project. The results presented centre upon a number of key migration-related issues, namely the presence or absence of geographical mobility intentions amongst the young people surveyed and their mobility decision-making processes.

In relation to descriptive statistics, 32 per cent of respondents stated that they had intentions to live outside their country of origin at some stage in the future, although there were no significant differences in respect to the mobility intentions of the young people surveyed and gender, age, socioeconomic background and academic background. We can however observe a significant disparity in respect to ethnicity, with young people from ethnic minority backgrounds being significantly more likely to be considering geographical mobility: 78 per cent, compared to only 24 per cent, in the majority community. This dichotomy however takes no account of differences between young people from dissimilar backgrounds within these groupings and should thus be treated with caution.

Considering the apparent absence of a relationship between these variables and mobility intentions, it may well be the case that other more subjective factors such as family and peer relationships or community attachments have more of a bearing upon mobility decision-making than age, gender, social class or educational background. This is a line of investigation consistent with conclusions from other studies of migra-tion decision-making, where close relatives and friends have been shown

Table 5.1 *Logistic regression analysis of statements relating to family by intention to be mobile*

Statement	β	Exp (β)
I have siblings who left home to live in other countries	1.171	3.224
My family would understand if I had to leave home to find a good job	0.802	2.231
I have siblings who left home to live in other parts of Portugal	0.533	1.703
It's good to live at home with your parents	0.116	1.123
My family need me to support them	−0.138	0.871
Having a good family life is more important than having a good job	−0.238	0.788
I need my family to support me	−0.380	0.684
I would feel incomplete without my family	−0.683	0.505
Most of my family live near me	−0.753	0.471

Source: Own calculation based on the CYFLO survey.

to be influential (Malmberg 1997, 41). These influences are thus explored in the following series of separate binary logistic regression analyses of responses made to various statements, utilizing the intention to be mobile as dependent variable.

Responses are presented to a number of statements relating to various aspects of family life. These statements range from subjective assessments of attachments and the importance of family to more factual statements on proximity to other family members, geographical mobility amongst siblings and family support. From the outcomes, we can immediately observe a number of significant factors which may have a bearing upon mobility intentions, in both positive and negative respects: in respect to the former, we can see that the potentially mobile young people in the sample are much more likely to have families who understand their need for movement and siblings who have left home to live in other countries or different regions of Portugal; regarding the latter, we can observe that the mobility-seeking young people are less likely to feel 'incomplete' without their families or live close to most of their family members.

How do peers react to declared intentions to be mobile? We can see that these responses mirror those made to the statements on family, with the potentially mobile more likely to have friends who live in other countries and/or regions of Portugal and have friends who would understand if they

Table 5.2   Logistic regression analysis of statements relating to peers by intention to be mobile

Statement	β	Exp (β)
My friends would understand if I went to live in another country	0.798	2.212
I have friends who live other parts of Portugal	0.644	1.904
I have friends who live in other countries	0.639	1.894
My friends would understand if I went to live in another part of Portugal	0.355	1.426
I see myself having many of the same friends in the future as I have today	−0.233	0.800
Having good friends is more important than having a good job	−0.256	0.788
I have many of the same friends today as I did when I was a child	−0.255	0.775
I would feel incomplete without my friends	−0.644	0.525
Most of my friends live near me	−0.644	0.525

Source: Own calculation based on the CYFLO survey.

went to live in another country; they are also less likely to feel 'incomplete' without or live close to their friends compared to their contemporaries who want to remain in Portugal indefinitely.

The relationship between responses made to various statements on community attachments and mobility, revealed some interesting outcomes in terms of dichotomies between the potentially mobile and immobile. The mobility seekers are revealed to be more likely to feel European and dislike the areas they live in; romance is also important to them, as they are more likely to consider having a relationship with someone even if it meant leaving their country. The potentially mobile are also less likely to feel at home in their country, to somewhat predictably want to leave their area and are less likely to socialize where they live.

· While the outcomes to these three different sets of statements are open to interpretation due to the subjectivity of young people's self-evaluations, for example, what constitutes feeling 'incomplete' without family and peers or being 'at home' may differ greatly according to personal circumstances, we are beginning to obtain an idea regarding what differentiates mobile and immobile youth, specifically the potentially mobile may have looser family attachments or families positively predisposed towards migration; they may be influenced by or even follow their peers or siblings

Table 5.3   Logistic regression analysis of statements relating to community attachments by intentions to be mobile

Statement	β	Exp (β)
I feel more European than Portuguese	0.393	1.481
I don't like the area I live in	0.373	1.453
I can name all the countries in the European Union	0.102	1.107
I think of myself first and foremost as an individual	−0.077	0.926
I know how many countries there are in the European Union	−0.169	0.844
I would not consider having a relationship with someone from another country if it meant having to leave Portugal	−0.477	0.621
I regularly socialize in my own area	−0.522	0.593
I always vote in elections	−0.537	0.585
I support my local football team	−0.616	0.540
I always want to live in my area	−0.804	0.447
I feel at home in Portugal	−1.556	0.211

Source: Own calculation based on the CYFLO survey.

Table 5.4   Logistic regression analysis of statements relating to Portugal by intentions to be mobile

Statement	β	Exp (β)
Salaries are too low in Portugal	0.610	1.841
Portugal has a good education system	−0.21	0.980
I have a fear of unemployment	−0.160	0.852
It's easier to find a good abroad compared with Portugal	−0.201	0.818

Source: Own calculation based on the CYFLO survey.

in their decision-making and have a much less profound attachment to their country of residence and a greater association with Europe.

Before proceeding onto the qualitative analysis, one further area of interest in this chapter concerns these young people's subjective evaluations of prevailing conditions in Portugal. How does their relationship to Portugal specifically relate to feelings on the Portuguese education system, salary levels and future employment and unemployment prospects?

While there is a significant dichotomy in respect to responses to the statement on salaries being too low in Portugal, with the potentially mobile less impressed with remuneration levels, the remaining outcomes seem relatively uninteresting. However, this is largely due to similarly very high or low responses to these statements, for example only 14 per cent of all young people surveyed thought that Portugal had a good education system.

5.4 QUALITATIVE ANALYSIS

While the quantitative analysis provides us with some important ideas as to the main influences upon the geographical mobility orientations of these young people, the results of the qualitative analysis enable us to observe what they actually think about the issue in question. The following case studies have been selected in order to provide specific insight into mobility and immobility orientations, illustrating how factors such as family and peer relationships, alongside community attachments, impact upon mobility orientations.

Luis is a 21-year-old second year anthropology student at ISCTE (Instituto Superior de Ciências do Trabalho e da Empresa), in Lisbon. Luis has always lived in the district of Vilha Franca de Xina in the same city with his parents, both of whom are civil servants, and his younger sister. He is generally satisfied with his present living situation and enjoys supportive relationships with his parents. Regarding his past travel experiences, Luis has yet to experience being abroad, preferring to take holidays with his family in Portugal. While having a preference to stay in Portugal in the future, Luis does have vague plans to work abroad at some point in the future as he realizes that opportunities for those in his academic field of study are limited at home; however, he is not as yet sure where he might go or when he might make a move. His family would also be sad to see him leave but would understand if an exit was necessary for reasons such as pursuing job opportunities outside Lisbon.

Catarina is a 24-year-old sociology student, studying, like Luis, at ISCTE. She also lives in Lisbon with her family in the Sao Jorge de Arroios district of the city. Her foreign travel experiences have so far been restricted to one visit to Spain and another holiday in the Dominican Republic, although she would like to travel further in the future. While Catarina has positive opinions on working and studying abroad, and some negative views regarding her own job prospects in Portugal, she does not see herself living abroad at any point in the future, feeling it would be too big a step for her to take. When pressed, she admits that she does not like the idea of having to be fluent in another language and would find it particularly hard to go somewhere like the USA.

Inês is a 19-year-old sculpture student at Art College in Chiado, downtown Lisbon. While she enjoys her studies and student life, Inês does find living with her parents a strain and would like to move out. However, her heavy workload and lack of finance dictate otherwise. Furthermore, the fact that Inês lives, and has always lived, within a short commuting distance of her place of study, in the Anjos district of central Lisbon, also means that it is convenient to remain living there, being only four stops away on the metro. While, like most of her contemporaries in the quantitative sample, Inês has negative views of her job prospects in Portugal, she also strongly stresses that in the future she wants to stay here, as 'I will never feel any sense of abandonment or helplessness.' Inês values her relationships with her family and her friends to the extent of feeling helpless without them. To consider breaking these ties through working or studying abroad is unthinkable. Furthermore, an interesting point Inês makes is that she feels that she would be letting her country down if she migrated. She is also optimistic about the future here: 'I think in the future that Portugal will become a good place in which to work. We all have to work together to do our best.'

One other case from the Lisbon sample is that of Maria, a 23-year-old fifth-year biomedical engineering student at the Technical University of Lisbon. Like Luis, Catarina and Inês, Maria lives in Lisbon with her parents and commutes daily to her nearby university campus. She enjoys a close relationship with her parents and admits that she depends on them almost totally to support her while she is studying and while not particularly well travelled, indeed her only experiences of being abroad are family holidays to Italy, Maria is open to the idea of living outside Portugal in the future and recognizes such a move as perhaps necessary if she is to have a career in her chosen field. She also feels that current salary levels in Portugal are much too low. Being a fluent English speaker, she would consider moving to the UK or another European country, although she would be less keen on moving to the USA.

5.5   CONCLUSIONS: THE 'RIGHT' PORTUGUESE?

In respect to moving towards an understanding of the geographical mobility orientations of these young people, we can observe that a range of factors, most notably family and peer relationships, along with community attachments, in many cases effectively negate migration intentions and, at a more existential level, 'represent a shield against social uncertainty

[and] anxiety about the future' (Leccardi 2005, 128). Furthermore, negative assessments of economic conditions in Portugal are not sufficient to promote feelings of dislocation (see Hadler 2006).

While the quantitative statistics provide us with an indication of how many of the young people surveyed are considering geographical mobility and possible reasons why, we can observe from the qualitative analysis more concrete reasons for the immobility of highly skilled Portuguese youth, with strong family, peer and community attachments demonstrated by Catarina and Inês. Meanwhile, those young people interviewed with mobility intentions, for instance Luis and Maria, have at best tentative plans rather than well organized migration strategies. There is thus an absence of information regarding how and when these young people would like to undertake mobility in the future.

In contextualizing these outcomes, there is an obvious parallel to be drawn with Thomson and Taylor's (2005) emphasis upon the significance of the value and 'fixity' of home for young people, while in respect to mobility, the relative paucity of mobility plans amongst these Portuguese youth, particularly those of a concrete nature, highlights a need for further investigation, perhaps amongst young people outside the major cosmopolitan centres in Portugal. In relation to the broader European context, we can observe the lack of impact of European Policy on mobility, implying a need for further measures to encourage youth movement which take account of local cultural phenomena such as strong family and peer relationships and seemingly unbreakable attachments to where these young people live.

NOTE

1. For example, in relation to the question of Muslims in Portugal, see Abranches (2007), Bastos and Bastos (2005), Fonseca and Esteves (2002), Gomes Faria (2007), Keshavjee (2000), Malheiros (1996), Tiesler (2005) and Vakil (2003).

REFERENCES

Abranches, M. (2007), 'Muslim women in Portugal: strategies of identity re(construction)', *Lusotopie*, **14** (1), 239–54.
Bastos, S.P. and J.G.P. Bastos (2005), *Filhos Diferentes de Deuses Diferentes*, Lisboa: ACIME/FCT/CEMME.
Biggart, A. and D. Cairns (2004), *Families and Transitions in Europe: Comparative Report*, Coleraine: University of Ulster.
European Commission (eds) (2001), 'European Commission White Paper: a new impetus for youth', Brussels: Commission of the European Communities.

Fonseca, M.L. and A. Esteves (2002), 'Migration and new religion townscapes in Lisbon', in M.L. Fonseca (eds), *Immigration and Place in Mediterranean Metropolis*, Lisbon: Luso-American Foundation, pp. 255–89.

Gomes Faria, R. (2007), 'Participação dos imigrantes marroquinos na construção da 'comunidade' muçulmana em Portugal', *Lusotopie*, **14** (1), 205–21.

Hadler, M. (2006), 'Intentions to migrate within the European Union: a challenge for simple economic macro-level explanations', *European Societies*, **8** (1), 111–40.

Huber, P. (2004), 'Inter-regional mobility in Europe: a note on the cross-country evidence', *Applied Economics Letters*, 11, 619–24.

Jamieson, L. (2000), 'Migration, place and class: youth in a rural area', *Sociological Review*, **48** (2), 203–23.

Jones, G. (1999), 'The same people in the same places? Socio-Spatial identities and migration in youth', *Sociology*, **33** (1), 1–22.

Keshavjee, F. (2000), 'A Índia em Portugal: concepções culturais da mulher islâmica', *Encontro Sobre Portugal e a Índia*, Lisboa: Fundação Oriente.

Leccardi, C. (2005), 'Facing uncertainty: temporality and biographies in the new century', *Young*, **13** (2) 123–46.

Malmberg, G. (1997), 'Time and space in international migration', in T. Hammar, G. Brochmann, K. Tamas and T. Faist (eds), *International Migration, Immobility and Development. Multi-diciplinary Perspectives*, Oxford and New York: Berg, pp. 21–48.

Malheiros, J.M. (1996), *Imigrantes na Região de Lisboa*, Lisboa: Edições Colibri.

Peixoto, J. (2001), 'Migration and policies in the European Union: highly skilled mobility, free movement of labour and recognition of diplomas', *International Migration*, **39** (1) 33–59.

Shildrick, T. and R. MacDonald (2006), 'In defence of subculture: young people, leisure and social division', *Journal of Youth Studies*, **9** (2) 125–40.

Thomson, R. and R. Taylor (2005), 'Between cosmopolitanism and the locals: mobility as a resource in the transition to adulthood', *Young*, **13** (4) 327–42.

Tiesler, N.C. (2005), 'Novidades do Terreno: Muçulmanos na Europa e o caso Português', *Análise Social*, **34** (173), 827–49.

Vakil, A. (2003), 'Muslims in Portugal: history, historiography, citizenship', *Euroclio Bulletin: Looking Outwards, Looking Inwards*, 18, 9–13.

PART II

Patterns of migration and mobility

6. Free-moving west Europeans: an empirically based portrait

Michael Braun and Ettore Recchi

6.1 INTRODUCTION

As the internal borders of the European Union are almost entirely removed, migration patterns within the continent take a different shape. Complementing free movement policies, cross-country transportations have expanded their scope and speed while lowering their prices. Eurostar trains, Ryanair planes, highways and highly improved roads are making it easy, as never before, to move across borders in Europe. Distances and costs are compressed, allowing Europeans to conceive of international mobility on a continental scale more flexibly and with diverse purposes. Yet, considerable increases in living standards and welfare entitlements in the traditional sending countries of southern Europe have at the same time reduced incentives for migration. The traditional migrant strategy of labour-led resettlement (which knew several variants in time and scope) is being supplemented, if not entirely replaced, by multifaceted life-plans and strategies of mobility. Perhaps the lifting of the Iron Curtain and the inclusion of eastern European countries into the EU have recently led to a revival of the traditional guest-worker migration, given the extreme wage differences between some new member states and western Europe. But it is also plausible that such movements will weaken progressively due to economic convergence between east and west and the low fertility of the sending countries.

6.2 STATISTICAL OVERVIEW

While there is a widespread awareness that this is the overall picture of the changing migration landscape within the EU borders, we know surprisingly little about the objective and subjective profile of the emerging population of free-moving Europeans. Official statistics, indeed, are at pains when trying to track down mobility flows within the EU – be it for the inherent difficulties of mapping immigrants of all sorts, for the

*Table 6.1   Stocks of all foreigners and EU15 non-nationals, 1990 and
2004 (in 1000)*

	1990			2004		
	Foreigners	EU	% EU	Foreigners	EU	% EU
Germany	4845.9	1516.8	31.3	7334.8	1767.3	24.1
France	3596.6	1321.5	36.7	3263.2	1195.5	36.6
Great Britain	2416.0	910.0	37.7	2760.0	1268.6	46.0
Italy	490.4	140.8	28.7	1334.9	132.1	9.9
Spain	398.1	245.8	61.7	2772.2	360.2	13.0

Source: Eurostat New Cronos Database and Eurostat Dissemination Database (see
Recchi *et al.* 2006); data for France from 1999, for Britain from 2003, for Italy from 2002.

inconsistencies of national statistical systems or for citizens' reluctance to
residence registration which is further boosted by the philosophy of free
movement (Poulain *et al.* 2006). Probably ex defecto, Eurostat indicates
that there were 6.3 million EU non-nationals living in the EU15 in 2004
(Recchi *et al.* 2006).

Immigration trends both from third countries and from other EU15
countries since the early 1990s vary considerably from one country to
another (Table 6.1). With regard to all foreigners, irrespective of geographic origin, in France, there was a slight decline (which, however,
might also have been affected by the relatively high number of naturalizations in France, in addition to a restrictive immigration policy) between
1990 and 2004. For Great Britain the numbers rose slightly by 14 per cent
and for Germany by 51 per cent. Figures in Italy and Spain, however, have
risen dramatically during this period. In Italy, the population of foreign
nationals nearly tripled, and in Spain it increased nearly sevenfold from
1990. Illegal residents, which tend to be numerous in Italy and Spain, are
not even included in these figures.

The number of EU15 foreigners was much lower in all of these countries
in 2004, ranging from 1.8 million in Germany to 132000 in Italy. Also, the
number of EU15 non-nationals since the early 1990s has experienced a
decline in France and Italy, and only a modest increase in Germany (16.5
per cent), Great Britain (39.4 per cent) and Spain (45.5 per cent). Overall,
the population of EU movers in the EU15 has increased by 21.1 per cent
since 1987.

When we look at combinations of the country of origin (hereafter:
CoO) and country of residence (hereafter: CoR), in 2002 the single largest
immigrant group is formed by Italians in Germany with more than 600000

Table 6.2   Stocks of movers from EIMSS countries, 2002

	Germans	French	Britons	Italians	Spaniards
Germany	–	86 696	99 587	644 955	115 818
France	76 882	–	75 546	200 632	160 194
Great Britain	266 136	96 281	–	107 244	54 482
Italy	35 091	29 313	19 957	–	12 327
Spain	78 020	46 894	94 862	36 815	–

Source: Eurostat Dissemination Database (see Recchi *et al.* 2006).

persons, followed by Germans in Britain with more than 260 000 and by Italians and Spaniards in France with some 200 000 and 160 000, respectively (Table 6.2.). The smallest groups are found in Italy, where none surpasses 35 000, and Spaniards constitute the smallest with some 12 000. In 2004, no group in Germany had less than 100 000 people (Eurostat 2006). These statistics reflect both the legacy of traditional guest-worker migration (movement exclusively from south to north) as well as more recent trends (movement increasingly also from north to south).

The sharpest rises can be found for Germans and Britons in Spain and France, while the number of Spaniards in Germany and France and of Italians in France has decreased, presumably as an effect of economic growth and convergence between these countries (Recchi *et al.* 2003). Migration to Britain has grown for all groups. These figures are compatible with a further decline of low-skilled labour migration and family unification and increases in highly skilled labour and retirement migration. Britain is presumably the target of highly skilled labour migration among our five countries, a result in line with past research (Salt 1992), while Spain is the target of retirement migration.

In spite of its interest for migration research (given its novelty) and EU studies (given its potential for Europeanization), the population of cross-state migrants within the European Union is scarcely investigated. Existing studies tend to concentrate on specific fractions of intra-EU movers. King *et al.* (1998, 2000) focus on retirement migrants along the north-south route. Their pioneer study shows the local impact and likely expansion of this migration pattern, as well as the status distinction associated with different areas of settlement – Tuscany being preferred by upper class British retirees and Costa del Sol by their middle class counterparts (more recently, see Huber 2004). Ackers (1998) examines opportunities and constraints for women's mobility across borders within the EU, finding that citizenship rights are likely to open new pathways to overcome gender-based glass ceilings in national labour markets. This same author has more recently studied scientists' mobility (Ackers 2005), in tune with a rising interest in high-skilled mobility, which is arguably boosted by the free movement regime in the EU. Perhaps Favell's (2004, 2006, 2008) research programme on 'Eurostars' – that is, free moving professionals in capital cities (London, Amsterdam, Brussels) – represents the most insightful exploration of high-skilled migrants in the EU. His in-depth interviews capture the subtle, entrenched and persisting local barriers to successful integration, even in apparently cosmopolitan milieus. A possibly more denationalized experience of border-crossing occurs with mobile students enjoying Erasmus and Socrates grants, even though their sojourn abroad is by definition time-limited and provisional, thus affecting their integration strategies substantially (King and Ruiz-Gelices 2003).

Until now, Verwiebe and Eder (2006) is the only study surveying a population of EU movers regardless of individual characteristics, albeit in a bounded locality (i.e. Berlin) and with a restricted set of nationalities (i.e. French, Italian, British, Danish and Polish). Using postal survey data and a control group design, this study shows that EU movers – and particularly those who settled in the last decade of the century – are relatively privileged people on the basis of their class origins, class destinations and education. Even more interestingly, this study finds that income inequalities are independent of nationality for British and French movers, whereas Poles and Italians suffer from lower economic returns to their mobility choice and Danes get, in fact, higher rewards compared to both structurally similar movers and German residents.

It is timely to broaden the focus and to investigate movements from different CoO to different CoR simultaneously. How do modern migrants fare in terms of structural and social integration? Are there differences between groups led by different motives to move? Are there special groups which assume the role as outliers or are all these groups blended into a highly Europeanized core? The reduction of economic differences – in terms of both employment opportunities and earning potential – between traditional sending countries and receiving countries makes it likely that CoO/CoR groups of movers become more similar over time, as long as getting more attractive and/or better-paid employment is their main migration motive. Free movers are, practically by definition, assumed to capitalize on individual opportunities – which are not necessarily connected to the state of whole economies. However, while labour migration should become more and more restricted to migration of the highly qualified inside Europe, we still expect remnants of the traditional guest-worker migration to be visible in single groups. Student and marriage migration should also show a strongly equilibrated pattern across countries and contribute to the forming of a Europeanized core. These two kinds of movers have neither a natural source nor a natural target (with the only exception of long-term student migration, for which the target in Europe might be Britain). Differences between CoO and CoR groups of movers might, however, arise by the dramatic increase in (pre-) retirement migration in recent decades, which is mostly generated by – still existing – differences of the physical climate between northern and southern Europe.

6.3 THE 'EUROPEAN INTERNAL MOVERS' SOCIAL SURVEY' (EIMSS)

The analyses presented in this chapter are based on the 'European Internal Movers' Social Survey' (EIMSS), conducted as part of the PIONEUR project in 2004. This is the first data set containing detailed information on an international sample of intra-EU migrants. Overall, the data set includes 4919 valid cases. In each of the five countries of the survey (Britain, France, Germany, Italy and Spain), approximately 250 telephone interviews were conducted with nationals of each of the other four countries who migrated there from 1974 through 2003, who were 18 years of age or older at the time of migration and have lived in the CoR at least for one year. By means of linguistic screening of names in constructing the sample, only migrants belonging to the main ethnic group of the CoO were considered. Thus, members of for example the German-speaking minorities in Italy and France who have migrated to other countries as well as former migrants and their offspring who have returned to the home countries of their parents or grandparents were excluded. In fact, migrants who have acquired the citizenship of the CoR are included, as this is a potentially important indicator of integration.

The selected sampling strategy was to combine telephone registers with linguistic information on names (Santacreu *et al.* 2006). Starting with the telephone directories of the countries of residence, linguistic units, that is family and Christian names, were ordered by frequency. For each country, the most frequent names were determined by a high frequency in at least one of their regions. The resulting list was manually checked by experts in each of the five countries to make sure that names which do not pertain to the main ethnicity are excluded (for example, Turkish names in Germany or Italian names in France). For all of the CoO/CoR subsamples, those names which are also very frequent in the other countries of residence were eliminated (for example, Maria which is very frequent in Spain, Germany and Italy). These names were then searched for in CoRs' telephone books.

Non-response bias is nearly impossible to quantify because, unlike in surveys of the general population, it cannot be assumed that the vast majority of those who could not be contacted or who refused belong to the target population. The target sample of the EIMSS survey is much smaller than the gross sample, even if the screening of ethnicities has worked perfectly. The reason is that the population was restricted to those who came to the respective countries of residence after 1973 and were 18 years old or older at the time of settlement, which is a much smaller group. As a consequence, what appeared to be a non-contact or a refusal could be neutral to the sample.

A standardized multilingual questionnaire was administered by bilingual interviewers. The average duration of the interviews was slightly less than half an hour. Aims were to collect quantitative information on migration experiences, political behaviour, attitudes and European identity.

The comparative design has several advantages. The study was conducted in five different countries and the same countries are used both as CoO and CoR. The studies of the five countries are comparable: in each country, random samples of the migrant populations were drawn according to the same sampling schema. In addition, the same questionnaire and the same kind of interviewers (bilinguals) as well as the same interviewer instructions were employed. Thus, after applying necessary controls, CoO and CoR effects can be separated. Finally, the data also cover additional individual-level variables which usually cannot be obtained from census data, such as interethnic friendships, communication and travel behaviour and a variety of attitudinal variables.

6.4 PROFILING FREE-MOVING WESTERN EUROPEANS

To describe the different migrant groups with respect to a variety of variables, one would usually produce large tables including all of the groups and all of the describing variables separately. In fact, what we try here is to give a general overview without going into too much detail. For this purpose, we will use multiple correspondence analysis (MCA, see Greenacre and Blasius 1994). MCA offers a geometric representation of rows and columns of nominal and ordinal data. This technique has also been referred to as 'principal component analysis for nominal data'. MCA offers a low-dimensional representation. However, while a more than two-dimensional representation might be more adequate for some data, we will use two-dimensional representations throughout. In MCA, these two dimensions are orthogonal, that is, independent of each other. Categories of a variable which are mapped widely apart have very different profiles to the other variables. In particular, migrant groups located in close proximity are similar with regard to (most of) the describing variables. Groups located close to the centroid (the intersection of the two dimensions) have an average profile. The same applies to the describing variables when they are located close to the origin. As far as the association of the categories of different variables are concerned, distance in the two-dimensional space is to be interpreted with care. If the category of a variable is located close to the origin, all its associations with categories of the other variables are small, that is, its distribution comes close to the marginal distribution. The highest associations are for categories which are far from the origin and are located in the same direction from the origin. The dimensions themselves need to be interpreted. Much like principal component analysis, this is determined by the categories which are located at the two poles.

We will now present a series of MCA representations starting with one which includes sociodemographic variables describing the migrant groups only (Figure 6.1). After having focused on these structural commonalities, we will turn to cultural and social integration (Figure 6.2). Then migration motives and identificational integration will be discussed. From these preliminary analyses we will infer which variables really matter and which do not (that is all of their categories are close to the origin). When we put variables of all three domains together, we therefore eliminate as much redundant information as possible (Figure 6.3). Finally, we will discuss separate MCA models for different periods of migration (that is from 1974 to 1983, from 1984 to 1993, and from 1994 to 2003).

Our strategy of analysis starts by examining *structural* commonalities among EU movers. To begin with, thus, we run a first MCA including the CoR/CoO combinations and demographic variables only:

- Gender: M = male, F = female;
- Migration period (abbreviated: mp): 1 = 1974–83, 2 = 1984–93, 3 = 1994–2003;
- Age at migration (abbreviated: ma): 1 = 18–29, 2 = 30–49, 3 = 50+;
- Education (abbreviated: ed): 1 = tertiary, 2 = higher secondary, 3 = intermediary secondary, 4 = lower secondary or less;
- Social class based on the Erikson-Goldthorpe (EGP, Erikson and Goldthorpe 1992) schema (abbreviated: e): 1 = service class, 2 = other non-manual, 3 = self-employed, 4 = qualified workers, 5 = unqualified workers, 99 = not classified;
- Ever worked in CoR (abbreviated: ev): 1 = yes, 0 = no;
- Ever lived in CoR before (abbreviated: lc): 1 = yes, 0 = no;

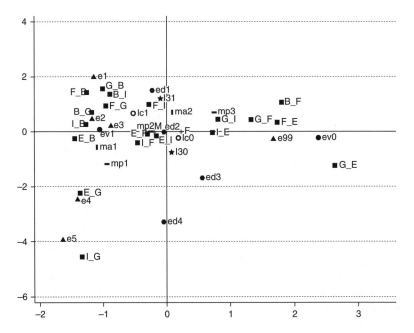

Figure 6.1   MCA of structural characteristics of EU movers

- Ever lived in third country before (abbreviated: l3): 1 = yes, 0 = no;
- As for CoO/CoR combinations, the first letter refers to CoO and the second to CoR: F = France, G = Germany, B = Britain, I = Italy, E = Spain. So, for instance, E_G stands for Spanish in Germany.

The outcome of this MCA is illustrated in Figure 6.1. We interpret it considering the vertical axis as a status axis. Higher education and upper social class categories lie on top. The horizontal axis unfolds along the age of migration and migration period: young migrants and the first migration period to the left and old migrants and the last migration period to the right. However, this axis can also be described in terms of structural integration in the labour market: all the EGP categories are to the left with the exception of unclassified migrants (that is those out of the labour market) who lie on the right-hand side. The information about work experiences in the CoR is located aside and in parallel: those who have had such experiences are on the left, the others on the right. Groups defined by whether they have lived for three months or more in the CoR or a third country before making the final move to the CoR are all located close to the centroid, that is, they do not contribute very much to defining the two-dimensional space. However, those who have previous migration experiences are located a bit more to the left. Both genders are also close to the centroid. Even if not discriminating, this is also a relevant finding: mobility within the EU is not structurally differentiated along gender lines.

Where do the CoO/CoR combinations fit in this space? The low pole of the structural integration axis has the Germans and the Britons in Spain and France, as well as the French in Spain. These are all more or less middle-level status groups. The latter also applies to the Italians and the Spanish in Britain, and the French and the Britons in Germany, but they are located closer to the high structural-integration pole. French and Germans in Britain as well as Britons in Italy are also highly integrated, but more to the high pole of the status axis. Perhaps these groups qualify as 'elite migrants' bringing about what Verwiebe and Eder (2006) call 'super-stratification'. In principle, their insertion in national labour markets can stretch pre-existing hierarchies of social inequality – for instance, by sustaining price levels especially in the housing market (on the transnationalization of inequality, cf. Weiß 2005). The same high status position is enjoyed by the French in Italy, though they enjoy a weaker level of integration (defined on the basis of our indicators). A combination of high structural integration in the labour market and lower status is, in fact, typical for the Italians and Spanish in Germany.

At this stage, we carried out a second MCA adding to the CoR/CoO combinations a set of variables measuring *sociocultural integration*:

- Language at the time of migration (abbreviated: lm): 1 = low, 2 = intermediate, 3 = high (originally measured on a 5-point scale ranging from 'no knowledge' to 'almost as well as native language'; the original categories 1 and 2 as well as 4 and 5 were collapsed into one category);
- Language at the time of the interview (abbreviated: l): 1 = low, 2 = intermediate, 3 = high (originally measured on a 5-point scale from 'no knowledge' to 'almost as well as native language'; the original categories 1 and 2 as well as 4 and 5 were collapsed);
- Friends from the CoO (abbreviated: fo): 0 = none, 1 = a few, 2 = several;
- Friends from the CoR (abbreviated: fr): 0 = none, 1 = a few, 2 = several;
- Partner status (abbreviated: p): 1 = partner from CoO, 2 = partner from CoR, 3 = partner from third country or no partner.

Findings of this second model are presented in Figure 6.2. Using just cultural and social integration as defining variables, it does not come as

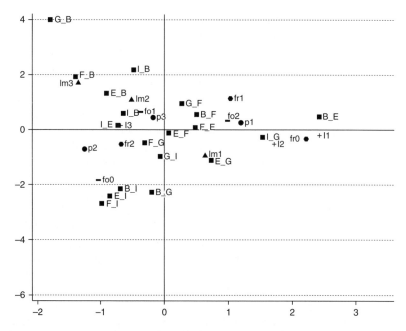

Figure 6.2   MCA of sociocultural characteristics of EU movers

a surprise that only the integration dimension – on the horizontal axis – seems to have a meaningful interpretation. On the low integration pole (right end of the graph), migrants have a low language proficiency at the time of migration, without any significant improvement during their sojourn. Furthermore, they do not have any friends from the CoR, but many from the CoO, and tend to have partners from their own home country. The reverse is true on the high integration pole (left end of the graph), where one finds respondents with high language proficiency, already at the time of migration, no friends from the CoO, but many from the CoR where their partner also comes from. Having a partner from a third country or no partner at all is close to the centroid, that is, this mating choice is not really distinctive among EU movers.

Which CoO/CoR combinations correspond to the low and high integration poles? Virtually all migrant groups to Britain and most to Italy are culturally and socially highly integrated. Of course, this similarity of integration levels can be (and is likely to be) achieved through dissimilar life arrangements – in particular, with a totally diverse emphasis on work contexts, taking into account that the labour market incorporation of movers to Britain and Italy are strikingly different (9.4 per cent of EU movers of working age in Italy were jobless in 2002 as opposed to 5.7 per cent in the UK: cf. Recchi *et al.* 2006). The opposition between movers to Britain and movers to Italy does give the vertical dimension a meaning. While the former are distinct by their high English language proficiency (which is required for participation in the labour force), the latter are distinct by not having CoO friends (which points to the fact that they do not live in ethnic enclaves). On the opposite pole, we have again the Germans and Britons in Spain and, again presumably for different reasons, the Italians in Germany. What keeps the latter group on the low cultural integration pole is not only their relatively poor command of German, but the preponderance of social integration into their own ethnicity in Germany compared to the destination country at large. Noticeably, Italians in Germany stand out as one of the better integrated migrant groups in structural terms – that is, mainly on the basis of their labour achievements and the persistence of their settlement. Their case highlights that structural and sociocultural integration do not necessarily overlap.

Now we switch to *identificational integration* – that is, a dimension of integration that touches upon identity and attachment to the CoR. First, we consider the sense of territorial belonging. Second, since our respondents are migrants, we deem that their identity is significantly shaped by the reasons they give for their mobility from one country to another – in particular, distinguishing between instrumental (work, study) and expressive reasons (love, quality of life). Their intention to stay or go back to their CoO (or elsewhere) is also a relevant indicator of their attachment to the CoR. Another indicator of identity orientation has to do with the kind of media preferred – namely, whether CoO or CoR TV channels are used.

The resulting picture is complex, as not all variables used here seem to have an impact in the same direction (not presented). In fact, a three-dimensional presentation would be better suited. In a two-dimensional space, however, the horizontal axis has the clearest interpretation: quality-of-life migrants are located on the right, while study-, work- and family-motivated migrants are found on the left. The former group comprises individuals who have mostly selected their given CoR out of free will, while the latter includes respondents who might have moved because their selected CoR had something valuable to offer (a job, a partner, a good university) but were less 'pulled' by the CoR itself. Consequently, they have a high return migration potential, which is virtually absent for quality-of-life migrants. The index of territorial identification is partially crossed with indicators of attachment measured by media usage. The quality of life motive is connected to a high sense of belonging to the CoR, but does not imply a high usage of CoR media. In fact, for the other migrant groups the reverse is true – they do not feel attached to their CoR, but watch the local TV chains.

Which of the CoO/CoR combinations are most clearly positioned? Again, Germans and Britons in Spain are characterized by a very low use of local media. French and Italians in Spain, Germans in Italy and Britons in France have a much stronger attachment to their CoR than their CoO. Low attachment to the CoR is especially found among Spanish movers nearly everywhere and Italians in Britain and Germany. Germans and French in Britain are characterized by a strong CoR media use – possibly a 'BBC effect'. What is of special interest is that attachment to the EU is virtually non-discriminatory. In other words, the combination of CoR and CoO attachment decides everything alone, whereas identification with Europe is a separate cultural dimension that responds to different logics.

We now proceed to the full model. Variables which did not contribute much to the definition of the semantic space in the models discussed so far are omitted: namely, gender, whether migrants have lived in the CoR or a third country before the final move and return migration intentions. We also exclude variables which are to some degree redundant: language proficiency at the time of migration (once language proficiency at the time of the interview is included), whether migrants have work experiences in the CoR (once the EGP missing category is included) and the number of friends from the CoO (this variable produces a mirror image to the number of friends from the CoR). For variables measuring identificational integration, categories are collapsed to produce fewer data points. Table 6.3 shows the abbreviations for the variables included in 6.3.

The status and integration dimensions emerge clearly. As in Figure 6.1, the status dimension is neatly defined by education and social class. In fact, the integration dimension seems to be more encompassing than structural integration. Social and cultural integration prove to have an even greater discriminatory power. Identificational integration, in contrast, seems to lack consistency: While TV usage follows the structural, cultural and social integration patterns, territorial identification turns out to be associated with status differences. Identification with the CoR prevails among the more educated and those with upper class jobs (or no job at all, perhaps because these include rentier-like people).

Some of the CoO/CoR combinations carve out their own peculiar location in the plot. In particular, on one hand, there are Italians (and Spanish) in Germany, who lie on the low-status end of the space, while showing an average level of integration. On the other hand, the Britons and Germans in Spain stand out as having the lowest integration, but occupy an intermediate position on the status dimension.

In a separate analysis (not shown), we ran the full models for each of the three migration periods (1974–83, 1984–93 and 1994–2003). In interpreting these models, it has to be noted that, in addition to a different intake of

Table 6.3   Variables used in Figure 6.3

Variable	Label	Codes
Demographic variables and structural integration		
Migration period	Mp	1 = 1974–1983, 2 = 1984–1993, 3 = 1994–2003
Age at migration	ma	1 = 18–29, 2 = 30–49, 3 = 50+
Education	ed	1 = tertiary, 2 = higher secondary, 3 = intermediary secondary, 4 = lower secondary or less
EGP class	e	1 = service class, 2 = other non manual, 3 = self employed, 4 = qualified workers, 5 = unqualified workers, 99 = not classified
Cultural and social integration		
Language proficiency	l	1 = low, 2 = intermediary, 3 = high
Friends for the CoR	fr	0 = none, 1 = a few, 2 = several
Partner status	p	1 = from CoO, 2 = from CoR, 3 = from third country or none
Migration motives and identificational integration		
Migration motives	m	1 = miscellaneous, 2 = work, 3 = family, love, 4 = quality of life, 5 = study
TV usage	t	1 = no TV or CoO/CoR TV equally, 2 = only or more CoO TV, 3 = only or more CoR TV
Territorial identification	tn	1 = equal CoO and CoR, 2 = more CoR attachment, 3 = more CoO attachment
CoO/CoR combinations	g	first letter = CoO; second letter = CoR; F = France, G = Germany, B = Britain, I = Italy, E = Spain

migrants in these three periods, the impact on selective return migration is much higher for the first than for the third period. This is simply related to the sheer length these migrants were exposed to the risk to return to their home countries.

What is most remarkable when comparing across migration periods is the behaviour of a couple of migrant groups. In the first period, Germans in Spain stand out as a very low integrated (but high status) group. In the second, but even more so in the third period, they are joined by the Britons. However, both groups (but in particular the Britons) have lost considerably on the status dimension over time. Retirement migration is becoming more 'democratic'. On the other hand, Italians and Spanish in Germany are distinct as low status, low integration groups in the first period. In the latter periods, the Italians in Germany are occupying a single position at

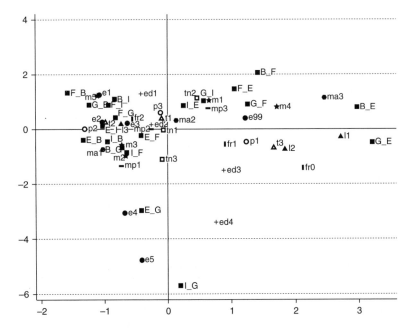

Figure 6.3   MCA model of structural, sociocultural and identificational characteristics

the low status pole while their integration has shifted towards the centre of the two-dimensional space. In contrast, the more recent arrivals from Spain to Germany have markedly improved their position both on the status and integration dimension.

6.5   CONCLUSIONS

In the face of the growing diversification of migration projects and trajectories, social scientists' efforts to generate empirically based and consistent classifications of migrant populations are rather rare (for an exception, cf. Düvell 2006). This chapter seeks to map out the objective and subjective differences within the rather loose category of intra-EU migrants on the basis of survey data on this population in the five largest EU15 countries (Germany, Britain, France, Italy and Spain). By using multiple correspondence analysis, we drew a parsimonious portrait of western European mobile citizens. This analysis led us to single out two key dimensions that seem to extract two basic inputs and outputs of individual migration choices – namely, social status and integration.

Migrants who originally came to study show the highest values on both dimensions. Those who came for love/family reasons are lower on the status dimension than those who came for work reasons, but both groups share an above average integration into the CoR. The most poorly integrated are those who moved exclusively to improve their quality of life. Among these movers, over time, we see generally decreasing values on the status dimension but some increase in integration.

We find most of the migrant groups defined in terms of CoO/CoR combinations to be rather similar: they have upper secondary or tertiary education and intermediary or good jobs. Their language proficiency is decent and they are relatively well integrated socially into their CoR. Having said this, we also have to point out that there are two markedly deviant cases: the first group is composed by the Italians and the first period Spanish migrants to Germany. They constitute remnants of the guest-worker migration age, characterized by very low values on the status dimension and an average position on the integration dimension. While low-skilled labour migration is a matter of the past among western Europeans, this kind of migration is likely to increase in the future, when eastern Europeans gain unrestricted access to the labour markets of the west. The second group, composed of the British and German migrants to Spain, shows the reverse picture: an intermediary position on the status dimension and a low position on the integration dimension. These migrants are mostly lower-middle class (pre-)retirement migrants. The Britons and Germans in France and the French in Spain resemble this pattern in a milder form. The remainder of the CoO/CoR combinations are not very distinct when regarded separately. However, when we focus on the CoR we can conclude that social integration is especially successful in Britain and Italy.

Of course, these divergent cases do not rule out the possibility of mixed configurations of intra-EU migrants. Equally, it would be misleading to consider these same configurations as being stable over time. Our analysis of different migration periods shows, for instance, that the status and integration characteristics of Spanish movers to Germany have changed noticeably from the 1970s onwards. We can speculate that such changes in the profiles of movers by country of origin and areas of settlement may even accelerate as free movement rights expand and become more easily accessible to EU citizens, especially with the significant enlargements of the EU in 2004 and 2007 (cf. Iglicka 2006). Adding to this the rapidly spreading networks of continental low-cost flights colonizing peripheral areas, as well as intensifying flows to major cities, we get a flavour of the wide and complex canvas of movements that are likely to blossom – possibly evolving towards shorter-term and shuttle forms of migration. More people, who are also more mobile, are a plausible scenario of geographical mobility in the EU in the years to come.

REFERENCES

Ackers, L. (1998), *Shifting Spaces: Women, Citizenship and Migration Within the European Union*, Bristol: The Policy Press.

Ackers, L. (2005), 'Moving people and knowledge: scientific mobility in the European Union', *International Migration*, **43** (5), 99–131.

Düvell, F. (2006), 'Polish immigrants: tensions between sociological typologies and state categories', in A. Triandafyllidou (ed.), *Contemporary Polish Migration in Europe: Complex Patterns of Movement and Settlement*, Washington, DC: Edwin Mellen, pp. 47–89.

Erikson, R. and J.H. Goldthorpe (1992), *The Constant Flux*, Oxford: Clarendon Press.

Eurostat (eds) (2006), *Population Statistics*, Luxembourg: Office for Official Publications of the European Communities.

Favell, A. (2004), 'Eurostars and eurocities: free moving professionals and the promise of European integration', *European Studies Newsletter*, 33, accessed at www.councilforeuropeanstudies.org/pub/Favell_jan04.html.

Favell, A. (2006), 'London as Eurocity: French free movers in the economic capital of Europe' in Smith, M.P. and A. Favell (eds), *The Human Face of Global Mobility*, New Brunswick, NJ: Transaction Publishers, pp. 247–74.

Favell, A. (2008), *Eurostars and Eurocities: Free Moving Urban Professionals in an Integrating Europe*, Oxford: Blackwell.

Greenacre, M. and J. Blasius (eds) (1994), *Correspondence Analysis in the Social Sciences*, San Diego, CA: Academic Press.

Huber, A. (2004), 'Geographical and ethnographic perspectives on the "rainbow" settlements of the Spanish coast' in Warnes, A.M. (ed), *Older Migrants in Europe*, Sheffield: Sheffield Institute for Studies on Ageing, pp. 35–9.

Iglicka, K. (2006), *Free Movement of Workers Two Years after Enlargement: Myths and Reality*, Center for International Relations reports and analyses 11/06, Warsaw.

King, R. and E.Ruiz-Gelices (2003), 'International student migration and the European "year abroad": effects on European identity and subsequent migration behavior', *International Journal of Population Geography*, 9, 229–52.

King, R., A.M. Warnes and A.M. Williams (1998), 'International retirement migration in Europe', *International Journal of Population Geography*, 4, 157–82.

King, R., A.M. Warnes and A.M. Williams (2000), *Sunset Lives: British Retirement Migration to the Mediterranean*, Oxford: Berg.

Münz, R. and H. Fassmann (2004), *Migrants in Europe and their Economic Position: Evidence from the Labour Force Survey and from Other Sources*, Hamburg, Germany: Institute of International Economics.

Poulain, M., N. Perrin and A. Singleton (2006), *THESIM. Towards Harmonised European Statistics on International Migration*, Louvain, Belgium: Presses Universitaires de Louvain.

Recchi, E., E. Baldoni, F. Francavilla and L. Mencarini (2006), 'Geographic and job mobility in the EU', report for the DG Employment, European Commission.

Recchi, E., D. Tambini, E. Baldoni, D. Williams, K. Surak and A. Favell (2003), 'Intra–EU migration: A socio-demographic overview', PIONEUR working paper 3, Florence: CIUSPO.

Salt, J. (1992), 'Migration processes among the highly skilled in Europe', *International Migration Review*, 26, 484–505.

Salt, J. (1997), 'International movements of the highly skilled', OECD Directorate for Education, Employment, Labour and Social Affair, International Migration Unit occasional paper no 3, Paris: OECD Publishing.

Salt, J. (2005), *Current Trends in International Migration in Europe*, Strasbourg: Council of Europe, accessed at http://www.geog.ucl.ac.uk/mru/docs/current_trends_2004.pdf.

Santacreu, O., N. Rother and M. Braun (2006), 'Stichprobenziehung für Migrantenpopulationen in fünf Ländern. Eine Darstellung des methodischen Vorgehens im PIONEUR–Projekt', *ZUMA–Nachrichten*, 59, 72–88.

Sopemi (various years), *Trends in International Migration*, Paris: OECD.

StataCorp (2007), *Stata Statistical Software*, release 10, College Station, TX: StataCorp.

Verwiebe, R. and K. Eder (2006), 'The positioning of transnationally mobile Europeans in the German labour market: an analysis of its causes and effects', *European Societies*, 8, 141–67.

Weiß, A. (2005), 'The transnationalization of social inequality: conceptualizing social positions on a world scale', *Current Sociology*, 53, 707–28.

7. A suspended status: the puzzle of Polish workers in the West Midlands

Guglielmo Meardi

7.1 INTRODUCTION

The enlargement of the EU in 2004–07 to the east set in motion a greater transnational mobility, which multiplied the economic and social interactions among people from different nationalities. This has had immediate policy implications at the EU level (for example the promotion of further mobility by the European Commission, debates on the ex-Bolkenstein directives, European Court of Justice rulings on labour disputes over 'social dumping') and at national levels (for example the 'transitory periods', the 'Polish plumber' media issue and its effect in the French referendum on the EU Constitutional Treaty, the anti-Romanian campaigns in Italy). But it also has deeper social consequences, requiring the revision of defining categories. Many commentators have seen intra-EU migration as a source of potentially disruptive tensions, others as a welcome influx of mobility and flexibility in labour markets – yet the phenomenon itself is not yet fully understood or even defined.

While a large amount of research has been undertaken on this topical issue (Anderson *et al.* 2006, Duszczyk and Wyśniewski 2007, Pollard *et al.* 2008), deeper debates on the conceptual and methodological implications for migration studies and for the understanding of the European labour market are still only beginning. This chapter will discuss how new approaches, linking migration and labour studies, are made necessary by the novelty of this migration wave. On the one side, migration studies still have not elaborated an adequate category for classifying this group of migrants and catching their specificity. The concept of 'transnational' migrants (Glick Schiller *et al.* 1995; Pries 1999; Cohen 2004) grasps many features of the phenomenon, but its application to the specificity of EU citizenship and freedom of movement is still explorative, in spite of some promising attempts (Pries 2003). On the other side, labour studies in Europe have focused on the mobility of capital rather than labour, on the assumption that only the former is the mobile factor benefiting from

Europeanization. The rare industrial relations studies on new intra-EU migration have focused on applied or trade union issues only (French and Moehrke 2007; Fitzgerald and Hardy 2007), with little integration into the broader labour market context. Taken alone, these two perspectives have failed to foresee and explain the current events. As an effect, there is currently a large knowledge gap on intra-EU migration, a phenomenon which cannot be easily understood on the grounds of models developed for other migration waves.

The utility of such a 'cross-contamination' of different perspectives (which, if taken alone, seem increasingly inadequate) is then shown through exploratory research on the extreme case of Polish workers in the West Midlands, the region with most immigrants from the new EU member states. Here we find the highest incidence of new migrants' temporary agency work within the UK, a phenomenon clearly calling for both cultural and labour explanations: as a growing form of employment, it responds at the same time to labour process dynamics of increased exploitation and to social dynamics of a new, ambivalent form of migration.[1]

7.2 THE INADEQUACY OF CLASSIC APPROACHES AND THE NEED FOR CROSS-CONTAMINATION

For regulatory but also cultural and political reasons, the movement of workers within the EU is different from classic migrations – to the point that most of the workers involved, staying abroad for less than 12 months, do not even qualify for the demographic definition of migrants. Images such as the 'Ryanair migrant' challenge the classical images of migration, but also the well-established representation of the EU labour market, long seen as an imbalance between capital mobility and labour immobility. In addition, this migration wave is different from previous European migrations (for example the Italians after World War II) for its gender composition and the large number of unmarried women (near half of the total), raising debates both on the nature of the European gender regime, and on the risks of a 'care drain', a sensitive issue in the USA but still understudied in the EU.

The novelty of the phenomenon is proven by the inaccuracy of the most authoritative forecasts from before 2004. The 'optimistic' forecasts (for example, Boeri and Brücker 2001, for the European Commission) not only foresaw an influx many times smaller than the actual one (812 000 instead of the expected 50 000 in the first four years in the UK according to the Worker Registration Scheme, 67 per cent of whom came from Poland[2,3]), but they mistook the trend as well: they expected an immediate decrease after the first year, while the number of workers coming to the UK kept increasing between 2004 and 2006, and only started declining in 2007, partly for demographic reasons (decline in the number of 'potential' migrants), and partly for exchange rate trends (the Polish złoty having gained nearly 40 per cent against the British pound between 2004 and 2008).[4] But the 'pessimistic' forecasts (for example Sinn and Ochel 2003, supporting the German decision of closing the borders) were equally wrong when expecting a movement towards social benefits (so-called 'social raids'), while in reality the flux has been nearly entirely for work (even in Sweden where social benefits are available for newcomers, or in the case of workers resident for longer than one year in Britain[5]). These forecasts, based on individualistic economic models, have failed to understand the social and cultural determinants of migration.

Another unexpected phenomenon is the apparent propensity of Polish workers in the UK and Ireland to join trade unions and mobilize for the defence of their rights. This contrasts with the frequently held assumption (although already proved false by the experience of countries such as the USA, UK and Italy) of a difficult relationship between migrants and trade unions. The European reality for a few years has shown that the opposite can be the case: trade unions (even if with some major ambiguities) can be at the forefront of migrants' defence and organization, in countries as different as the UK (Avci and McDonald 2000) and Spain and Italy (Watts 1998).

Even more it challenges the insiders/outsiders models of labour markets, currently often used to promote labour law deregulation in the EU. While the segmented labour market theory (Piore 1979) holds a number of useful insights on migration, pushing it to an insider/outsider dichotomy raises theoretical and political problems. The ideas of 'outsiders' (in a way similar to the sociological concept of 'underclass' or race) were first developed out of a 'progressive' concern for the conditions of the most vulnerable parts of the population, but have been embraced by the political Right to attack existing worker rights. Challenging these models as empirically ungrounded (because migrant and local workers' conditions and aspirations are more similar than opposed) has therefore an important political and theoretical dimension. In particular, it would help to overcome muddled debates such as those on so-called 'social dumping', which often blame the poorest workers without identifying the specific social processes in place.

There are indeed aspects of the migration phenomenon which are reminiscent of social dumping in the sense of the employers' (rather than employees') intentional strategy of putting pressure on local labour conditions. A Home Office report on the employers' use of migrant labour, besides praising migrants for their prodigious contribution to the British economy, reported among the many employers' tributes to migrants the following: 'the more favourable work ethic of migrant workers had the effect of encouraging domestic workers to work harder' (Dench *et al.* 2006, 13). While this may sound a patent admission of social dumping, the subjective side of migration is missing in all social dumping talks: migrants' hopes and strategies, which may have nothing to do with 'social dumping'.

Integration between industrial relations (study of associations, of conflict, and the ethnography of the workplace) and sociological migration studies (cultural, social and economic aspects) is particularly useful to filling this knowledge gap. Industrial relations studies can contribute through their critique of economic models of the labour market (Kaufman 2007), which currently dominates in the perception of the migrant as 'closest living embodiment of *Homo œconomicus* – that rational, self-seeking, amoral agent that propels economic models of human behaviour' (McGovern 2007, 218). Specifically, that industrial relations' focus not only on state regulations, but also on employers' strategies and on associations (trade unions, employer associations) adds a dimension migration studies have largely neglected by focusing on the individual and/or on families. Through the study of conflict, mobilization and resistance industrial relations avoid the dichotomy between structural and subjective models that exist in migration studies (for example all is due either to capitalist interests, or to migrant preferences). As McGovern (2007) argues, it combines the strengths of institutional economists' focus on demand (the employers) with the sociologists' interest in supply (the workers). Given that work is the main concern of migrants, and that migration is such a big preoccupation for workers, the reciprocal relative ignorance between industrial relations and migration studies is rather striking.

In the EU enlargement, trade unions and employer associations have had an important role in shaping the migration patterns (for example Meardi 2002, Bohle and Husz 2005, Gajewska 2006). Also relevant is the patrimony of studies on self-organization of women in trade unions (for example Colgan and Ledwith 2002), a phenomenon in many ways similar to that of the current Polish self-organization in British trade unions. In addition, through the study of conflict, mobilization and resistance, industrial relations avoids the dichotomy between structural and subjective models that exists in migration studies (for example all is due either to capitalist interests, or to migrant preferences).

On the other side, the expertise of migration studies, cultural studies and gender studies is a necessary contribution to the understanding of labour market processes of socialization, segregation and discrimination, as industrial relations have been for long gender- and ethnicity-blind, as still seen in the mistaken expectations that migrants would not join trade unions. The recent emerging industrial relations studies of migration have provided good examples of innovative qualitative research (for example Milkman 2006, Waldinger and Lichter 2003). The neglected role of labour market institution has been proven to be important by Erne's (2008) study of the role of 'corporatism' in explaining the more open Swiss labour market in comparison to the German market, which would not be explained by cultural or political factors. More generally, the large scale of migration from the new member states (NMS) to the UK involves a major shift in the power balance of employment relations, as exemplified by the Bank of England's governor's declaration in August 2007 that immigration is limiting wage growth, and by the Polish government's efforts to retain workers. Such power dynamics require specific industrial relations interpretative tools, such as the 'exit and voice' concepts (Hirschman 1970).

There are some important questions raised by the new wave of intra-EU migration. While different, they can be covered by the same, broad research question: are the workers moving from the new to the old member states 'migrants' – that is marginalized foreigners in the way described by Sayad (1999) in the case of Algerians in France, who are neither in France nor in Algeria – or rather new 'EU-cosmopolitans', combining experiences and networks in more than one country, in the way suggested by Cohen (2004)? Within Europe, this question is parallel to that raised by Habermas a decade ago: will the increased interactions between eastern and western Europeans (especially in the workplace) lead to social and political mobilization and exclusion that contribute to foster the dividing premises of segregation, marginalization and exclusion, or common shared grounds of a transnational and European citizenship (Habermas 1996, 506)? This question has two corollaries. First, are we seeing a new divide between western and eastern European workers (Meardi 2000), or the emergence of some sort of EU-citizenship with potentials for new, cross-border forms of socialization, mobilization and communication? Second, are these migrants clearly different from extra-EU migrants, or do hidden factors (both formal and informal) perpetuate their discrimination or segregation in spite of the EU principles of free mobility?

7.3   EMERGING EMPIRICAL ISSUES

The Effect of 'Open' Borders

The early experience of 2004–06, as assessed by the European Commission (2006), shows that the 'transitory periods' selectively applied by some countries have had a strong impact on distorting migration flows, notably replacing Germany and Austria with the British Isles as preferred destination countries. Statistics are unfortunately of little reliability within countries, and heterogeneous among countries, so precise comparisons are impossible. According to available figures, the difference is, however, quite striking: Germany and Austria, which by 2004 already hosted the large majority of accession countries' migrants and were predicted (Boeri and Brücker 2001) to receive 90 per cent of the new flows, in the two years after the enlargement seem to have received only 82000 and 8000 NMS migrants respectively, against the 265000 and 63000 of UK and Ireland, which are also smaller countries (Barrell *et al.* 2007).[6]

The impact of free movement is not only quantitative, but also depends on the 'quality' of migration. It increases the amount of short-term movement, as there are fewer risks involved: 60 per cent of the NMS workers registering in the UK declare the intention to stay for less than 3 months, 24 per cent do not know how long they want to stay, and only 12 per cent want to stay for longer than a year (Home Office 2008).

In the EC's eyes, it also appears that 'opening' the borders to the NMS' workers is only beneficial. On one side, the transition periods introduced in some countries such as Germany generate illegal employment and pseudo self-employment in the form of service provision. As these forms of employment are outside the reach of trade union organization, in the long term this reinforces the barriers between unions and immigrants, who come to perceive the local unions as hostile. When the media (for example Gazeta Wyborcza) in the spring of 2007 revealed the extreme exploitation of Polish migrants in the factories of the largest German meat-packing company, Tönnies, the striking thing was not the exploitation itself (€3.5/hour pay, 84-hour working week), as such can be probably found in extreme cases in all countries. It was rather that this large company had no union at all, and that it did not deny the facts and did not see anything wrong in it, as these were not its own employees, only the employees of a Polish contractor. It was only in September 2007 that German inspectors and trade unions managed to sue Tönnies, after elaborating a particularly complicated argument on the 'fictitious' nature of the service contracts with Polish providers.

On the other side, a country like the UK has seen extensive complementary migration, leading to increased growth, tax revenue, pension funding and inflation control. The Bank of England, employers and government are particularly satisfied, and no particular social problems have arisen (unemployment is growing the least where immigration is strongest).

This experience has contravened another forecast of Boeri and Brücker, after that of limited migration flows: that of a 'race to the top' among countries in restrictive regulations (Boeri and Brücker 2005). In 2006, the majority of EU countries followed the British example by lifting restrictions (Portugal, Spain, Italy, Finland and Greece) or at least easing them (Belgium, Denmark, France, Luxembourg and the Netherlands). France decided to open its borders in 2008. However, little is known about the link between restriction and integration patterns. Even in the UK, popular fears are high, as implicitly admitted by the government when closing the borders to Romanians and Bulgarians, who are restricted to agriculture and self-employment.

The specificity of EU status does not appear to involve economic privileges, though. A total of 70 per cent of NMS workers arriving between April 2007 and March 2008 earn between GBP4.50 and GBP5.99 per hour, the minimum wage being GBP5.52 (GBP4.60 for the under-22s) (Home Office 2008), and new migrants constitute one of the largest groups of 'vulnerable workers' (TUC Commission on Vulnerable Workers 2008). Notably, newly arrived Poles earn several pounds less than immigrants in the same jobs who came to the UK before 2000: the lowest rate paid to all 26 nationalities studied, including Somalis, Turks and the Chinese (Eade *et al.* 2008). The fact that in many cases new EU migrants appear to have replaced previous migrant groups, now more integrated, suggests a demand-based, structural hypothesis of extreme segmentation employer strategies, frequently substituting workforces in the search for ultimate vulnerability.

The Gender Dimension

The large number of young women involved (nearly 50 per cent of the total) and their strong representation in sectors such as health and hospitality (including homes for the elderly) raises the question of a possible 'European care chain', even if it is clear that most of the personal care sector involves women from outside the EU. One issue for research includes to what extent women in the NMS are being replaced by immigrants from further east (for example Ukraine) in such a 'care chain', and with what consequences. More broadly, the expansion of the sector and its tight connection with immigration raises issues on working conditions in these sectors, characterized by low visibility, difficult social control and personal power relations. It is already known how deskilling and exploitation of migrants follow gender-specific forms (Kofman 2000) and this is confirmed in the case of the Poles (Currie 2007). There are implications not only for career opportunities but also for mobilization. There are signs that the mobilization of domestic workers and similar is possible (Schwenken 2005), yet its forms and conditions are still to be identified.

In addition, there is a broader issue on the gender identities and cultures of migrants, as researched by the seminal work by Passerini *et al.* (2007) on Hungarian and Bulgarian women migrants. Gender arrangements are in some regards different in the new and old member states, as a legacy of full female employment under communism and traditional values in some countries such as Poland. It may be expected that through migration these different cultures get in contact with potential for change, for example when Polish women return to their home country. Any evidence of improved equality expectations by returning migrants would support the hypothesis of a potential European space which workers can use to their advantage comparing conditions and upgrading their expectations – the opposite of what the 'social dumping' scenario suggests, and something similar to what multinational companies do on the opposite side.[7]

The Role of Temporary Work Agencies

The issue of temporary agency work has political (the proposed EU directive on temporary agency work, on which interestingly the UK and Poland are allied in opposing equal rights for agency workers) and symbolic implications. A total of 39 per cent of registered A8 migrant workers work in 'Administration, Business and Management' (Home Office 2008), but this denomination includes all agency workers regardless of the actual job performed. The data on jobs confirm that only a tiny minority is actually in management or professional business jobs (less than 1 per cent). Moreover, the share of workers in this 'ABM' sector is constantly increasing: it is not a temporary phenomenon. In terms of contracts, 53 per cent of NMS workers are in temporary contracts and 43 per cent in permanent (Home Office 2008).

Does the fact that about a third of workers from the NMS in the UK receive their first job through agencies stem from choice (flexibility, short-term commitment, cosmopolitanism) or rather from fate (new form of labour market segregation)? In some sectors, especially local public services but also food industry and manufacturing (the media reported thousands of underpaid agency workers at each of the large companies such as BMW, Coca Cola, Corus), trade unions point at an 'apartheid' of migrant workers, through their segregation in agency employment, and early evidence shows that some migrants perceive agency work (with the reduced rights and pay it entails) as a form of discrimination. Do employers pursue a strategy of segregation by perpetuating a discriminatory stereotype of immigrants as people for whom responsibility should be left to agencies? Temporary work agencies may emerge as both a segregating institution, and as a contested terrain for social mobilization around the issue of migration. Indeed, migration can also, rather than simply jeopardize worker rights, act as a catalyst for more mobilization and political action for the improvement of all workers' rights. This seems to have been the case in the UK, where the Trade Union Congress created a Commission for Vulnerable Workers and increased its political pressure over the temporary work agencies issue, obtaining, in May 2008, the government's promise of new legislation giving more rights to agency workers with more than three months' employment.

Mobilization Between Exit and Voice

The contested nature of temporary work agencies leads us immediately to the next issue, that is the mobilization potential of new migrants. Trade unions have increasingly focused on groups outside their core constituencies. This has followed 'contested' as well as 'invited' patterns, and resulted in 'autonomous' organizing (separate organization or special structures) or 'mainstreaming' (Colgan and Ledwith 2002). The former strategies (for example feminist initiatives in Italy in the 1970s, or class, gender and sexual orientation groups in the UK in the 1990s) necessarily call into question the meaning of 'class unity' and cause reactions which may be mediated later. Such strategies are potentially important for migrants, both in improving the respect of their rights, and offering them opportunities for 'active' organizing and self-representation. The case of the Poles in the UK is innovative on two points. First, the role of cross-border linkages (cooperation between Trades Union Congress and *Solidarność*) raises the issue of a possible EU public space usable by workers (does such cooperation increase the assertiveness of trade unions in Poland?). Second, the experiences of special Polish-language union sections (the first in Southampton) are an interesting case of community unionism, but raise particularly deep questions on class unity, given the role of language as a barrier and the potential for conflicting interests between Poles and locals. There are also the side-questions of the situation of the other EU migrants who do not have the 'critical mass' for separate organizing, and of the relations with other, older ethnic minorities.

Within the Polish community, there is also the interesting theoretical issue of the class-ethnicity intersection on employment issues: the old Polish migrants (wave of 1945) being culturally distant from the current one, but cooperating on trade union initiatives.

An additional implication is the effect of migration for mobilization in the country of origin. The link between emigration and mobilization can be conceptualized through the link between 'exit' and 'voice' in the labour market, as two shifting and mutually enforcing responses to dissatisfaction (Hirschman 1970, 1982).

'Voice' has been weak in post-communist Europe (Meardi 2007). With trade union density and collective bargaining figures very low, workers are left to react to problems at work through 'exit', that is – in Hirschman's dichotomy – individual, market-logic options. There are many forms of 'exit' among central eastern European workforces, including informal economy, exit from the labour market, populism, abstention, riots, organizational misbehaviour, turn-over (Greskovits 1998). It is migration which has peaked most visibly following EU accession, in spite of improved economic conditions in the NMS. Seen from the perspective of the countries of origin, migration to western Europe is more important than for the host countries. In the period up to June 2007, 2.5 per cent of active Poles, 2.4 per cent of active Slovaks, 3.1 per cent of active Latvians and 4 per cent of active Lithuanians had registered for work in the UK only (Home Office 2008). Numbers are much lower for other NMS. The total share of workers who have chosen to 'exit' their countries, at least temporarily, after 2004 may be over 10 per cent in the case of the Baltic States and only slightly less in that of Poland and Slovakia. This contrasts with the old member states, where mobility since the creation of the European Economic Community only affected less than 2 per cent of the workforce.

Such macroscopic exit affects the balance of power in employment relations in the home countries. Both real and potential worker mobility (the right to legal employment in other EU states) after 2004 affects employers less than capital mobility affects employees, as capital remains inherently more mobile than labour. Still, labour shortages are complained of in all NMS, and employer organizations are requesting the easing of migration barriers to workers from their eastern neighbours (Belarus, Russia and Ukraine). The exit threat also forces employers and governments to make concessions they had been unwilling to make before. Wages have been increasing quickly since 2004, even if less than productivity and therefore without damaging the competitiveness of these countries: between 2000 and 2006, by 50.6 per cent in Poland, 59.3 per cent in Lithuania, 60.4 per cent in the Czech Republic, 88.9 per cent in Slovakia, 97.8 per cent in Hungary, 100.4 per cent in Estonia and 118.3 per cent in Latvia, as against 26.3 per cent in the Euro area (Eurostat data). However, inflation is marginally higher, and productivity increase much higher in the NMS. This means that actually there is much more wage moderation in the NMS than in western Europe (Van Gyes *et al.* 2007). Interestingly, these figures are roughly inversely correlated to collective bargaining coverage (higher in Poland and Slovakia than in the Baltic countries), and wage drift (the difference between actual pay and collectively agreed pay) is greater than in western Europe. This means that formal industrial relations are not the driving force behind them.

Wage increases are granted not because of union power, but because of exit threats: not surprisingly, they are most generous in sectors such as construction and transport, where employees are most mobile. National and regional governments have also needed to take measures against emigration. Apart from easing immigration from eastern neighbours, they have proposed a number of disparate incentives and policies to 'bring people back'. For instance, the Polish government promised graduates a two-year exemption from social contributions and 20,000-PLN (about 5,000 Euro) grants to set up companies.

Such massive 'exit' may in turn promote 'voice', as voice becomes more attractive when exit opportunities become more 'sticky'. In the current situation, the attractiveness of migration seems bound to decline (in spite of a likely wave at the end of the German and Austrian transitory periods), as suggested by the declining 2007 WRS data: the wage gap between east and west is narrowing, and migrants are discovering, with time, the discrimination and segregation barriers as well as the extra costs they face in the host countries. Many examples of worker resurgent assertiveness across the NMS suggest that such a shift from exit to voice might be starting (Meardi 2007).

7.4   THE WEST MIDLANDS CASE

This section combines the Worker Registration Scheme data (Home Office 2008) with early findings from research (interviews, case study) on Poles in the West Midlands. The Midlands (east and west) region was second after East Anglia (where migration is more frequently seasonal and in agriculture) in number of registered migrants from the NMS. This combines in the Birmingham area with a considerable 'old' Polish community, the World War II veterans who preferred England to communist Poland in 1945. This case is particularly interesting because in this region the share of Poles working through temporary agency employment is the highest (61 per cent, against a national average of 39 per cent). The issue of temporary agency work has political (the proposed EU directive on temporary agency work, new legislation in the UK) and symbolic implications: does it stem from choice (flexibility, short-term commitment, cosmopolitanism) or rather from fate (a new form of labour market segregation)? Finally, the Midlands has also a relatively high share of NMS' migrants working in manufacturing (8.3 per cent against a national average of 7.5 per cent, but the West Midlands are much more industrialized than the East), the most unionized sector in the country; it is therefore where relations with the unions may be the most developed.

The exploratory research covered the observation of a cooperation project between the Trade Union Councils and the Polish Club in Birmingham, the analysis of a survey conducted within the same project, and ten semi-structured interviews with male and female migrants.[8]

Union-ethnic Cooperation

The cooperation project between the TUC and the Polish Club covers information and advice primarily on basic social and employment rights, with the secondary aims of recruiting and organizing migrants into the unions as well as creating capacities (in terms of organization and expertise) within the Polish Club to pursue such activity autonomously in the future. In practice, it mostly consists in surgeries offered by union experts within the Polish Club one afternoon per week, with translation provided by volunteers of the Polish Club.

The project is interesting, first of all, for the interaction between cultural/ethnic associations and class-based ones. The Polish Club in Birmingham (officially named Polish Catholic Association) was created by World War II veterans in the post-war period and it has had a mostly cultural and religious function so far (it includes a Church and the most attended event is the Sunday Mass). There is a large generation and cultural gap between that generation of Polish refugees and the current generation of migrants. The old generation's identity was based on staunch anti-communism, and an idealized version of patriotism which is alien to the new generation. The old generation did not even recognize the People's Republic of Poland as a legitimate state – while the new generation was born in it and, generally, it accepted it as a matter of fact. The borders of Poland have also changed so much after 1945 that the two generations may often refer to different homelands: the old one mostly coming from the eastern territories that now belong to the Ukraine or Belarus.

This cultural and generational gap seems to have been bridged, however, by the emergence of the large number of young Polish migrants coming to the Club with requests for help. The Club, lacking the necessary expertise and capacity, turned to the Trades Union Congress which, coincidentally, was keen on starting a project on migrant workers. The project seems to have met the approval of workers and the surgeries enjoy certain popularity. Questions are raised as to the degree to which the secondary aims have been reached, though. Recruitment has been meagre, and the unions have doubts about the autonomous capacities of the Polish Club. By contrast, the Polish translators know the needs and are able to answer (even more quickly and effectively) queries without the presence of the union experts.

Within the project, a questionnaire was distributed to the workers attending the surgeries. In 2006, 100 questionnaires were filled in. The results confirm a marginal labour market position: one-third of the respondents was employed by agencies, 30 per cent did not have a written employment contract (compulsory in the UK) and 22 per cent did not even have, nor had they requested, a National Insurance number, and were therefore working illegally.

Migrants' Voices: A Suspended Status

Ten semi-structured interviews on the migration and employment experience were conducted in May 2007 with ten Polish migrants who arrived after 1 May 2004 and were working in the low-pay sector. The sample included five female and five male respondents in order to investigate possible gendered processes. Six interviews were conducted with a specific group, cleaners from one organization, and four at the Birmingham Polish Club during the mentioned surgery hours. The interviews lasted 50–60 minutes, were conducted in Polish, fully recorded and transcribed, and covered by a confidentiality and anonymity agreement.

The first, clear observation refers to the specific nature of the migration experience of these workers. The migrant status is often 'fluid', unplanned, corresponding to the typology of 'transnational' migrants (Pries 2003). Unlike other groups for which migration is an important, difficult life-choice, for all the interviewees the choice was casual or even unconscious, given the ease of moving between Poland and the UK.

I came with a friend and at the beginning it had to be just a 2-month holiday job experience [. . .] during those 2 months I was without work, I didn't speak English [. . .] After nearly 2 months we found a job as room attendants in a hotel. Then my friend returned to Poland, I stayed and so I didn't finish university [. . .]
How long do you plan to stay?
No idea. But I suspect that I will stay for longer. For a really longer time (female cleaner, 21).

At the beginning it was just . . . I wouldn't say gambling, but curiosity to see how things are here [. . .]
How long do you plan to stay in this country?
Oh, I don't know how to answer this one . . . Really difficult to say . . . I can only say that as long as I have a job here certainly I don't return to Poland (male cleaner, 37).

The first person who came here was my daughter, who signed a contract in Poland to work here. She was in the first year of English at the university and decided that she rather wanted to learn the language here. [. . .] After 6 months I came to visit her [. . .] In half a year she had managed to save a good sum, while I was working in Poland for 800zł [£140] monthly. I was shocked. [. . .] This consideration convinced me to stay (female cleaner, 49).

While decisions come accidentally and are varied in their form, the underlying reason is constant and is financial, combined in some cases with interest in the language. But even the financial aims themselves are varied, including raising the money for a flat, for paying back car accident damage, or for a pension.

The 'suspended' nature of this migration is confirmed by the very frequent contacts with Poland through telecommunication, usually on a daily basis and with text messages as the most frequent channel. Respondents also use Polish media and information sources regularly, especially the media and satellite TV. In one case, the respondent has Polish satellite TV at home, but no British TV.

How Migrants Compare Countries

Some respondents compare the UK with other western countries they have experience or knowledge of, usually Germany. Maybe surprisingly from a labour rights point of view, they all prefer the UK to Germany. Two factors seem to play a role: a historical/cultural one (the Polish hostility to Germany) and a recent regulatory one of free access to employment. The resulting opinion is to consider the UK more employee-friendly.

> Sure, one can go to Germany, but there it is worse, they treat workers worse (female cleaner, 23).

> I am a carpenter and I worked for a long time in Germany. In Germany I have been many times, in various companies and regions and it was varied, things I haven't seen here.
> *In what sense it was 'varied'?*
> Apart from all, financially. There was no trust, work was not entirely legal, it wasn't registered in Germany. This was in the 1990s. [. . .] So far I really praise Britain (male cleaner, 37).

The praise for Britain is overall, however, very instrumental, as the following quote reveals strikingly.

> it was an undeclared job so I resigned. [. . .] I am keen on working legally because I want to stay for 5 years and get the citizenship [. . .]
> *You said you will apply for citizenship?*
> Yes, because in the future I'd like to go to Australia, and with the British citizenship it's easier.

Why leave England?
Because here I don't like anything (male kitchen aid, 35).

The Gender Dimension

The interviews reveal quite a striking similarity between female and male migrants: the choice of migrating takes the same form, and women are as proactive as men, including when it is a couple moving. Female respondents are keen to stay on in the labour market, even when they have children or are pregnant. A possible difference is, however, in the age groups: female migrants are either very young or in their 40s (more rarely migrating with children in school age), while men often migrate in their 30s. It should be remembered, however, that, according to Home Office data, this migration wave is overwhelmingly very young: 43 per cent are between 18 and 24, 39 per cent between 25 and 34 (a further implication of which is that nearly none of these migrants had work experiences under communism). In terms of age, the overall split is 57 per cent men and 43 per cent women (Home Office 2008).

The focus on cleaners also reveals that Polish male migrants are ready to cross gendered lines in the labour market, which they would probably not cross in Poland. As a result of this redefinition of gendered roles, which quite typically for migrants puts a higher weight on instrumental than symbolic value of work, interviewees may even perceive gendered labour demand as incongruous.

In hotels, they don't take men. Even if they ask (female cleaner, 23).

Temporary Work Agencies

The UK has the largest use of temporary work agencies in the EU, and has the softest regulations and the fewest employment rights for agency workers (at least until proposed new legislation in 2008). It has been reported that in some sectors (especially privatized public services) a very large use of agency workers results in a 'Balkanization' of the labour market separating indigenous and migrant workers. With few exceptions naming specific agencies that proved useful, migrants have an overwhelmingly negative opinion about them.

These agencies are all one big fraud, exploiting people. When there was work, this agency would require 100 people, although it could only employ 20, but with some guarantee of work continuity. And the agency recruited 100, who would compete to work as long as possible, while the agency was only interested in getting the contract as quickly as possible, at the cost of the employees (male cleaner, 34).

They take the transaction fee from everybody. After 6 months you have to renew the contract and they take the fee again. They also take the first week of salary. Even if it is not actually them who found me the job, they just gave me the information. [. . .] I wanted to leave the agencies, they pay only the minimum wage (male waiter, 29).

These agencies are of no use. [. . .] Any agency you walk into, they just sit and drink coffee. Maybe they have some state subsidies because otherwise they would not survive. I didn't receive any phone call from any agency for six months (male kitchen aid, 35).

Agencies often take on as many people as they can and pay less than the minimum wage or the going rate. I received an offer for £4.47. The agency sacked me when they discovered that I was pregnant. They simply told me that since I am pregnant, I cannot work [. . .] I know that there is a very good protection for pregnant workers with a permanent contract, but nobody cares about those from agencies such as me. Protection for pregnant agency workers simply does not exist (female warehouse operative, 21).

Respondents detect here some national dividing lines, both in terms of discrimination and segregation.

Two years ago some agencies didn't look positively at Polish job-seekers (male cleaner, 37).

These agencies simply make money on us, for as long as 6 months. They take provisions out of our pay. Not just a transaction fee. I don't have good opinions about them. The worst is, that firms don't want to employ without the intermediation of agencies. It's a self-enforcing business (male driver, 40).

Such decisively negative views challenge the argument of deregulated agency work as opening opportunities to, and therefore benefiting, migrants (and outsiders as a whole: as the previous quote shows, female migrants suffer even more from agency employment). Although many migrants manage to escape agency work, it is not an easy process and employer preference for it probably combines ethnic prejudice with abuse of flexibility. Other research, as well as the media and social organizations, have documented exploitative practices by some agencies, such as illegal pay deductions under the form of accommodation or other social expenses (French and Möhrke 2006). This is clearly a point where more research, covering not just the supply but also the demand of agency work, is required.

Mobilisation

The issues emerging from the Polish Club-TUC cooperation can be further examined through migrants' answers. Most migrants have no experience and nearly no interest in trade unionism. According to the TUC survey, 10 per cent have been trade union members in Poland, and 3 per cent are members in the UK. Respondents seem to put more hope and trust in Polish organizations rather than in local trade unions.

> First of all, the initiative for helping Poles should be taken by the Polish club (male cleaner, 37).

However, the weak interest in trade unionism should be contextualized and not treated as inherent to migrant or Polish workers. Low unionization is normal for low-pay young employees in temporary employment, whether migrants or not. Some respondents actually express some appreciation for trade unions, while others point at the difficulty in organizing in sectors where the employers are anti-union.

> Generally it's always good if there is an institution or a trade union which represents the employees (female cleaner, 49).

> There is such a tyrannical management that there is no chance for a trade union. They would sack half of the people (male driver, 40).

> There was a trade union but when I arrived it didn't exist anymore. The people who had created it had been sacked, as simple as that. [. . .] it would be certainly useful, thanks to the union we got a half-hour break (female warehouse operative, 21).

More difficult to understand is the very low interest in unions among the cleaners, given that the workplace is unionized. Here a combination of low attention to diversity by the union, and the relative feeling of privilege enjoyed by the migrants may explain the situation, which might change over time. This is, however, a workplace where some respondents claim to be discriminated against (in comparison to indigenous workers) in the allocation of harder jobs.

7.5   CONCLUSIONS

The example of the Poles in the West Midlands is symptomatic of the need for integrated (supply and demand, social and cultural) explanations of the current innovative migration wave. Migration strategies appear to be very instrumental and therefore economically rational, but they are also shaped by social and cultural perceptions of opportunities (as seen in the Polish-specific way of comparing destination countries) and by institutions such as agencies, employer strategies and government policies. Mobilization creatively combines unionism with ethnic association, and creates challenges for both. Temporary agency work combines employers' segmentation strategies with the extreme flexibility of this group of workers.

A broad theoretical framework is needed to appreciate how unprecedented this migration wave is. Although it is impossible to generalize, the majority of new Polish migrants to the UK correspond more to the idea of 'transnational migrants' than to that of 'classical migrants', as their lives are organized across borders. While the concept of 'transnational migration' has been developed by studying of Mexicans in the USA, the enlarged EU, with freedom of movement and low transport costs, is the privileged terrain for such a form of worker mobility. It may be even argued that these workers are of a newer type, as they enjoy EU citizenship. Interviews in this research have shown how 'volatile' these workers can be, but also how they are able to claim their rights. However, the chapter, by focusing on the employment situation, shows how such EU-citizen status does not prevent segregation and exploitation. They are already at the bottom of the labour market in terms of pay. As the UK government's immigration policy shifts to requiring an English proficiency test to any prospective migrant from outside the EU (such a requirement would be illegally discriminating against EU citizens), workers from the NMS could become the lowest strata in the British labour market, offering unskilled labour without the language proficiency needed for either developing a career, or claiming rights and mobilizing within the local space. Such a status – particularly 'free', but also often particularly exploited – for so many people is likely to become a crucial test for EU policies and labour market regulations.

NOTES

1. The author is grateful to a number of colleagues, and in particular Roland Erne, David Lane and Ludger Pries, for their precious comments and suggestions at different stages of this chapter's drafting. An earlier version was published as 'The Polish Plumber in the West Midlands: Theoretical and Empirical Issues', *Review of Sociology of the Hungarian Academy of Sciences*, 13 (2), 39–56.
2. The data of the WRS include many workers who have worked in the UK only for a short time and may have returned to their home countries, but do not include self-employed nor informal employment (Home Office 2007).

3. The data of the WRS include many workers who had arrived before 2004, or who have worked in the UK only for a short term and may have returned to their home countries, but do not include self-employed nor informal employment (Home Office 2008).
4. The number of successful applicants was 125 880 in 2004 (May–December), 204 965 in 2005, 227 850 in 2006, 210 575 in 2007, and 42 790 in the first quarter of 2008 (Home Office 2008). The number of National Insurance numbers issued to new member states (NMS) citizens in the same period, which should also include self-employed, was 875 000.
5. There is indeed an increase in registered workers with dependents in the UK: in 2004 only 4.4 per cent of newly registered workers from the A8 had dependents, but in 2007 the number was already 9.5 per cent. The successful applications for child benefits from NMS citizens have increased more than fourfold between 2005 and 2007 (from 10 363 to 44 029). However, the number of National Insurance numbers allocated for benefit or tax credit purposes is only 2.2 per cent of the total allocated to NMS citizens, the remaining being for employment purposes. The number of approved income-related benefits, including unemployment benefits (restricted to those who have stayed for at least 12 months), has rapidly increased from 171 in 2005 to 3077 in 2007, but remains extremely low at about 0.7 per cent of registered workers (Home Office 2008).
6. Flows do not only depend on regulations, but also on other factors such as proximity, labour market opportunities, and cultural/language proximity. The latter two factors would explain the proportionally much higher inflows in Ireland, and much lower in Sweden, despite these two countries having opened their borders at the same time as the UK.
7. A sub-question which deserves analysis relates to the specific, but telling, case of homosexuals, where the gap in treatment is even higher. It is probably impossible to produce quantitative estimates, but the phenomenon of homosexual professionals fleeing Poland (reported by the media for example M. Jarkowiec, Bóg kocha w Londynie, Gazeta Wyborcza, 19 May 2007) seems an extreme occurrence of employees 'voting with their feet' when confronted by hostile systems. Emerging phenomena require investigation, and specifically interpretative research.
8. This part of the research could not have been conducted without the precious co-operation of Laura Moczarska who carried out the interviews.

REFERENCES

Anderson, B., M. Ruhs, B. Rogaly and S. Spencer (2006), *Fair Enough? Central and Eastern European Migrants in Low-wage Employment in the UK*, York: Joseph Rowntree Foundation.

Avci, G. and C. McDonald (2000), 'Chipping away at the fortress: unions, immigration and the transnational labour market', *International Migration*, **38** (2), 191–212.

Barrell, R., J. Fitzgerald and R. Riley (2007), 'EU enlargement and migration. Assessing the macroeconomic impact', NIESR discussion paper 292.

Boeri, T. and H. Brücker (2001), 'Eastern enlargement and EU–labour markets: perceptions, challenges and opportunities', IZA discussion paper 256.

Boeri, T. and H. Brücker (2005), 'Migration, co-ordination failures and EU enlargement', IZA discussion paper 1600.

Bohle, D. and D. Husz (2005), 'Whose Europe is it? Interest group action in accession negotiations: the cases of competition policy and labor migration', *Politique Europeenne*, 15, 85–112.

Cohen, R. (2004), 'Chinese cockle-pickers, the transnational turn and everyday cosmopolitanism: reflections on the new global migrants', *Labour, Capital and Society*, 37, 130–49.

Colgan, F. and S. Ledwith (eds) (2002), *Gender, Trade Unions and Diversity: International Perspectives*, London: Routledge.

Currie, S. (2007), 'De-skilled and devalued: the labour market experience of Polish migrants in the UK following EU enlargement', *International Journal of Comparative Labour Law and Industrial Relations*, **23** (1), 83–116.

Dench, S., J. Hurtsfield, D. Hill,and K. Akroyd (2006), *Employers' Use of Migrant Labour. Summary Report*, London: Home Office.

Duszeyzyk, M. and J. Wyśniewski (2007), *Analiza spoleczno – demograficzna migracji zarobkowej Polaków do państw EOG po1 Maja 2004 roku*, Warsaw: Instytut Spraw Publicznych.

Eade, J., S. Drinkwater and M. Garapich (forthcoming), 'Poles apart? Enlargement and the labour market outcomes of immigrants in the UK', *International Migration*.

Erne, R. (2008), *European Unions: Labor's Quest for a Transnational Democracy*, Ithaca, NY: Cornell University Press.

European Commission (eds) (2006), 'Report on the functioning of the transitional arrangements set out in the 2003 Accession Treaty (period 1 May 2004–30 April 2006)', Brussels.

Fitzgerald, I. and J. Hardy (2007), 'Trade union cross border collaboration and Polish migrant workers in the UK', paper for the British Universities Industrial Relations Association's Conference, Manchester.

French, S. and J. Möhrke (2007), *The Impact of New Arrivals upon the North Staffordshire Labour Market*, Keele: University Press.

Gajewska, K. (2006), 'Restrictions in labor free movement after the EU-enlargement 2004: explaining variation among countries in the context of elites' strategies towards the radical Right', *Comparative European Politics*, **4** (4), 379–98.

Glick Schiller, N., L. Basch and C. Blanc-Szanton (1995), 'From immigrant to transmigrant: theorizing transnational migration', *Anthropological Quarterly*, **68** (1), 48–63.

Greskovits, B. (1998), *The Political Economy of Protest and Patience: East European and Latin American Transformations Compared*, Budapest: Central European University.

Habermas, J. (1996), *Between Facts and Norms: Contributions to a Discourse Theory of Law and Democracy*, Cambridge, MA: MIT Press.

Hirschman, A. (1970), *Exit, Voice, and Loyalty: Responses to Decline in Firms, Organizations, and States*, Cambridge, MA: Harvard University Press.

Hirschman, A. (1982), *Shifting Involvements. Private Interest and Public Action*, Princeton, NJ: Princeton University Press.

Home Office (2007), 'Accession monitoring report, May 2004–June 2007', London.

Home Office (2008), 'Accession monitoring report, May 2004–March 2008', London.

Kaufman, B. (2007), 'The core principle and fundamental theorem of industrial relations', *International Journal of Comparative Labour Law and Industrial Relations*, **23** (1), 5–33.

Kofman, E. (2000), *Gender and International Migration in Europe: Employment, Welfare and Politics*, London: Routledge.

McGovern, P. (2007), 'Immigration, labour markets and employment relations: problems and perspectives', *British Journal of Industrial Relations*, **45** (2), 217–35.

Meardi, G. (2000), *Trade Union Activists, East and West: Comparisons in Multinational Companies*, Aldershot: Gower.

Meardi, G. (2002), 'The Trojan Horse for the Americanization of Europe? Polish industrial relations towards the EU', *European Journal of Industrial Relations*, **8** (1), 77–99.

Meardi, G. (2007), 'More voice after more exit? Unstable industrial relations in central eastern Europe', *Industrial Relations Journal*, **38** (6), 503–523.

Milkman, R. (2006), *LA Story: Immigrant Workers and the Future of the US Labor Movement*, New York: Russell Sage Foundation.

Passerini, L., D. Lyon, E. Capussotti and I. Laliotou (eds) (2007), *Women Migrants from East to West: Gender, Mobility, and Belonging in Contemporary Europe*, New York: Berghahn Books.

Piore, M. (1979), *Birds of Passage: Migrant Labour and Industrial Societies*, Cambridge: Cambridge University Press.

Pollard, L., M. Latorre and D. Sriskandarajah (2008), *Floodgates or Turnstiles? Post-EU Enlargement Migration to (and from) the UK*, London: Institute for Policy Research.

Pries, L. (ed) (1999), *Migration and Transnational Social Spaces*, Aldershot: Ashgate.

Pries, L. (2003), 'Labour migration, social incorporation and transmigration in the old and new Europe. the case of Germany in a comparative perspective', *Transfer*, **9** (3), 432–51.

Sayad, A. (1999), *La Double Absence: Des Illusions de l'Emigré aux Souffrances de l'Immigré*, Paris: Seuil.

Schwenken, H. (2005), '"Domestic Slavery" versus "Women Rights": Political Mobilizations of Migrant Domestic Workers in the European Union', Center for Comparative Immigration Studies working paper 116, University of California.

Sinn, H.-W. and W. Ochel (2003), 'Social union, convergence and migration', *Journal of Common Market Studies*, **41** (5), 869–96.

TUC Commission on Vulnerable Workers (2008), *Hard Work, Hidden Lives*, London: TUC.

Van Gyes, G. and T. Vandenbrande (2007), *Industrial Relations in EU Member States, 2000–2004*, Dublin: European Foundation for the Improvement of Living and Working Conditions.

Waldiger, R. and M.I. Lichter (2003), *How the Other Half Works: Immigration and the Social Organization of Labor*, Berkeley, CA: University of California Press.

Watts, J. (1998), 'Italian and Spanish labour leaders' unconventional immigration policy and preferences', *South European Society and Politics*, **3** (3), 129–49.

8. Turkey, the new destination for international retirement migration

Canan Balkır and Berna Kırkulak

8.1 INTRODUCTION

International Retirement Migration (IRM) is a new form of international human mobility which entails the movement of elder people in their later lives to the places with favourable characteristics in the pursuit of a better life. The IRM literature has heavily focused on western Mediterranean countries such as Spain, Portugal, Malta and Italy as the first wave countries. Despite some early twentieth century residents in Italy and later in the French Riviera, the figures only became significant in the 1960s. Williams *et al.* (1997) cite four main reasons for the overall growth of IRM. The first two are the increase in longevity and the decline in the legal age of retirement, which together have extended the duration of retirement (Commission of the European Communities 1994, 33). Growing numbers of people have been able to anticipate longer periods of active post-work life in their 'third age'. A third reason is the increase in the lifetime flow of earnings and in the accumulation of wealth in the aftermath of World War II, thus enabling escalating numbers of individuals with sufficient resources, to consider a range of retirement strategies, including migration abroad. Of course, the growth of foreign travel also facilitated the first phase of tourism-related migration. The fourth factor is 'the changing patterns of lifetime mobility' which provide more knowledge and experience of living in foreign countries. A repeated holiday visit to the same place has functioned as a stepping-stone to permanent emigration of retirees.

O'Reilly (1995) provides a five-fold typology based on the sense of commitment and relative orientation towards host and origin countries. The categories are differentiated as expatriates (permanent, identify with host country); residents (in terms of orientation and legal status, seasonally visiting the country of origin for 2–5 months); seasonal visitors (orientated to the country of origin, and spending 2–6 months at the destination each year); returnees (usually second home owners, who visit irregularly);

and tourists who (identify with the area initially discovered as a holiday destination).

The role of tourism in expanding the potential places of retirement for migrants has been widely discussed in the literature. Retired people would seem to be at the forefront of this wave of 'settled tourism' also referred to as 'retired migration' (Casado-Diaz *et al*. 2004, Ackers and Dwyer 2004). The push and pull factors determining international retirement migration have also been widely discussed in studies concerning IRM to Southern Europe. Serrano MartõÂnez (1992) associated the massive concentration of foreign residents on the coast rather than the interior of Murcia with the knowledge of the area from previous tourist visits. Salvà Tomàs's (1996) study in Mallorca explains the links between tourism and inward migration as well as emphasizing the evolution of settlement. The first foreign residents who were looking for peaceful landscapes either bought homes in new coastal estates or restored old houses in the mountains. However, it was after the second half of the 1980s that the number of foreign migrants increased significantly, mainly driven by the previous tourist experience and appreciation of Mediterranean climate and lifestyle. In Italy and Malta the peak of IRM was earlier than in the Costa del Sol and Algarve. More and more, retirement began to be seen as an opportunity for trying a new lifestyle in the sunny coasts of the Mediterranean. The relaxed lifestyle free of formalities and time restrictions, and the favourable climate and landscape have all been valued as ideal for retirees.

Southern Europe or, specifically, the Mediterranean has been popular as a retirement location for north Europeans since the 1960s. Spain's Costa del Sol, Portugal's Algarve, Italy's Tuscany, and Malta have been popular mass-retiree destinations. Mediterranean tourism is also expected to grow further in the future and this will have important implications for future patterns of IRM. The retirees seeking sunshine, a healthy climate and outdoor lifestyle have bought, or rented, property where they reside year round or for a large portion of the year. They do not settle only on the coast, there is increasing evidence in Spain and Portugal of buying property inland. In most cases, the Mediterranean destinations of IRM have either been a former colony of European countries or have historical connections in terms of culture or religion.

However, Turkey, in the last decade, and recently Bulgaria and Romania, the latest EU members, with cheap property prices have also joined the list of destination countries. Northern Europeans are buying property either for use as holiday homes; to live in for a large part of the year; to settle permanently; or merely for investment purposes. Although Bulgaria and Romania are also somewhat different from northern Europe in religious and cultural terms, Turkey is definitely different in terms of culture and religion. Thus the impact of IRM both to the receiver and the sender country deserve to be studied ever more intensively.

This chapter is an attempt at providing the key issues and themes that need to be considered with reference to IRM in Turkey, based on the case study of Antalya and its districts, the Mediterranean province which hosts the retirees. There are an increasing number of European retired settlers in Turkey, although this increase is modest when compared with other Mediterranean countries. But, nevertheless, there are two crucial issues that have to be answered concerning European retired migrants in Turkey and the current study tries to gather and analyse data for this purpose. The first issue concerns the settled European retirees, their demographic and socio-economic characteristics, reasons for moving to the destination area, their mobility patterns, residential choices in Antalya and the economic and social ties that they have established with the host community. The second issue concerns the local host community, their sensitivities concerning IRM and inquires to what extent the host community is prepared for the influx of European retired migrants.

The issues discussed in the chapter are based on the findings of a study funded by TUBITAK (National Scientific and Technological Research Council of Turkey), in which the authors took part.[1] The research is among the first attempts to describe the profiles of the retired European migrants and their interaction with the local community. The study includes a questionnaire-based survey and in-depth interviews both conducted with the retired migrants and the local community.

There is an increasing trend in the contributions of Turkish academics to the literature on IRM in Turkey. Turan and Karakaya (2005) studied the demographic characteristics, motivations, economic contributions of the British living in Didim. Südaş and Mutluer (2006) and Unutulmaz (2006) studied Alanya, looking at the cultural and economic impact of the settled foreigners. There are other studies concerning the social integration of foreigners, such as the UK citizens settled in Muğla-Gökova region carried by Muğla University. Another study on the territorial effects of IRM in Turkey has been carried by Koç University Migration Centre. There are also studies looking at Turkey as the destination country/transit country by Kaiser (2003, 2004, 2007), Kirişçi (2003), Mutluer (2004), Akgün *et al* (2004), and Yılmaz (2005). Also, the second house ownership of foreigners has been a recent research topic (Mutluer and Südaş 2005, Kurtuluş 2006, Tamer-Görer *et al.* 2006).

8.2 INTERNATIONAL RETIREMENT MIGRATION IN TURKEY

Today, Turkey has become a popular European retirees' destination, particularly for British, German, Dutch and Nordic citizens. Kirişçi (2003) states that Turkey is traditionally known as an emigration country, but a lesser known fact is that Turkey and its predecessor, the Ottoman Empire, have always been countries of immigration and asylum. However, the main immigration flows then tended to consist of Muslim and/or Turkish expatriates. Being culturally alike, these people have not found it difficult to be 'integrated'. Today the retired migrants are coming from different cultural and religious backgrounds, and this is a challenging experience not only for the migrants, but also for the local community.

As is the case in other countries, it is extremely difficult to enumerate the settled foreigners in Turkey. The main reason being that the settled foreigners do not have to acquire a residence permit, and can choose to stay in the country on a tourist visa valid for 90 days, leave the country when that expires, and collect a new visa on instant re-entry. As of 1 March 2007, according to the records of the General Directorate of Security, 202085 foreigners have residence permits in Turkey, not including those with expired visas or residence permits, and also those who may have entered the country illegally in the first place. The highest number of foreign residents is in Istanbul with 106156, followed by Bursa with 16772; Antalya with 12832 and Ankara with 12157. The ones who are settling in cities such as Istanbul or Ankara have diplomatic, business, education or other motives compared with the retired Europeans settling in the tourist regions of south-western Turkey, including Antalya. A total of 93724 residence permit holders are from EU countries,[2] with 51787 from Bulgaria (people of Turkish origin), 9902 from Germany and 7940 from Britain.

Turkey's political and economic liberalization in the 1980s and its bid for full membership of the European Union has made it an attractive destination for European tourists and migrants (Kaiser 2004). The IRM to Turkey has been concentrated in several destinations, mainly western and southern coastal towns and cities. The districts most favoured by foreigners are Alanya, Fethiye, Didim, Bodrum and Kuşadası along the coastline, as well as Ürgüp in Anatolia. It looks as if age, economic status and the previous location of holidays in Turkey are all factors considered in the decision of where to settle in Turkey. The people, who prefer to settle at a location within easy reach of an international airport, might settle in Fethiye on the Mediterranean coast, which is only 20–30 minutes from Dalaman Airport. Others who prefer a quiet and isolated life choose Kaş. Along the Mediterranean, Alanya is a particularly preferred location for

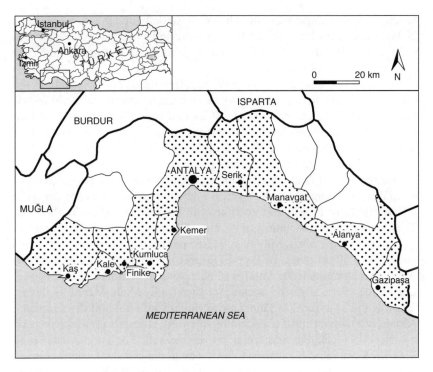

Figure 8.1 Map of the research area

Germans and Scandinavians, while the British purchases of property are highest in Fethiye and Didim.[3]

Antalya, the Turkish Riviera

Antalya is currently the most important international tourism destination in Turkey with a share of almost one-third of total international arrivals. Therefore, tourism has played a central role in the development of this region and most of the migrants had experienced the area as tourists before they became residents. The Mediterranean climate and the style of life in coastal towns such as Alanya, Kaş, and Kemer have attracted many elderly tourists. In Alanya alone, foreigners of 38 different nationalities have settled (Yiğit 2008). The rapid growth of the tourism sector since the early 1980s, liberalization in tourism services and the strong European currencies *vis-à-vis* the weak Turkish lira all had a positive impact on the number of incoming tourists. It is also probable that the rapid transformation of the country after it had acquired EU candidacy status had an encouraging impact on the choice of settled foreigners (Unutulmaz 2006). Foreigners have begun buying land and property and settling in the coastal area and in the meantime running small businesses and even printing their own local journals.

As mentioned above, the tourism migration nexus is very strong in the case of Antalya where the Mediterranean climate and the relaxed lifestyle have attracted the elderly tourists. Repeated tourist experiences[4] end up in providing a certain level of emotional attachment, establishment of personal contacts and a sense of familiarity with the surroundings. This usually culminates in the decision to purchase a second home.

The province of Antalya is 2051 square kilometres, with a population of 1 726 205 according to the 2000 census. The retired migrants are scattered all over Antalya Province from Alanya in the east to Kalkan in the west. They are concentrated mainly in the city of Antalya itself (36.4 per cent); in Alanya (33.09 per cent), Manavgat (11.82 per cent), Kemer (10.2 per cent) and Serik (5.80 per cent).[5] It takes 2.5 hours to travel from Antalya centre to Alanya and 4 hours from Antalya to Kaş. Alanya became a tourist attraction in the 1960s after the opening of the Antalya-Side-Mersin highway. The town has a typical Mediterranean climate with hot and dry summers. Along with banana and citrus farming, there are greenhouses which provide a variety of vegetables and fruits in every season. The poor coastal road between Kemer and Kaş seems to be the main reason why fewer foreigners come to Kaş. There are important residential areas like Kumluca, Demre and Finike on the coastal road between Kemer and Kaş, but these areas are more concerned with farming citrus and greenhouse crops than tourism.

European retiree profiles for Antalya City, Kemer and Manavgat are similar to those of Alanya. Based on the number of residence permits, the Germans are the biggest community, followed by the Dutch, Norwegian and British. On the other hand, the majority of the retirees living in the south-eastern towns such as Kaş and Kalkan are British. While British people prefer to live along the south-western coastline, Germans prefer the south-eastern coast. This confirms the widespread view that foreigners from different countries of origin are becoming geographically segregated. This regional segregation of different nationalities also occurs at the level of housing complexes, where foreigners live with people of their own nationality.

It has been observed during a field study in Manavgat that retired migrants prefer to live in seaside districts like Belek and Side rather than Manavgat town centre. Resident foreigners in Kemer do not live in multi-storey buildings like the ones in Alanya. Kemer municipality's critical approach towards multi-storey structures coincides with the single-storey luxury villa choices of foreigners. There is a similar situation in Kaş.

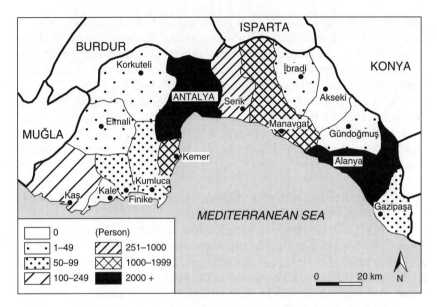

Figure 8.2 Distribution of foreigners with residence permit in Antalya province

8.3 METHODOLOGY AND FINDINGS

Data collection was challenging as it was difficult to locate the target population group in the absence of reliable population lists. Thus, the data was collected through interviews conducted with the officials, real estate companies, friendship associations and local restaurant and bar owners; a method that has been used in other studies on IRM (Casado-Diaz *et al.* 2004; Casado-Diaz 2006). The questionnaire for the retired migrants was drafted in English/German and was filled in with the help of a professional employee of the survey company. The questionnaire for the local community was in Turkish. The survey sample was 500 for retired European migrants and 500 for local Turkish people. The survey was conducted in Antalya Centrum, Alanya, Kaş, Kemer, Manavgat, and Kalkan, the most populated municipalities with respect to settled European retirees, from April to May 2007. The questionnaire addressed to the local community was also executed in the same towns with the addition of Korkuteli, a district with no settled foreigners, in order to see the difference in perception due to interaction between the two communities. The questionnaire was administered to European retirees aged over 40,[6] who live in Antalya and its surroundings for at least six months a year. In-depth interviews were conducted with retired European migrants, local people, and key bureaucrats at the municipalities and other public institutions, managers of real estate companies, board members of the chambers of commerce and industry, and the leading figures of the civil society.

The survey provided data on the demographic characteristics of retired migrants such as the age distribution, social status, citizenship, education and the length of the time spent in Antalya, and on the economic and social impact on the host society. Some of the specific questions considered are:

- What are the motivating factors of European retired migrants to settle down in Antalya and its districts?
- What is the average income of retired migrants in Antalya?
- What is the distribution of expenditure categories in the monthly income?
- What is the ownership status of the house in which they live?
- Are retired migrants satisfied with their lives in Antalya and do they recommend it to their friends and relatives as a retiree destination?
- How readily do retirees adapt to their new destination, for example by learning the local language?
- What are mobility patterns after retiring to Antalya, such as visits to country of origin?
- What kind of problems do the retiree migrants encounter?
- What kinds of factors affect retirees' decisions to go back to their home countries?

The survey also examined the interaction and dialogue between the retirees and local people. Do they have a 'cultural communication' problem, which is more vital than the basic language difference? Are the European retiree populated towns enjoying multiculturalism or are they becoming areas of conflict with potentially adverse consequences for the future? How does the local community view the different lifestyle of the settled retirees; issues concerning neighbourhood and social togetherness; the property purchase by European retirees; the contribution of retirees to the local economy and their impact on local social life?

Demographic Characteristics of European Retired Migrants

Out of the survey sample of 500 retired migrants, the findings indicate that 24.2 per cent of the respondents were British, 22.6 per cent Germans, 13.2 per cent Dutch, 12.6 per cent Norwegian, 10.2 per cent Danish (10.2 per

Table 8.1   Demographic characteristics of IRM in Antalya province

Gender	%	Age	%	Marital status	%	Education	%	Turkish partner	%
–	–	40–54	25.4	single	17.8	university	57.0	–	–
Male	55.0	55–60	25.4	married	74.2	high school	40.6	yes	13.0
Female	45.0	61–65	23.0	other	7.4	–	–	no	78.6
		66+	25.2	no answer	0.6	primary school	1.6	no answer	8.4
		no answer	1.0			no answer	0.8		
Total	100		100.0		100.0		100.0	Total	100.0

Source: Project SOBAG-105K156.

cent), 5.8 per cent Belgian, 3.0 per cent Swedish, 2.8 per cent Irish, 1.8 per cent Swiss, 1.4 per cent Austrian and 1.2 per cent Finnish. There are also retired migrants from Iceland, Luxembourg, Italy and Poland; however, their number is very low. This chapter will focus only on the retirees of the nationalities representing a minimum 10 per cent of the sample. Thus the retirees from UK, Germany, Holland, Norway and Denmark, consisting almost 83 per cent of the total sample, will be evaluated.

While more than half of the residents interviewed were under 61, approximately one-quarter of the sample were over 65 (Table 8.1). Furthermore, the respondents, on average, report a high level of education, 57 per cent having university degrees and 41 per cent having high school diplomas. It was found that 52 per cent of the respondents have a residence permit, while 45 per cent have tourist visas. A total of 69.4 per cent of the retired migrant families have two members in the household, 9 per cent have three members, 6 per cent have four or more members, and 14 per cent live alone. More than two-thirds (74.2 per cent) of the respondents are married, 17.8 per cent are single. A total of 13 per cent have a Turkish partner. The proportion of single-member households is considerably lower than in the findings for other Mediterranean IRM case studies (King *et al.* 2000; Rodríguez *et al.* 1998). The male-female ratio is almost balanced, with a slight majority of men (55 per cent) in the sample.

Almost 41 per cent of the respondents have been living in Antalya for more than 5 years. In particular, the interest of Germans in the region started about 15 years ago. The high interest rate policy designed to attract the foreign currency savings of Turkish workers in Germany, had a positive impact on the German citizens' choice of investing their savings in Turkey. This, in turn, paved the way to their decision to retire in Turkey.

In towns like Alanya, where the most populous settled group is German,[7] most of the shops, restaurants and cafes use the German language on their signboards and employ people who know German. The German language has become the 'second language' and many German retired residents do not feel the need to learn Turkish. These developments, in turn, have made Alanya emerge as an unproblematic and almost a protected place to live for German retirees.

Considering the demographic characteristics of the local host community, 51.7 per cent was born in Antalya, and those not from Antalya have been living there for a long time (62.3 per cent over 15 years); 71.7 per cent were over the age of 30; 76.6 per cent married; and 51.3 per cent male. Concerning the educational level, primary school graduates (40.6 per cent) were the majority and those with higher education was only 10.9 per cent. Their level of education is considerably lower than the level of education of the European retirees.

When we look at the similarities to IRM in the Mediterranean, it is mainly couples who decide to retire to a new destination, they are mostly in their late 50s and early 60s, relatively well-off, searching for a better quality of life, and generally have a previous experience of living or working abroad. In the Turkish case, although most of the similarities are there, the choice of destination is clearly based on the tourism-migration nexus.

Pull and Push Factors

What are the pull and push factors of the Turkish case? The decision to migrate to a foreign country whose religion and culture is different is not easy. There has to be a combination of factors that affect this decision. Settled retirees state their reasons for living in Antalya as 'the sunshine, climate, lower cost of living, natural beauty, good social relationships, respect for elders, security and a peaceful lifestyle' (Table 8.2). Europeans can buy and maintain a house at a more reasonable cost, compared with that of their country of origin.[8] Thus, coming from the lower and middle income bracket, these people can own a house with a swimming pool, something unimaginable in their home countries. Many pronounce that the other Mediterranean destinations such as Spain have become expensive after joining the EU and this had an impact on their choice to settle in Turkey. The marketing of Alanya as 'the same sun, the same sea, why pay more?' describes clearly this economic reasoning.

A total of 63.8 per cent of the respondents cite 'climate' as being the most important factor in their decision to migrate. The Mediterranean lifestyle is closely associated with a warm climate, which facilitates a

Table 8.2   Motivating factors for moving to Antalya

Reasons	Not important	Less important	Moder- ately important	Important	Very important	No answer	Total
Climate in Antalya	0.2	2.6	14.2	16.0	63.8	3.2	100.0
Climate in retiree's home country	4.4	6.8	23.8	13.6	47.4	4.0	100.0
Social/human relations in Turkey	6.0	13.8	20.4	24.8	31.2	3.8	100.0
Lower cost of living	8.0	17.2	24.2	18.8	27.8	4.0	100.0
Historical/cultural attractions in Turkey	12.4	12.4	23.8	27.8	19.0	4.6	100.0
Social/human relations in retiree's home country	19.6	18.2	27.4	12.6	17.8	4.4	100.0
Marriage/ relationship	69.8	4.4	8.4	6.2	5.4	5.8	100.0
Political/ administrative circumstances in retiree's home country	59.6	14.0	14.4	4.6	2.2	5.2	100.0
Business	63.8	7.0	13.4	4.8	1.8	9.2	100.0
Other	2.8	0.0	0.4	0.2	0.8	95.8	100.0

Source: Project SOBAG-105K156.

more active outdoor social life. The lower cost of living makes going out to restaurants, cafes and bars more affordable than in the migrants' home countries. These findings are consistent with those of the other Mediterranean countries (Williams *et al.* 1997, Rodríguez *et al.* 1998, King *et al.* 2000, Rodríguez *et al.* 2001, Casado-Diaz 2006). In all these studies, the Mediterranean climate is the main pull factor, although this needs to be understood more as an enabling factor (for a particular outdoor lifestyle) as much as the direct enjoyment of a particular type of climate.

The adverse evaluation of the climate of the home country, such as being 'cold or rainy and cloudy most of the year', can be taken as a push factor. The Mediterranean climate makes one feel much better and enables one to spend a great amount of time outdoors. This implies a more lively social life, in which the retirees also become part of the community and do not have to stay alone in the house. However, merely good climate and low-cost living do not explain the whole situation. Without enjoyable social relationships and Turkish hospitality, would they mean anything? Hospitality is another pull factor cited in the interviews. This concept which has been utilized for tourism promotion of Turkey has also proved to be an important pull factor for the elderly migrants. They point to the fact that countries like Spain, which have already got their share of migrants did not really care about them anymore. However, in Antalya, migrants still enjoy Turkish hospitality.

Although the Mediterranean climate is the main pull factor, the heat and humidity in the mid-summer is not favoured by many foreign residents, who often spend July and August in their home countries. They then leave home countries in September as the cool autumn begins and return to Antalya where the weather is milder. Generally, they come in September and stay till mid-December. Towards the end of the year, they return to their home countries for Christmas, a time for being together with family members and friends. As the majority of the retired settlers in Antalya are married couples, they retain strong links with their home countries and families. After the New Year's festivities end, they return to Antalya and stay untill the hot days begin.

IRM involves retired people who are not working and who rely on their savings or pensions. However, there are many migrants in Antalya and its coastal surroundings who run their own restaurants, cafes and pubs, serving the cuisine of their own countries.[9] Sometimes they provide a goods or a service that the local people detest performing, such as the case of the German butcher in Alanya who sells pork. The target consumer group of these small businesses is not only the migrant settlers but also tourists from European countries during the holiday season.

Income and Expenditure

Concerning the average income of the retirees, it was difficult to get answers. As most of the retirees were reluctant to answer this question; the percentage of the replies is too low to make general conclusions about the real purchasing power of the retirees. Among the ones who did respond, the majority belonged to medium-level income group. As was expected, very few retirees (4.2 per cent) earn over 5000 Euros per month. Thus, lower costs of living had played a crucial role in their decision to settle in Antalya and it is clear that retirees cannot get a similar quality of housing and living with the same level of income in their home countries. The survey results show that those retired migrants with a monthly income of 2000 Euros and above own the house they live in.

Concerning the expenditure pattern of the retired migrants, the category 'others', in the monthly budget has the largest share, followed by food, leisure, health/rent and international travel/domestic transportation. The reason for leisure having such a great share in the budget for the elderly is that the majority of retirees enjoy outdoor life and eat out.

It is interesting to note that retirees spend almost equal portions of their incomes on local and international transportation. There are low-cost charter tickets available all year round, from Antalya to European cities, which facilitates visiting their home countries. However, retirees travel to Antalya centre for bureaucratic procedures and they also like discovering different regions of Turkey and thus spend money on local and domestic transportation.

Housing

Williams, King and Warnes (2004) studied retired British people with second homes who became residents in four Mediterranean settings. According to their findings, more than one-third of the respondents had owned a second-home in the area before they migrated or moved their principal home to the new destination. In the case of Antalya, survey findings show that almost half of the respondents (47.6 per cent) own a house, while the other half (48.6 per cent) rent. The settled retirees with an income lower that 1000 Euros, prefer to reside in rentals, whereas 70 per cent of the retirees with an income of 2500 Euros or more prefer to own the house. The real estate sector oriented towards the retired migrants is so attractive that many small- and medium-sized hotels are selling their places to multi-storey apartment buildings. High-rise developments are permitted in some regions, where banana gardens are being uprooted to build apartment complexes.

Furthermore, the in-depth interviews revealed that some of the retirees are in the business of sub-letting their houses to friends and relatives, thus earning unregistered income. In particular, hotels are adversely affected by this practice, but the municipality finds it very difficult to take the necessary precautions.

There has been an increasing trend in the real estate industry due to foreigners. After the 1999 Helsinki Summit in which Turkey was granted EU candidacy status, there was an enormous increase in the residential permits in Antalya. Many Turkish firms partnered with foreign firms in the construction industry to meet this increasing demand. The harmonizing of Turkish legislation with the EU has had a positive impact on

European interest in Turkish real estate market. The devaluation of the Turkish lira by dropping the property prices in foreign currency boosted the sales.

While high-income foreigners still prefer to buy independent villas on hillsides, the retired migrants of the low-income group prefer three-storey buildings. The 80–90 m^2 plots are usually enough for a dwelling with two bedrooms and a living room, but if retirees have children they prefer bigger houses. Villa-type houses are generally 100 m^2 in size and cost about 200 000–300 000 Euros. Land registration, air conditioning, electricity and water connection costs and the prices of household appliances such as refrigerators and washing machines are included in the sale price. Houses in a complex, called a 'gated community', with fitness centre, pool, landscaped gardens and a security system are usually preferred. The property developers are creating these residential complexes, with marketing primarily aimed at European retirees. Performing the management of these complexes as well, they are also creating monthly revenue for the company. The gated community is becoming a preferred option of the settled retirees who choose to live with their fellow nationals.

For the foreigners who are on the verge of making a decision to settle in Turkey, there are tours arranged under the coordination of construction companies and travel agents including free accommodation and return flight tickets to and from Antalya, based on the condition that the outcome of the trip is finalized with the purchase of property.

Concerning the opinion of the local Turkish people, the findings show that approximately 63 per cent of the local respondents do not approve of foreigners buying property in Turkey. A total of 73.1 per cent of the respondents stressed that they preferred to sell property to Turkish people, while only a small group (4 per cent) claimed their preference in selling property to foreigners.

Satisfaction and Integration

The survey results present a sense of satisfaction with the experience of settlement in Antalya province. Almost 59 per cent of retirees expressed that they were satisfied with their decision to live in Antalya and their decisions have a positive impact on their friends and relatives to do the same. Through their contacts with friends and relatives and visits to their home country at least once a year (43.7 per cent), they are generating potential tourism.

The preference of neighbourhood is an important issue and can be perceived as an indicator of retirees' willingness to integrate into the local community. Contrary to the practice of living in a gated community, 69.6

per cent of retired migrants indicated that they are indifferent concerning neighbourhood preference and it does not matter with whom they live in the neighbourhood. Only 13.6 per cent of the retired migrants preferred to live with the local host inhabitants, 3.8 per cent prefer to live with compatriots, 9.2 per cent with Europeans in general. In the cross-nationality comparison, there were important differences. British were most indifferent concerning neighbourhood preference (79.3 per cent) and also had the highest percentage preferring the locals as neighbours (16.5 per cent). Germans had the highest percentage in preferring to live with people from their country (7.1 per cent). Danes preferred to live with the migrants from EU countries, followed by Dutch, Norwegians and Germans. The segregation according to nationality within the region is also evident in other aspects of daily life. British citizens prefer to dine and be entertained at places run by the British themselves and Germans go to places run by Germans.

As for the preference of the local people concerning the neighbourhood in which they would like to live, the results are more startling. Although from the outset, it looks as if there is no problem, the results of the questionnaire show that 61.6 per cent of the local population does not prefer to reside in foreigner populated neighbourhoods although almost the same percentage (60.4 per cent) does not support the gated community intended for foreigners. A total of 52.9 per cent of the locals also do not prefer to go to the same entertainment places as foreigners go.

Another main indicator of integration with the local community is learning the language of the host country. The survey results show that a large majority of the respondents have very limited, or no knowledge of Turkish (Table 8.3). Their poor language skills are partially explained by the widespread use of either English or German and the difficulty of learning a new language at an older age. On this issue, the retired migrants in Antalya are similar to the retired migrants in Spain, who have low language skills and are integrated little with the host society. In contrast, retired migrants in Tuscany who would like to be part of the Italian lifestyle learned to speak fluent Italian and are well integrated in the host society (King and Patterson 1998).

The European migrants also have a handful of publications in their mother tongue, the main ones being Alanya Bote (in German, biweekly), Alanya News, Orange (in German and English, weekly), Dutch Talk (in Dutch, monthly), Primaleben Turkei, Antalya Times, Hello Alanya Magazine (in English and Dutch), Riviera News (biweekly), Die Brücke e.V. (German Culture and Charity Association publishing); and a TV Channel A (news in German every Tuesday and Fridays). The local municipalities also make their announcements in several languages.

Table 8.3   Overcoming the language barrier

If you don't speak Turkish, how do you manage daily routine?	Frequency	Percentage
Many people speak my language	295	59.0
I can sustain my life with my own countrymen	89	17.8
I find a person who knows my language	55	11.0
I speak English	11	2.2
No answer	137	27.4
Total	587	117.4
Base	500	100.0

Source: Project SOBAG-105K156.

Another important indicator which shows that the European retirees are not really integrating with the Turkish community is hidden in the replies that 79 per cent of the respondents do not intend to become a citizen of the Turkish Republic even if they can keep their current citizenship. The majority of those who consider becoming Turkish citizens while keeping their own nationalities are females (68 per cent). The majority of the retired migrants with a residence permit consider acquiring Turkish citizenship, where the majority of the retired migrants with a residence permit are British.

However, the findings also show that 84.8 per cent of the settled retirees are at an outstandingly supportive position of saying 'yes' to Turkey's membership in the European Union and 79.8 per cent of the participants also approve the free movement of Turkish citizens in their home countries, although this percentage shows a striking difference with respect to nationalities.

On the issue of satisfaction with their new life, it is important to reveal the main problems faced by the retired migrants. According to the findings, one of the main problems is bureaucracy in administrative issues. They come into contact with bureaucracy and red tape when purchasing a property, getting a work permit, renewing their residence permit, and so forth. There are two sorts of problems encountered by migrants related to the issue of residence permits. The first one is related to the fact that the Turkish state does not grant a permanent residence permit (Kaiser and Friedrich 2004). Residence permits are granted for different time periods of up to five years. Given the bureaucratic procedures mentioned above, this situation creates problems for elderly migrants. In addition, especially for certain nationalities, residence permits are quite expensive. The cost of a residence permit is also determined in a reciprocal manner between

Table 8.4   Reasons for returning back to home country

Reasons	Stay in Antalya	Move to another place in Turkey	Return to my country	Go to another EU country	No answer	Total
Reduced personal mobility	8.2	6.6	64.0	3.4	17.8	100.0
Serious health problems	5.2	4.0	68.6	5.0	17.2	100.0
Death of a partner	17.4	5.8	57.0	1.6	18.2	100.0
Urban security problems	5.4	9.4	56.8	10.8	17.6	100.0
Decline in income	18.0	5.2	53.8	2.4	20.6	100.0
Other	1.0	0.2	2.2	0.6	96.0	100.0

Source: Project SOBAG-105K156.

the countries. The other problem with the residence permits is the fact that the renewal office is in Antalya, which means a trip of at least a few hundred kilometres each way. Fortunately, this problem has been solved for those living in Alanya by the efforts of the German-Turkish Friendship Association. This is in line with the survey result concerning the assistance received in solving difficulties encountered, where personal relationships are ahead of official institutions such as consulates. The retired migrants avoid establishing links with their embassies or consulates as they do not want to be bothered for tax purposes or other reasons.

The findings also show that retirees do not have problems concerning practising their religion, despite the fact that they are Christians living in a Muslim country. There are already several active churches in Antalya City, Side and in Alanya.

The survey also provided some information concerning the reasons given by retirees for a possible return to their home countries in the future (Table 8.4). The results are consistent with the findings of Rodríguez *et al.* (1998) for the situation on the Costa del Sol, where the retirees would consider the possibility of moving back to their countries if their health worsened, there was a decline in personal mobility, the death of a partner or decline in income. However, some of the retirees expressed the opinion that that they would move to any other EU country in the case of urban security problems. One must take these results as tentative since they represent intentions, and individuals may behave differently when confronted by real life situations.

The over-ageing of local demographic structure on public services is another important issue which has not been studied much in Turkey, but which is expected to affect the life quality of both retired migrants and the local community in the near future.

8.4   CONCLUSION

The literature on IRM is heavily oriented towards the western Mediterranean countries such as Italy, Portugal, and Spain, while this chapter is designed to gain insight into the IRM to the southern coast of the Turkish Mediterranean, namely Antalya and its districts. There are many striking results that are consistent with those of other IRM destinations in Europe. There is rapid urbanization associated with residential tourism; residential segregation according to nationality within the region, for example, the British tend to be concentrated around Antalya, Germans in Alanya and the north Europeans in Alanya and in Kemer; and the situation is predominantly a European retiree migration, mainly British, German and Dutch. People from Scandinavian countries follow them numerically. Retired migrants choose Antalya because of its Mediterranean climate, lower cost of living and warm social/human relations. The tourism-migration nexus is very strong in the case of Antalya.

Concerning integration with the local community, there are certain factors that hinder their fuller integration. The first factor is the language barrier. The elderly retirees do not show much interest in learning the language, most often because they can carry out most aspects of everyday life in their native language, due to English or German being spoken by many in the locality. They can keep up-to-date with the news in their own language through satellite television and foreign newspapers. Another important factor which hinders social integration is the cultural difference between local people and retired Europeans, as well as between different nationalities of retirees. Thus each nationality usually interacts mainly with its own people.

The foreign retirees are generally reluctant to give information about their income, but in-depth interviews reveal the fact that most of the retirees are from lower and medium income brackets. Despite this fact, they inject money into local economies through property purchases and day-to-day spending. Almost half of the retirees own their own home, and spend their incomes mainly on food, leisure, transportation and health insurance. The ones with a monthly income of 2000 Euros and above invest in Turkey. As for the locals' perception of the impact of retired migrants on business and working in Antalya, more than half of the locals

(59.2 per cent) do not prefer to work with or establish a business with a migrant and 65.1 per cent of the locals indicated that migrants working in Antalya have a negative impact on the local population's employment opportunity. The locals do not prefer to marry foreigners and also appraise the developments with regard to foreigners acquiring property in Turkey unfavourably. There is a valid need for further analysis covering the medium- and long-term impact of IRM on the local community, on the local economy and on the social and cultural structure of the host community.

NOTES

1. Research team: Canan Balkır, Zerrin Karaman Toprak, Berna Kırkulak, and research assistant Ilkay Sudaş. The chapter draws on the data gathered through TUBITAK (National Scientific and Technological Research Council of Turkey) funded research project (SOBAG-105K156). The authors acknowledge the invaluable work of Prof. Dr. Zerrin Karaman Toprak who has worked as a researcher on the same project, looking at the relations of the settled European retirees with the local administration and issues of citizenship; and research assistant Ilkay Sudaş for his support during the project. The questionnaire was prepared by the research team and field survey conducted by Consensus Research and Consultancy.
2. This is very small when compared with IRM in Spain which is cited as 958 311 for EU15.
3. Between 2003–05, 15 842 properties have been acquired by non-Turkish legal or private persons in Turkey. The purchasers constituted a total of 18 959 legal or private owners or co-owners from a total of 58 different countries.
4. In order to overcome the definitional challenge with respect of differentiating tourists from migrants, the criteria of the length of residence in Antalya, which is not less than a period of six months was considered in the survey.
5. Serik, a district mostly populated with Russian workers, not Europeans, was not included in the survey.
6. The age 40 is young compared with other studies on IRM but the pre-survey investigation in Antalya and its district, showed that there are many early retired migrants in the region.
7. Germany is the biggest trading partner of Turkey and its investments also rank at the top of FDI in the country. There is also a steady increase in Turkish-German marriages. Thus along with German tourists who decide to retire to Turkey, many of the bi-national families also set up a home in Turkey (Kaiser 2004).
8. The principles governing purchase of property by foreign (i.e. non-Turkish) nationals in Turkey is governed by the 1934 Property Act (Law Nr. 2644, dated 22 November 1934), which was modified by a by-law (Law Nr. 4916, dated 3 July 2003). This law was predicated on a reciprocity clause; that is to say, citizens of countries whose governments allow Turkish nationals to purchase real estate in their country are to be allowed to purchase real estate in Turkey. The modifications brought by the 2003 by-law were declared as void by the Turkish Constitutional Court on 26 April 2005, in a decision which was to come into effect as of 27 July 2005 and the purchase of real estate by foreign nationals was suspended until a modified law, dated 7 January 2006 was implemented. This current law brings the following amendments, especially with regards to size limitations: A foreign national cannot purchase more than 25 000 m² (6 acres) of land (built on or otherwise) in Turkey without special consent from the Turkish Council of Ministers.

The Council of Ministers is authorized to increase this limit up to 300000 m² per person; foreign national ownership of real estate cannot exceed 5/1000 of land in any designated province; the property also has to be within a municipality. Foreigners cannot buy in villages. The land or property must not be in a sensitive military area, and the individual must be considered as suitable to own real estate in Turkey.

9. According to an interview made with Antalya Chamber of Industry and Commerce, there is no reliable data about the small sized foreign-owned businesses operating in Antalya province. However in Alanya, district of Antalya, where statistics are available, there are 669 small companies from 23 countries (Yiğit 2008).

REFERENCES

Ackers L. and P. Dwyer (2004), 'Fixed laws, fluid lives: the citizenship status of post-retirement migrants in the European Union', *Aging and Society*, **24** (3), 451–75.

Akgün, B., Z. Şahin and A. Hermancı (2004), Türkiye'dekı Yabancılar (Arastırma Raporu), National Geographic Türkiye, Kasım sayısı: 26–28.

Casado-Díaz, M.A. (2001), *From Tourists to Residents: International Retirement Migration to Spain*, Becas Turespana: Spanish State Secretary for Tourism, Industry and SMEs.

Casado-Díaz, M.A. (2006), 'Retiring to the Costa Blanca: a cross-national analysis', *Journal of Ethnic and Migration Studies*, **32** (8), 1321–39.

Casado-Díaz, M.A., C. Kaiser and A.M. Warnes (2004), 'Northern European retired residents in nine southern European areas: characteristics, motivations and adjustment', *Aging and Society*, **24** (3), 353–81.

Commission of the European Communities (eds) (1994), *The Demographic Situation of the European Union: 1994 Report*, Brussels: Commission of the European Union.

Cribier, F. and A. Kych (1992), 'La migracion de retraite des Parisiens, une analyse de la propension au depart', *Population*, 47, 677–718.

Kaiser, B. (2003), 'Lifeworlds of EU immigrants in Turkey', in E. Zeybekoğlu and B. Johansson (eds), *Migration and Labour in Europe: Views from Turkey and Sweden*, Istanbul: Muteir ve Nial.

Kaiser, B. (2004), 'German migrants in Turkey: the "other side" of the Turkish-German transnational space', in T. Faist and E. Ozveren (eds), *Transnational Social Spaces*, Avebury: Ashgate.

Kaiser, B. (2007), 'Türkiye'deki Avrupa Birliği Yurttaşları: Siyasal ve Toplumsal Katılım önündeki Engeller. Kökler ve Yollar: Türkiye'de Göç Süreçleri, in A. Kaya and B. Şahin, (eds), *İstanbul Bilgi Üniversitesi Yayınları*, Istaubul: 159, 475–89.

Kaiser, C. and K. Friedrich (2004), 'Migration decisions, living environments and adjustments to changing needs of elderly Germans on Mallorca', in A.M. Warnes, (ed.), *Final Report ESF-Network*, Sheffield.

King, R. and G. Patterson (1998), 'Diverse paths: the Elderly British in Tuscany', *International Journal of Population Geography*, **4** (2), 157–82.

King, R., A.M. Warnes and A.M. Williams (2000), *Sunset Lives: British Retirement to Southern Europe*, Oxford: Berg.

Kirişçi, K. (2003), *Turkey: A Transformation from Emigration to Immigration*, Washington, DC: Migration Policy Institute.

Kurtulus, H. (2006), 'Turizm Bölgelerinde "Kıyısal Kentleşme" ve Uluslararası Göçlerde Yeni Boyutlar: Muğla Kıyılarının Avrupalı Sakinleri', paper presented at the 6th Türkiye Şehircilik Kongresi, Izmir: Dokuz Eylül Üniversitesi.

Mutluer, M. and İ. Südaş (2005), 'Yabancıların Türkiye'de Mülk Edinimi: Coğrafi Bir Yaklaşım', *Ege Coğrafya Dergisi*, **14** (1–2), 45–55.

Mutluer, M. (2004), 'Migrations vers la Turquie: survol des prosessus historiques et des données récentes', in A. Manço (ed.), *Turquie: vers de nouveaux horizons migratoires?* Paris: L'Harmattan.

O'Reilly, K. (1995), 'A new trend in European migration: contemporary British migration to Fuengirola, Costa del Sol', *Geographical Viewpoint*, 23, 25–36.

Rodríguez, V., G. Fernández-Mayoralas and F. Rojo (1998), 'European retirees on the Costa del Sol: a cross-national comparison', *International Journal of Population Geography*, **4** (2), 183–200.

Rodríguez, V., P. Salvà-Tomàs and A.M. Williams (2001), 'Northern Europeans and the Mediterranean: a new California or a new Florida', in R. King, P. de Mas, and J.M. Beck (eds), *Geography, Environment and Development in the Mediterranean*, Sussex: Academic Press, pp. 176–95.

Salvà Tomàs, P.A. (1996), 'The Balearic Islands: a new "California" for the European people', paper presented to the 8th International Geographical Union Congress, Den Haag, 4–10 August.

Serrano MartõÂnez, J. M. (1992), *Jubilados Extranjeros, Residentes en la Costa Calida*, Murcia: Universidad de Murcia.

Südas, J. and M. Mutluer (2006), 'Immigration européenne de retraité's vers la "Riviera turque": le cas d'Alanya (côte méditerranéenne)', *Revue Européenne des Migrations Internationales (REMI)*, **22** (3), 203–23.

Tamer-Görer, N., F. Erdoğanaras, Ö. Güzey and Ü. Yüksel (2006), 'Effects of second home development by foreign retirement migration in Turkey', paper presented at 42nd IsoCaRP Congress, Istanbul.

Turan, A.H. and E. Karakaya (2005), *Türkiye'ye Yabancı Emekli Göçü: Didim Örneği*, KEAS'05: Kentsel Ekonomik Araştırmalar Sempozyumu, II, Denizli.

Unutulmaz, K.O. (2006), 'International retirement migration in Turkey: case of Alanya', unpublished research paper presented to Florence School on Euro Mediterranean Migration and Development, Florence.

Williams, A.M., R. King and A.M. Warnes (1997), 'A place in the sun: international retirement migration from northern to southern Europe', *European Urban and Regional Studies*, **4** (2), 115–34.

Yilmaz, H. (2005), Avrupalılarin Türkiye'nin Gündelik Hayatı Hakkındaki Anlatıları: Türkiye'nın Avrupalılarla Yapılan Görüşmeler', in H. Yılmaz (ed.), *Avrupa Heritasında Türkiye*, Istanbul: Boğaziçi Üniversitesi Yayınevi.

Williams, A.M., R. King and A. M. Warnes (2004), 'British second homes in southern Europe: shifting nodes in the scapes and flows of migration and Tourism', in M. Hall and D. Muller (eds), *Tourism, Mobility and Second Homes: Between Elite Landscape and Common Ground*, Clevedon: Channel View Publications, pp. 97–112.

Yiğit, F. (2008), 'Profile of settled Europeans in Alanya', presentation at workshop on *Economic and Social Impact of International Retirement Migration (IRM): Turkey, an Emerging Destination in Southern Europe*, 7 April 2008, Antalya.

9. Recent migration from the new European borderlands

Claire Wallace and Kathryn Vincent

9.1 INTRODUCTION

The enlargements of the European Union (EU) in 2004 and 2007 led to the incorporation of twelve new member states, eight of them bordering countries that were part of the Soviet Union and are now referred to as NIS (Newly Independent States). This has created a new borderland between east and west with new flows of goods, people and capital. Despite the imposed migration regulations (stricter and more rigid than before), there are significant and increasing flows of migrants from the NIS into the EU and elsewhere in the world (Israel, USA, Canada and Russia). While the new member states were originally the target of this migration (before their incorporation into the EU) migrants now head increasingly for other destinations in Europe and elsewhere. In this respect both new and old EU member states are targets of migration (Drbohlav 1996, Bedzir 2000, Stola 2000, Dietz and Segbers 1997, Iglicka and Sword 1998, IOM/ICMPD 1999).

This chapter relates to the new migration situation between NIS countries and the enlarged European Union. The chapter focuses upon the following factors: the characteristics of different kinds of migrants; their destination countries; the activities and financial situation of migrants and finally the role of social capital and gender in determining these patterns.

9.2 THE NEW FAULT LINE

The new European borderland represents a geographical fault line in several respects. Although economies have improved in most of the NIS countries since the turn of the century, living standards are still low in comparison with the EU and many households in the NIS depend upon the remittances from migrants. As a result of their incorporation into the EU, the rising living standards in the new EU member states have created even greater contrasts along the borderlands. Particular countries and regions belonging to the NIS have established a tradition of migration, some of it to old European Union countries (Germany and southern European countries such as Portugal, Spain and Italy) some to new European Union countries such as Poland, the Czech Republic, Hungary and Slovakia (King 2001, Wallace and Stola 2001).

The character of migrations has changed in relation to earlier periods of migration, such as the recruitment of labour migrants in some western European countries in the mid-twentieth century, which was focused upon industrial workers. Alternatively, emigration to the New World or out of communist eastern Europe was normally one way and permanent (Castles and Miller 1993). People from the post-communist countries now had more opportunities to travel and did so in great numbers after the collapse of communism going to buy and sell goods as 'suitcase traders' or going as labour migrants to the EU or to the central European accession states. They no longer carry out industrial work, but rather reflecting changes in the post-industrial labour markets of Europe, there is a demand for short-term and flexible services workers or an expendable workforce in industries such as construction, catering, tourism and agriculture.

In addition, the changing domestic arrangements in western European households mean that there are more elderly people and children to be cared for as women go out to work and 'outsource' their former domestic roles to cleaners, babysitters, care workers and so forth, and this is also a consequence of the lack of welfare coverage in places such as southern Europe, forcing families to find 'private' solutions, often ones involving eastern European care workers (Ehrenreich and Hoschild 2003, Bakan and Stasiulis 1997). There are thus both male and female migrations taking place independently. In this context the domestic organization of the household in the sending country is important for understanding how migration operates as a 'household work strategy' both socially and economically (Wallace 2002, Stark 1991). Arlie Hochschild has argued that this represents a 'care chain' in which the children of the affluent west are cared for by female migrant workers and then their children are in turn cared for by someone else (Ehrenreich and Hochschild 2003). The darker side of these movements is the trade in human trafficking, the sex industry and the migration of criminal individuals or organized groups, where migrants from the east have been prominent (Lazaridis 2001). This new migration situation in the eastern borderlands of the European Union has hardly been researched at all and thus it is important for yielding new empirical findings for social science and policy makers.

9.3   THE RESEARCH PROJECT

Based on an ethnosurvey funded by the International Association for Cooperation with Scientists from the former Soviet Union (INTAS; Grant no. 04-79-7165) at the European Commission between 2005 and 2007, the authors explored the migration of people into the EU and elsewhere using a survey of their homelands combining quantitative and qualitative methods. The research questions reflect the preliminary exploratory investigation of these migration processes trying to understand descriptively what patterns are emerging and comparing them with what is known about previous migration.

Research Questions

What are the motivations of migrants? The first and maybe the most important research question can be answered very precisely. One clear reason for migration is economic. The collapse of the economic system in the former Soviet Union in the early 1990s meant that large proportions of the populations of eastern and central Europe lost their economic security and were plunged into poverty. Unable to make a living at home, many of them turned to migration.

However, other possible reasons for migration include ethnic and civil strife, ecological catastrophe and political persecution. In the region we are considering, there were several civil and ethnic wars in the post-Soviet period. For example, in Moldova the secession of Transnistra and the tension between Romanian and Russian populations led to an armed conflict in the early 1990s which is still not entirely resolved. Transnistra operates as a more or less separate state outside the control of the Moldovan authorities. In Armenia the civil war over Ngorno-Karabackh led to waves of refugees from Azerbaijan in the early 1990s and this is also unresolved. In Georgia the secession of South Ossetia and Abkhazia led to large numbers of displaced persons (they still occupy the main hotels in Tbilisi) and continued conflict in regions not controlled by the Georgian state. The proximity of Georgia to Chechnya means that they are inevitably drawn into that conflict too. Ukraine and Belarus have avoided any violent conflict despite the significant number of ethnic minorities living in those countries. However, there has been environmental devastation through the Chernobyl nuclear explosion in 1988, leaving many regions still contaminated by nuclear fallout which we might expect to provoke migration of people. Therefore, in all these countries there are plenty of reasons for migration due to ethnic and political conflict or environmental damage.

What are the characteristics of migrants? Migrants are usually male and young, although increasingly women migrate as well. Therefore, we would expect to find migrants with these kinds of characteristics. Education might also play a part in migration with migrants being slightly better educated than other population groups. We might also find some ethnicities more likely to migrate than others.

What is the role of migrant networks and social capital? Studies of migration have tended to emphasize the 'chain' effect of settlement patterns. Migrants from one country follow their countrymen to a new destination. The kinds of networks that people have can be characterized in terms of their 'social capital'. Yet many of the countries that people from NIS countries migrate to are entirely new ones, where they may not have contacts. Therefore, it is not clear how initial migration patterns are established or how they continue.

What role does the financial situation of households play? We were also interested in the extent to which the financial situation of the individual migrant might influence migration. In particular, is it poverty that encourages people to migrate? Given the substantial economic insecurity in the region, we might expect this to be a strong reason for migrating. Perhaps the lack of a secure future for young people may play a role in this too.

What are the destination countries of migrants from the new European borderlands? Traditionally Europe, especially Germany, was seen as a destination country for work migration and the New World countries were seen as countries for emigration. However, Russia also attracted many migrants from NIS countries. On the other hand, the opening of labour markets in Sweden, the UK and Ireland may have also attracted migrants from outside the EU.

What activities do migrants undertake in their destination countries? Migrants traditionally work in sectors of the economy where temporary work is required and where an illegal status can go undetected. However, this may differ between countries, especially east and west. We might assume that the activities would differ between destination countries and that women might be carrying out different activities to men.

Methods of Research

The new migrations from countries belonging to the NIS into the EU are under-explored because migration data have not been collected systematically and comprehensive survey research has been lacking. Although migration potential surveys have been long used as instruments for estimating migrations, they have deficiencies. The advantage of such surveys is that they provide systematic, statistically testable data. The disadvantage is that they survey only the people who are still at home, not the ones who have left and the percentage of real migrants picked up in such surveys is rather low. Thus, they can ask people only to think hypothetically about migration, something which has grave methodological problems.

Ethnographic studies of migrants themselves carried out by researchers who conduct lengthy unstructured interviews after winning the trust of the (often illegal) migrant and talking to them in their own language provide richer more and accurate data. But it is unsystematic and there is the problem of finding the migrants who may be in any one of several countries across Europe. For this reason, we sought a form of data collection that could combine the systematic and statistical reliability of the standard survey with the accuracy and depth of the ethnographic study. We term this the 'ethno-survey' and it is adapted from the surveys developed by Douglas Massey for studying border regions between the USA and Mexico (Massey *et al.* 1987, Massey and Espinosa 1997, Massey and Zenteno 2000). This survey enables us to compare systematically migrants with non-migrants in the same regions.

The ethno-survey involved questioning a sample of 400 respondents drawn from two regions with high rates of migration in each country (although in Moldova they were drawn from everywhere). The survey was carried out by partners in the respective countries using a random routing method along with a multi-stage random sample. Twenty households were chosen from the ones that had migrants in them and these were interviewed using in-depth methods. This chapter concentrates only upon the quantitative study, although it is informed by our reading of the qualitative interviews. It was not difficult to find households with migrants in them because the numbers of migrant households was quite high. However, the numbers are much reduced compared with the full sample with only 8 per cent having actually migrated, a total of 161 individuals. Of the different nationalities, 3.3 per cent of Armenians were migrants, 10.8 per cent of Belarusians, 1.8 per cent of Georgians, 13.5 per cent of Moldovians and 11.3 per cent of Ukrainians.

The sample survey was followed up with 20 in-depth interviews with (re-)migrants in each country. These were transcribed and translated into English. Here we have analysed only the interviews from Belarus, Moldova and Ukraine since the interviews from Georgia were lost and those from Armenia have not yet been coded. The analysis was carried out using the framework analysis method designed by Ritchie and Spencer, which involves coding and charting interviews according to dominant themes and then comparing them (Ritchie and Spencer 1994).

In this chapter we focus upon the people who actually migrated in the sample since 2004. These are necessarily temporary migrants because they were interviewed after their return to the country of origin.

Table 9.1   Basic demographic factors of returned migrants

Factor	Category	Migrants %	Non-migrants %
Country**	Armenia	8.1	21.0
	Belarus	26.7	19.5
	Georgia	4.3	21.5
	Moldova	33.5	18.9
	Ukraine	27.3	19.0
Gender**	male	55.9	34.6
	female	44.1	65.4
Age*	young	54.7	46.6
	middle aged	45.3	53.4
Education* *	low	9.9	4.5
	medium	63.4	57.5
	high	26.7	37.9
Regional type*	urban	62.7	69.1
	rural	37.3	30.9
Religion**	Orthodox	66.5	67.7
	Catholic	14.9	5.8
	non-believer	6.2	2.6
	other faith	12.4	23.9
Financial situation**	below subsistence	4.3	12.9
	subsistence	37.9	52.2
	financially stable	56.5	32.8
	unanswered	1.2	2.1
Migration networks*	yes	62.2	51.8
	no	39.8	48.2
N		161	1.823

Note:
Question was 'Do you have any friends or family living abroad who could help you to migrate?' ** high significant and * significant differences between the migrant and non-migrant population.

Source: Own survey; INTAS-Grant no. 04-79-7165.

However, they can give us a picture of actual patterns of migration in the recent past.

Results

From the sample population of 2003 participants and 1984 valid interviews, 161 had travelled to another country for more than a month for temporary work or study since 2004. Belarus, Moldova and the Ukraine constitute the largest groups of immigrants with 26.7, 33.5 and 27.3 per cent of the (re-)migrant population respectively. Armenia and Georgia contributed only 20 migrants in total. However, this seriously underestimates the number of migrants from Georgia and Armenia. It would seem that this kind of ethno-survey is not a good way of capturing the patterns of migration in those countries, although it works better for Moldova, Belarus and Ukraine.

Demographic characteristics

Age was coded into three groups. Those participants between the ages of 18 and 35 were classified as young, participants 36–55 were middle aged and 56 plus were regarded as retired, but with such a small number (19) they were excluded from the analysis. Education was coded into the following categories: those who finished less than tenth year were classified as having low education, those finishing secondary school (12 years) or vocational training were medium educated and those with any University education were highly educated. Missing data were excluded. In addition, we included religion as a factor since this is a way of indicating which ethnic group a person belongs to. Finally, we included an account of their financial situation, coded as below subsistence for those whose household could not afford basic food and clothing, subsistence for those who could, and financially stable for those who could afford the above basics plus consumer goods like televisions and even larger items such as cars or a home.

In terms of demographic characteristics, women are under-represented in the returned migrant population as they constitute only 44.1 per cent compared to 55.9 per cent of men. Younger people are significantly more likely to remigrate as are the lower educated, which was also unexpected. There appeared to be more remigrants from rural areas than urban ones, which is an unusual finding. However, these are very small numbers and the samples were not representative at a national level, so we should be cautious about drawing conclusions too readily.

Reasons for leaving

The questionnaire asked a range of questions about motivations for migration, which can be broadly broken down into political motivations and economic motivations.[1] In order to better understand the motivation behind the actions of migrants and non-migrants, respondents were asked a series of questions about the more popular perceived reasons for migration.

The predominant belief is that people migrate from their countries in order to improve their economic situation. This reason is followed by

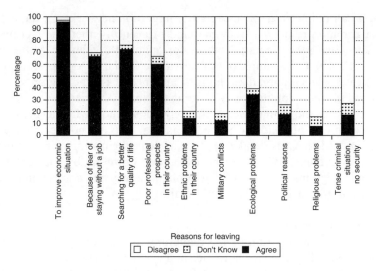

Source: Own survey; INTAS-Grant no. 04-79-7165.

Figure 9.1   Reasons for leaving

three additional economic factors, including fear of unemployment, better welfare facilities, and professional development, each of which more than 60 per cent of the population agree are significant factors. Meanwhile, sociopolitical reasons such as ethnic problems, military conflict, political difficulties, religious tensions and crime are considered important causal factors by less than 20 per cent of the population. Hence, although there are abundant reasons for ecological and conflictual migration from this region, this motivation is not predominant.

The importance of networks
Migrant social networks were coded by assigning the designation 'yes' to all participants who answered that they had a friend or family member abroad who was willing to help them migrate. It did not distinguish how many contacts each migrant had abroad. Migrants were significantly more likely to have friends and family abroad than non-migrants. However, we note that at least half of the non-migrants also had social networks abroad.

When we turn to the qualitative analysis we find a different story. Of the 60, 16 respondents reported using friends as a way of migrating and a further 16 mentioned that family contacts were used (often a spouse who was already in the destination country). Hence, more than half used social capital of some kind. However, what is perhaps more surprising is that nearly half did not use social capital or migration networks. Of these, the most common resort was to some kind of agency, either one recruiting workers, one recruiting students or for 'cultural exchange'. Altogether one-third (19) of the sample of 60 interviewees had used agencies. In some cases these agencies organized housing and income for the migrants – and this was the most common way of going to North America.

The sample shows that overwhelmingly, those who are financially stable are migrants, while those who need financial help are not very likely to migrate, and they also make up an almost negligible minority amongst returned migrants. This may be explained, however, by the fact that returned migrants have most likely brought money and goods home with them, thus increasing their family's wealth.

Destination countries
The favourite destination of the remigrants in the surveyed region was overwhelmingly Russia for both men and women, though in a greater proportion for men. Poland and the US were also both popular destinations for female remigrants. Men were spread thinly over a larger number of destinations. However, given that each of the countries under consideration has a different historical relationship to both east and west Europe, it seemed worthwhile to break the information down by country of origin, despite the small numbers.

Both men and women of Armenia preferred Russia as a destination for migration. Women equally preferred Turkey and Great Britain as destinations, while men spaced themselves out widely in Italy, Germany, Great Britain and other countries. Belarusian men also prefer Russia, though the women do not. The men also show a preference for Germany and Great Britain, as well as some interest in the US, Czech Republic, Italy, Poland and other places. Women, however, are concentrated in the USA, followed by Poland and Great Britain. However, the small numbers of migrants makes generalizations difficult for this portion of the analysis.

Men from Georgia stray from the pattern of moving to Russia, like citizens of the previous two countries as they only moved to Turkey and France. Georgian women are more spread out between Turkey, the US, Russia and Greece. As only seven people migrated from Georgia, it is difficult to generalize from these findings. Moldovians, both male and female, overwhelmingly choose to move to Russia, though a larger proportion of women chose to go. Both genders had representatives in Italy, France and the Ukraine. Only men migrated to Greece, Germany and Great Britain, while only women migrated to Portugal and Turkey. As there were a larger number of Moldovians to migrate than Georgians or Armenians, these results are more accurate.

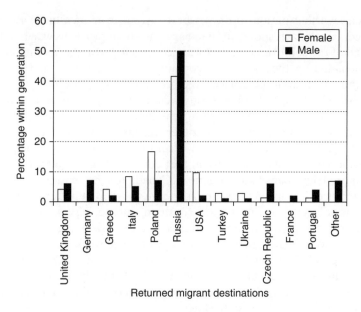

Source: Own survey; INTAS-Grant no. 04-79-7165.

Figure 9.2   Returned migrant destinations

The most preferred destination for Ukrainian women was Poland, followed by Russia and Italy. Men from the Ukraine were more spread out. Though they did migrate to Russia and Poland in significant numbers, they also went to Portugal as well as a number of other European countries and the US.

Migrant activities
An important category of migrants was students. Students went to Russia in some cases, but also to the US, Sweden, the Netherlands, Germany, China, the Czech Republic, the UK and in the case of Moldovians, some went to Romania to study. In most cases the students also worked in a variety of service occupations such as bartender, book keeper and waitress. In some cases the terms of the grant covered all their expenses, but in most cases this was not so. Therefore, students shade into workers, even if the purpose of their migration was not mainly to work.

As we saw above, many migrants went to Russia before they remigrated. They worked either selling on the market (Moldovians sell fruit) or, for men, it was construction work that drew them there. Women were more likely to work in a shop or a kitchen. It seems that the economic improvements in

Russia lead that nation to draw workers from their own 'near abroad'. Indeed, one of the respondents had bargained to improve his wages. Given that all of the countries we are concerned with had Russian as a main or a second language, the problems of communication were minimal. However, respondents from the Caucasus faced problems of prejudice.

Those who went to the US mostly went on academic grants or cultural exchange programmes. Although they might have worked while they were there, they were mainly invited for other reasons. However, one Ukrainian went to Canada as a construction worker on his own initiative, helped by the large Ukrainian community in that country. It is perhaps surprising that more Ukrainians had not gone to Canada for this reason.

In terms of European migration, there was a different pattern. The main destination region in Europe was southern Europe, especially Italy, but also Portugal, Spain and Greece. In these countries six of the nine respondents were women and they were employed as care workers, looking after elderly people. The men worked as builders or gardeners. Often migrants were a husband-wife team. They were recruited entirely through informal networks and began their stays as illegal workers, although they often managed to legalize their status later.

The central European new member states attracted some people. Of the 11 who went to these countries, four were Moldovians going to Romania, where they had common language links, and the rest were Ukrainians and Belarusians going to Poland where they worked either trading on markets or as agricultural workers, continuing a pattern established early in the 1990s (Iglicka 1999, Sword 1999). Agricultural work such as fruit picking as well as work in construction, bars, restaurants and shops were the kind of activities that they carried out.

Those going to northern Europe mostly went through agencies or on temporary workers or student schemes of various kinds (such as by becoming an *au pair* or temporary agricultural worker). They mainly carried out agricultural or construction work and, in most cases, this work was arranged by an agency who dealt with the travel and immigration problems. Although many went to northern Europe as students, the student schemes were often a disguised way of recruiting workers, since they did not attend language schools, but rather worked on farms, speaking mainly to other migrant workers. Students were not necessarily unhappy about this since it expanded their personal experience and brought them money.

Hence, we see a distinct pattern whereby migrants going to North America mainly went on temporary grants and cultural exchange schemes. Those going to northern Europe went with agencies of various kinds, either to study or to work. Those going to southern Europe did so by informal networks and the women worked as care workers while the men did agricultural or construction work. In Russia it was likewise construction work or catering that drew migrants there.

Logistic regression
Finally, we put all this together in a logistic regression model to see which factors were most important in determining migration. In this case, the dependent variable was whether respondents had migrated or not and hence a logistic regression was necessary.

In order to better understand the effect that each of the previously mentioned independent factors had on the probability that a respondent has migrated, a binary logistical regression was conducted. In the first block, the demographic variables of age, education, religion, gender, country of origin, and regional type are set as independent with the enter method. For the second, a backward stepwise likelihood ratio method was used with social capital, social capital in NIS countries, social capital in EU countries and social capital in other countries as the additional independent variables. In the third block, financial situation was added as the independent variable.

According to the Negelkerke R Square, the factors in block 1 explain 12.1 per cent of the variation, a significant portion. By examining the p-values for each individual factor compared to the reference category, one finds that Catholics were more than twice as likely to migrate as Orthodox and men were twice as likely to migrate as women. Armenians and Georgians were significantly less likely to migrate than Ukrainians.

In block 2, social capital values were added. However, as they were of very low significance, all but the factor 'social capital other' were rejected from the analysis, leaving an R^2 of 0.124. At the end of this block, 12.4 per cent of the variation was explained. The important variables stayed the same as before, though Armenia lost some significance.

In block 3, financial situation was added. According to the Chi-squared values, those who are financially stable are significantly more likely to have migrated. In addition, those of a lower educational background were significantly more likely to remigrate than those of higher education. Men and Catholics were still more likely to remigrate, though the gaps between them and the reference categories shrank. In the end, 14.8 per cent of the variation was explained by these variables.

9.4   CONCLUSIONS

First we need to sound a note of caution in the interpretation of these data. The number of actual remigrants in our sample was small in comparison

Table 9.2   Logistic regression for returned migrants

Factors		N	Block 1: odds ratio	Block 2: odds ratio	Block 3: odds ratio
Age	young	937	1.279	1.252	1.168
	middle aged	1046	1.0	1.0	1.0
Education	low	98	1.80	1.846	2.194*
	medium	1151	2.0	1.311	1.419
	high	734	1.0	1.0	1.0
Religion	Orthodox	1341	1.0*	1.0*	1.0*
	Catholic	129	2.483*	2.447*	2.475*
	non-believers	58	1.696	1.675	1.750
	other	455	1.176	1.095	1.153
Gender	male	721	2.092**	2.084**	1.857**
	female	1262	1.0	1	1
Country	Armenia	396	0.354*	0.336*	0.441
	Belarus	399	1.190	1.192	1.078
	Georgia	399	0.216**	0.213**	0.264**
	Moldova	399	1.641	1.502	1.958*
	Ukraine	390	1.0*	1.0	1.0**
Regional	urban	1359	1.0	1.0	1.0
	rural	624	0.870	0.895	0.873
Social capital	yes	1042	-	Rejected	-
	no	941	-		-
Social capital NIS	yes	493	-	Rejected	-
	no	1490	-		-
Social capital EU	yes	578	-	Rejected	-
	no	1405	-		-
Social capital Other	yes	285	-	1.0	1.0
	no	1698	-	0.670	0.710
Financial situation	below subsistence	243	-	-	1**
	subsistence	1011	-	-	2.175
	financially stable	689	-	-	4.176**
	unanswered	40	-	-	1.607
R-Squared			0.121	0.124	0.148

Source: Own survey; INTAS-Grant no. 04-79-7165.

with the population in general so that in analysing a total number of 161 respondents for all countries, most findings were non-significant. We should also be aware that even these were not representative at a country level. In order to find suitable respondents we focused the sample in regions that were likely to have higher numbers of migrants within each country. The sample that we have greatly underestimates the migration from these countries in general. It reflects only those who had returned and who happened to be there at the time of interview. Many more may be absent or away for longer periods.

However, the advantage of this kind of survey is that it is the nearest thing to a representative sample survey of migrants, which makes quantitative analysis possible in a way that cannot normally be done. It also enables us to make systematic comparisons with non-migrant populations in the same regions. There are a number of conclusions that we can draw from this analysis.

First of all, we can confirm that the motivations to migrate were mainly economic ones rather than political ones. Political factors played a very small role in this kind of migration despite the ample reasons for political as well as environmental migration from these regions and the large numbers of refugees and displaced persons living there. We found that the financial situation of migrants was very important since migrants were significantly better off then non-migrants (indeed they were more than four times as likely to be better off). However, this also reflects the fact that households with migrants in them were better off as a result of migration rather than this being a cause. Therefore migrating was an important source of household financial well-being.

Social networks were barely significant in determining migration according to the quantitative analysis (the significance, in fact, disappears in the logistic regression once we control for other factors), but the qualitative analysis showed that informal networks were the main channel of recruitment to southern Europe while for northern Europe and North America it was agencies of various kinds, where social networks were unnecessary.

In terms of destination countries, Russia was overwhelmingly the main destination, although Poland was also important, especially for women; Italy and Great Britain also featured. Russia was the most important destination among all national groups, although among the Georgians, France, Turkey and Greece were important and among the Ukrainians, Poland, Italy and to some extent Portugal were too. For Moldovians, Romania was an important destination country due to the fact that Moldovians and Romanians share a common language and history. We could therefore see that there was a significant flow of migrants to the east. In terms of new destination countries, those in southern Europe were becoming more important for some countries and Britain was also visible as a destination, but mainly, in this sample, through various kinds of recruitment or student agencies.

There are some general implications to be drawn. First of all, we need to expand our idea of migration. It is not only one way and permanent, but includes the circulation of people around Europe and the world. Many of these migrants are students, which seem to represent an important kind of migration. Although the main reason for these people to move was to study and improve their human capital, in fact, students mostly either worked to support themselves or the student migration scheme was actually a disguised way of recruiting workers.

Second, not all migration is only or even mainly into the European Union. The most common migration is to Russia, reflecting the booming economy in that country, the relaxation of migration restrictions and the fact that it was easier for migrants to travel and adapt to life in that country. Even of the migrants going to the west, a popular destination is the United States, using various kinds of temporary schemes.

Third, the main countries attracting migrants are not the traditional ones (Germany, France, the Netherlands) but rather non-traditional ones such as those in southern Europe and the new member states. In southern Europe the care of the elderly was a major reason for recruiting female migrants from eastern Europe, something we might term 'care migration' which is a response to the limited provision of welfare in southern European countries alongside an ageing population.

As predicted, there is an ambiguous overlap between what is legal and what is illegal and this tends to reflect the migration regime of the receiving country. In the southern countries migrants start as illegal and then regularize their status over time. In North America and the northern European countries, migrants have to find some other 'gateway' to migrate and this is usually through legitimate means, even if they later work illegitimately.

What we did not find was some of the patterns we might have expected. Since women were not usually caring for children (except in the case of the two au pairs one of whom was a man) we did not find the feminized 'care chains' described by US scholars. Secondly, we found that migration networks were important only in some circumstances because many of the destinations of the migrants were new ones, to countries where there was no previous cultural link. In this respect, various kinds of agencies step in to facilitate migration. In circumstances where migration is more and more circumscribed by various regulations, the agencies are often in a better position to deal with immigration.

Pulling all this together, it would seem that those western countries with a long tradition of migration (such as the US, the UK and Germany) have effectively closed their gates to new migration from the east. The only way to enter those countries is through designated schemes and agencies. However, those countries where migration is a relatively new phenomenon (southern Europe, new member states) have not yet been able to close all the migration gates effectively and so in these countries migration is relatively common and more irregular, using social networks as a main mechanism.

The implication of this analysis is that the European Union will need to compete with other more open and easier destinations such as Russia or even the US to attract future migrants from the border regions of Europe. Once the supply of workers in the new member states dries up due to demographic and economic changes, it is possible that the new wave of potential migrants from further east will have already departed for other destinations. Given the xenophobic backlash against eastern European migration in recent years within the EU, it is possible that the member states of the EU will not even notice this problem until it is too late.

NOTE

1. Question: To what extent do you agree or disagree with the fact that people from your country go abroad for the following reasons? To improve economic situation (their own or their family's); because of fear they will remain without a job in their native land; searching for better quality of life (medical services, pensions, social insurance); poor professional prospects in their country; ethnic problems in their country; military conflicts; ecological problems; political reasons; religious problems; tense criminal situation, no security guarantees. Answers were coded according to a four point scale.

REFERENCES

Bakan, A.B. and D. Stasiulis (1997), *Not One of the Family: Foreign Domestic Workers in Canada*, Toronto: University of Toronto Press.

Bedzir, V. (2000), 'Migration from Ukraine to Central and eastern Europe', in C. Wallace and D. Stola (eds), *Central Europe: New Migration Space*, London: Macmillan.

Castles, S. and M.J. Miller (1993), *The Age of Migration*, London: Macmillan.

Dietz, B. and K. Segbers (1997), 'Policies toward Russia and other successor states', in R. Münz and M. Weiner (eds), *Migrants, Refugees and Foreign Policy*, Providence RI and Oxford: Berghahn Books.

Drbohlav, D. (1996), *Labour Migration in Central Europe with special reference to Poland, the Czech Republic, Slovakia and Hungary, Contemporary Trends*, Prague: Charles University.

Ehrenreich, B., A. Hoschild and A. Russel (eds) (2003), *Global Woman. Nannies, Maids and Sex Workers in the New Economy*, London: Granta.

Iglicka, K. (1999), 'The economics of petty trade on the eastern Polish border', in K. Iglicka and K. Sword (eds), *The Challenge of East-West Migration for Poland*, London: Macmillan.

Iglicka, K. and K. Sword (1998), *The Challenge of East-West Migration for Poland*, London and New York: Macmillan/St. Martins Press.

IOM (1998), *Migration Potential in Central and Eastern Europe*, Geneva: International Organization for Migration.

IOM/ICMPD (1999), *Migration in Central and Eastern Europe: 1999 Review*, Vienna: International Organisation for Migration and International Centre for Migration Policy Development.

King, R. (eds) (2001), *The Mediterranean Passage: Migration and New Cultural Encounters in Southern Europe*, Liverpool: Liverpool University Press.

Lazaridis, G. (2001), 'Trafficking and prostitution: the growing exploitation of migrant women in Greece', *European Journal of Women's Studies*, 8, 67–102.

Massey, D.S., J. Alarcon, J. Durand and H. Gonzalez (1987), *Return to Aztlan: The Social Process of International Migration from Western Mexico*, Berkeley, CA: University of California Press.

Massey, D.S. and K.E. Espinosa (1997), 'What's driving Mexico-US migration? A theoretical, empirical and policy analysis', *American Journal of Sociology*, 102, 939–99.

Massey, D.S. and R. Zenteno (2000), 'A validation of the Ethno survey: the case of Mexico-US migration', *International Migration Review*, 34, 766–93.

Okolski, M. (1997), presentation at migration conference, Warsaw.

Pilkington, H. (1998), *Migration, Displacement and Identity in Post-Soviet Russia*, London and New York: Routledge.

Portes, A. (1995), *The Economic Sociology of Migration*, New York: Russell Sage Foundation.

Portes, A. (1997), 'Immigration theory for a new century: some problems and opportunities', *International Migration Review*, 31, 799.

Ritchie, J. and L. Spencer (1994), 'Qualitative data analysis for applied policy research', in A. Bryman and R. G. Burgess (eds), *Analyzing Qualitative Data*, London: Routledge.

Sassen, S. (1988), *The Mobility of Labour and Capital*, Cambridge: Cambridge University Press.

Stark, O. (1991), *The Migration of Labour*, Cambridge, MA: Blackwell.

Stola, D. (2000), 'Two kinds of quasi-migration in the middle zone: central Europe as a space for transit migration and mobility for profit', in C. Wallace and D. Stola (eds), *Central Europe: New Migration Space*, London: Macmillan.

Sword, K. (1999), 'Cross border "suitcase trade" and the role of foreigners in Polish informal markets', in K. Iglicka and K. Sword (eds), *The Challenge of East-West Migration for Poland*, London: Macmillan.

Wallace, C. (2002), 'Household strategies: their conceptual relevance and analytical scope in social research', *Sociology*, 36, 275–92.

Wallace, C. and D. Stola (2001), *Patterns of Migration in Central Europe*, Basingstoke: Palgrave.

10. The entry of female immigrants into personal home care services in Spain

Raquel Martínez Buján

10.1 INTRODUCTION

On 1 January 2007, according to the census, Spain had approximately 2 124 000 female foreign dwellers. This number is threefold that of six years before, in 2001, when the presence of the female foreign community amounted to 650 000 people. In the beginning of the 1990s, when Spain became an established immigration receptor country (Izquierdo 1992), the absolute number of foreign women approached 180 000, meaning a weight of 51.1 per cent in the total foreign population (year 1991). However, the relative number of females has decreased since the beginning of the 1990s, to 47.0 per cent.

Male migration flows in recent years have resulted in the decrease in that percentage of foreign women. Nevertheless, that amount must not divert attention from the fact that part of that male settlement is caused by the family joining their female relatives who migrated in the first place and became head of their families. Such a situation is particularly relevant for the population of Latin American origin whose presence has always had a strong female ratio in Spain. The latest data reveal that women make up 54.6 per cent of the population of Latin American origin but, when measured separately, numbers show a tendency to male predominance among those nationalities that have been settled for longer in Spain.

Foreign women have made themselves visible as active agents in the economic support of the household members and their decisions have been the element that has forced the family to embark on migration. Despite this assumed 'power' as agents of their destinies in the host countries, women are imported to be employed as cheap labour for those occupations relegated to females, which their native counterparts are no longer willing to perform.

The insertion of immigrant women within an international division of reproductive work must be considered a global phenomenon that in Europe attains particularly to Spain and the countries in the south of the continent (Greece, Italy and Portugal). In fact, although in Spain it is still a novel matter for research, outside its borders relevant literature has developed, analysing female migration flows as a resource of developed countries to fill those gaps left by indigenous women within households. These not only include taking care of basic cleaning housework, but also those tasks which involve looking after children, the sick, the elderly and the disabled. Because of this, some new terms have been created recently: 'servants of globalization', coined by Rhacel Parreñas (2001); 'global chains of affection', used by Hochschild (2000) and that of 'global women' referring to female immigrants working as nannies, nurses and maids (Ehreinreich and Hochschild 2004).

The irregularity of domestic service and its insertion in the black economy suggest that statistics do not offer reliable data regarding both activities . In Spain, all activities connected to the performance of repro-ductive tasks are officially counted as part of the domestic service, without differentiating the variety of occupations included in that sector. Thus, numbers cannot reflect the fact that, parallel to the increase of foreigners into domestic service, there has been a change in the activities for which, traditionally, a maid was employed. Looking after dependent individuals is becoming the occupation that starts the working path of immigrant women in Spain (Martínez Buján 2005).

These activities are carried out in most cases as 'housework' and are regulated under the working, economic and legal terms and conditions existing for that job. The sector of care within households lacks a legal framework, as it is regarded as an activity equal to cleaning the house. This lack of recognition in the care sector culminates with no proper name to designate this activity, so it is considered in all cases 'domestic service'.

This chapter is based on in-depth interviews with three foreign women's collectives involved in care for the elderly (30 interviews), families employ-ing carers (20 interviews) and interviews with workers for associations, non-governmental organizations (NGOs) and other institutions such as employment agencies offering care work to foreigners (20 interviews). The geographical area for the research was limited to the cities of La Coruña and Pamplona, although some other contacts were established in Madrid and Barcelona.

10.2   AGEING, DEPENDENCE AND PUBLIC CARE PROVISION: A QUANTITATIVE APPROACH

The two demographic factors that explain why ageing is on the increase amongst the population are: the drop in fertility, which is presently 1.3

Table 10.1   Growth of the elderly population in Spain by age group 1900–2000

	Total Spain	65 and over		80 and over	
	absolute	absolute	%	absolute	%
1900	18618086	967754	5.2	115365	0.6
1910	19995686	1105569	5.5	132615	0.7
1920	21389842	1216693	5.7	143014	0.7
1930	23677794	1440739	6.1	177113	0.7
1940	25877971	1690388	6.5	222498	0.9
1950	27976755	2022523	7.2	272478	1.0
1960	30528539	2505165	8.2	368975	1.2
1970	34040657	3290673	9.7	523656	1.5
1981	37683363	4236724	11.2	725131	1.9
1991	38872268	5370252	13.8	1147868	3.0
2000	40499790	6842143	16.9	1545994	3.8
2007	45116894	7529879	16.7	2046275	4.5

Source: Personal compilation of data. IMSERSO (2007): Informe 2006. Las personas mayores en España (Report 2006 Elderly People in Spain); INE Municipal Register of Inhabitants 1 January 2007.

offspring per woman (below the generational replacement level of 2.1) and the rise of life expectancy, which is now at 80.2 years (74.7 for men and 81.9 for women) (IMSERSO 2002). Ageing means the end of the demographic transition and the Spanish situation is characterized by an ageing process among the most elderly:

> While the number of young elderly has grown by 90 per cent, the number of octogenarians has increased by 195 per cent. We are witnessing an aging process within the elderly population, which is an important characteristic of the ageing phenomenon. The number of octogenarians is increasing at an annual cumulative rate of 3.7, which is a great deal higher than the growth of the rest of the elderly population or other age groups for that matter. (IMSERSO 2002: 32)

Since 1900 the number of people over 65 has progressively increased (Table 10.1). There was a surge in this increase in the 1990s, although in 2005 the numbers seemed to stabilize. The percentage was at 5.2 per cent at the beginning of the century, in 1950 at 7.2 per cent and in 1970 at 9.7 per cent. In 2000, it reached 16.9 per cent and, in 2007 had decreased slightly to 16.7 per cent.

Table 10.2   Population with some type of disability and population over 65
with some type of dependence

	Frequency	Percentage
Total population 1999	40 350 974	
Population >65 1999	6 790 852	
People with some kind of disability	3 528 221	8.7
People with some kind of ADL disability (dependents)	2 285 340	5.6
People over 65 with some kind of disability for AVD (elderly dependents)	1 464 815	21.6

Source: Personal compilation of data from EDDES, 99; INE, Padrón Municipal de
Habitantes (Municipal Register of Inhabitants) (population data calculated for mid-year).

The small 'demographic breathing space' that has taken place in the
last five years does not mean a decrease in absolute numbers of elderly
people. Its only significance is that there has been a relative decrease due
to the growth in number of other age groups in this period. The arrival of
foreigners has caused a growth in the workforce available, which has led
to a small relative decrease in the number of elderly people. Thus, the sta-
bilization of percentage growth amongst the elderly population in the last
five years is a reflection of the growth in international migration in the
same period.

However, the effects of international immigration do not go far enough
to offset the growth in the number of octogenarians, which is the main
characteristic of Spanish ageing. In the mid-twentieth century only 1.0 per
cent of the population was over 80, in 2000 this number was 3.8 per cent
and in 2007 reached 4.5 per cent. This sharp increase of ageing amongst
the oldest sector of the population has been caused by a growth in longevity, the consequence of which is the appearance of an ever more dependent
population.

The Survey entitled Discapacidades, Deficiencias y Estado de Salud
(Disabilities, Deficiencies and State of Health) (1999) shows that there
are more than 3.5 million disabled people in Spain, representing approximately 9 per cent of the total population. In the over-65 age group this percentage increases to 30.5 per cent. Of these individuals with some form of
disability or other, 21.6 per cent are in a dependent condition as a result
of their disability. In other words, nearly a quarter of those over 65 years
of age are dependent and need help from a third party to be able to carry
out their activities of daily living (Table 10.2).

Dependency is closely linked to the age factor, and this can be seen in the fact that as people get older their care needs increase. Figures show that amongst the over-80 age group lack of autonomy is present in 39.3 per cent of the population, while this number drops to 16.3 per cent in the 65 to 79 age group. Another significant factor is gender. Life expectancy is higher amongst women and this brings about a higher level of ageing and consequently a greater need for personal care for this gender. A total of 80.0 per cent of octogenarians that require help from a third party to be able to carry out daily activities are women. The fact that ageing in Spain is related to a growth in the number of people over 80 not only means more people with dependencies, it also means people with more severe or profound dependencies. A total of 71.6 per cent of the people in the over-65 age group are severely or totally dependent, and this figure rises to 78.4 per cent amongst octogenarians (IMSERSO 2004a).

The demand for personal caring services should be understood within this context of ageing and increasing dependence. It should also be considered that 21.6 per cent of old people in Spain are unable to cope by themselves without the help of a third party, and that 70 per cent of this age group with a lack of autonomy suffer from severe or total dependence. Public service provision covers only 12.3 per cent of the elderly population (IMSERSO 2007), which means that only 63.0 per cent of elderly people with some form of dependence where ADLs are concerned can count on public institutional help for their caring needs. Furthermore, these figures are only correct when applying the hypothesis that all the places offered by government are for dependent people. However the 'real supply' is also available to people defined as 'valid' (personally autonomous). In fact, only half of the residential places (138 354) are available to people with low incomes, which means that the availability of public care services to elderly dependent people is the considerably lower figure of 27.3 per cent. Institutionalization still implies internment without care and is often given to elderly people in socio-economic difficulties, but without autonomy problems.

This conception of centres for the elderly has made it difficult for the residential centres to adapt to the new social service concept known as 'ageing at home'. The ratios of provision regarded as desirable by the *Plan Gerontológico Nacional* (National Plan for the Elderly) in 1992 (INSERSO 1993) show that all the public resources destined for care did not reach the expectations or figures established for the year 2000. The home help service is the resource that most significantly fails to achieve the designated directives as defined by the plan. The proposal was to reach a level of 8.0 per cent of welfare provision in the home, and in 2004, barely 3 per cent of the elderly population was actually provided for. Within the European context of home hospitalization, the Spanish situation is quite saddening,

Table 10.3   Users and provision of some caring resources, 2006

Caring resources	Users and provision		Provision considered desirable by Government
Home help service	Users	305 801	*Plan Gerontológico (Escenario 2000)* (Plan for the Elderly, Situation 2000)
	Provision*	4.1	Provision: 8.0
Day centres	Users	261 433	Informe Defensor del Pueblo (*Ombudsman's Report*)
	Provision	3.5	Provision: 2% of those living alone
Residential centres	Places	47 624	*Plan Gerontológico (Escenario 2000)* (Plan for the Elderly, Situation 2000)
	Provision	0.6	Provision: 4.5

Notes: * Provision has been calculated by dividing the number of users by the number of people over 65 (7 529 879 people according to the census of 1 January 2007).

Source: IMSERSO (2007): Informe 2006. Las personas mayores en España (Report 2006. Elderly people in Spain).

given that home care provision in Spain is the lowest in the OECD, the average of which is around 9.1 per cent. It is also a country where, together with Switzerland and Ireland, institutional services (residential centres) are a more common care resource than home help (Huber 2005).

10.3   THE ISOLATION OF THE FAMILY IN CARE PROVISION

The absence of a public service network for the care of dependents places the responsibility for care firmly in the hands of the family. All recent surveys on informal support for elderly people (EDDES 1999, IMSERSO 2004b) coincide in highlighting the central role of the family in care provision, which in most cases is a solitary exercise with no external help forthcoming or offered. According to IMSERSO (2004b), 8.3 per cent of families providing care receive no type of public or private support for provision of care to dependents. Even when some type of social service is available for people to help them with reduced capacities, the service always requires an informal support network so that the rehabilitation and maintenance programmes can function effectively (with the exception of residential centres where elderly people without families are often sent). The family plays the main role where care for the elderly is concerned. In some cases it is the sole provider of care and attention, and in others where some type of public help is forthcoming, this help has a complementary function. Family support is the buffer against possible adversities for the elderly in Spain.

Spanish Constitutional legislation recognizes the important role of the family in caring for dependents, although at the same time it sees the need for developing a social services network that can provide adequate care for this group. The current conflicts that families have with the legislative apparatus arise when changes occur in the family that affect the 'care work' structure in the home. The steady ageing of the population, the inclusion of women into the labour market, and the change from extended to nuclear families have created new expectations and roles that are incompatible with previous ones. The problems that arise can be summarized as:

● The existence of a family network is not complemented by the development of a social service network that can help to keep the elderly person at home and provide a framework for family care provision.
● Another problem is that when the family is referred to as a care provider for the elderly, in reality it is not the entire family institution that fulfils this service. The weight of care provision is normally in the hands of just one person. Women are the main service providers in this context. The inclusion of women into the work place has generated conflict over the domestic tasks that normally were seen as their responsibility in the home. There is a new generation of women that can no longer continue with the traditional roles of domestic workers and carers that previous generations of women fulfilled.

Several surveys coincide in concluding that the family is the central institution for care provision, also concurring where the profile of the main care provider within the family is concerned. The EDDES (1999) and the IMSERSO (2005b) agree that informal care providers are mostly women over 50, married, who left school after receiving primary education, and whose main occupation is domestic work (IMSERSO 2005b).

The Spanish care system is based on unpaid work provided by women who have not been able to find a place in the labour market, and the public provision of help to the sector of the population with fewest resources. The Spanish Welfare State is therefore welfare-based and familistic, and falls into the framework of what is commonly referred to as the Mediterranean or Latin Welfare system.

> The family (organised as an informal network in which the central node is usually the woman, whose main task is care provision) is the basic social structure for personal care. It is based on the woman as an unpaid worker whose main job was being a housewife, but who more recently has decided to increase her presence in the job market. (Cabrero 2005)

The load that falls on carers' shoulders can be most clearly seen in the intensity and frequency of care work. In 84.6 per cent of cases, care work is a daily task of some 11 hours on average. (41.4 per cent spend more than eight hours a day on care work). The average total time spent on care provision is more than six years. The costs that this represents for leisure time, health and other professional work are not to be underestimated. For 63.4 per cent of women carers, the provision of their services has affected their professional and economic lives (from reducing their working hours to being unable to work out of the home).

If the profile of the typical carer is that of a housewife who consequently has limited activity in the formal work market, it remains to be seen if the new generations of women are willing to continue to provide the service of full time carer. The inclusion into the labour market of present generations of women is on the increase, and will surely mean that the time they can dedicate to caring for the elderly will decrease (CES 2003).

10.4   THE EXTERNALIZATION OF WELFARE AND THE EMPLOYMENT OF FEMALE IMMIGRANT CARERS

A situation of demographic ageing, the growth in numbers of elderly people needing personal care, the lack of adequate public services for geriatric care and the decrease in numbers of full time 'housewives', mean a growing number of families employ someone to take care of a dependent person. There are various ways to externalize care services, which range from residential centres to home help service companies to the use of support from the traditional domestic service provider, a post occupied by a large number of immigrant women. This latter option is the primary route for the privatization of 'care work'. Only 0.4 per cent of the families with care needs commercialized the service through private companies, while 7.0 per cent employed a home worker to fulfil this function.

The working characteristics of domestic service mean that there is more flexibility in timetables, caring time and other domestic tasks. There is the added benefit of having a live-in carer who is attentive to the elderly person's needs 24 hours a day at an average salary of 600 Euros. The financial costs of private companies that offer care provision are so high that few family budgets can cope with them. Another factor is that the hours and frequency that these companies offer do not cover the needs of the dependent population. Families looking for a carer need someone whose job goes beyond the purely personal care of an elderly person, from the 'physical work' of cleaning the home to the 'emotional work' involved in being constantly present and the attendant need to provide wellbeing and affection.

> No one from here would do this job. I know of some companies that do morning, afternoon and night duty but they're very, very expensive. We're talking about 3000 Euros every month. And no one can pay that. And so what with one thing and another and with what we had we decided to employ someone from abroad. (female employer of immigrant carer, Pamplona, 2004)

> I got them (referring to carers) through an agency and they look after elderly people and so 'don't you worry because no one will let you down'. That's why at the beginning I decided to go through an agency. It shows through the salary, which is higher, but the salaries were similar, but the thing is one girl did seven hours and the other did the whole day. And where the salary's concerned I've always let myself be guided by the association rules because they're the same for domestic employment in Spain. (female employer of immigrant carer, Pamplona, 2004)

The inclusion of women into the labour market and the lack of sexual equality when sharing domestic tasks at home practically ensure that the demand for female carers will increase. According to data from the Consejo Económico y Social (Economic and Social Council) (CES 2003), despite the growth in the number of women in employment, there has not been a corresponding decrease in the number of women doing two jobs or two shifts, and instead this figure has remained constant. In 1993, 63.3 per cent of employed women also carried out domestic tasks, and in 2003 this figure stood at 61.1 per cent. Responsibility for domestic tasks and the care of dependent people is still seen as 'women's work'.

The families employing immigrant carers for the elderly point out that the main reason for employing the person was that the woman in the family could no longer take on what was previously assumed to be her duty to care for the elderly dependent. The lack of a female presence in this case could be caused by her inclusion into the labour market , by the necessity for her to be with members of her direct family or for both reasons. Questions of social policy and the absence of a social service network were not seen as especially vital. It seems that the factors that really motivated the family to employ a female carer were related to aggravations of pre-existing dependencies and the inability to cope with care requirements for work motives.

All of the families interviewed identified the appearance of a health problem that increased the dependence of the elderly person (an embolism, a fall and so forth) as the factor that sparked off the search for and employment of a carer. However, this situation is linked to other related factors. The move to employ a female carer is a response to a family strategy for a situation in which there is an elderly person to live with and be cared for. The person deemed responsible for this task is the woman, who at that moment is entering the labour market .

In this respect, questions such as where the elderly person lives, and who with, become relevant. If the elderly person lives alone because he/she does not have a partner or because he/she lives a long distance away from the family (for example, in a village), the most frequently demanded resource is a live-in carer. The family members themselves may not be able to reach agreement about where the person should live, or the person him/herself may not want to leave his/her home. When the elderly person lives within a family unit (with offspring or another member of the family) the reason for employing a carer is often related to the woman's situation: she has entered the labour market and finds herself responsible for caring for the elderly person. The difficulties inherent in reconciling work and family life are thereby resolved by externalizing the care. In this case, the type of employment is mostly on an hourly basis.

> Why? Because there were two of us here in Pamplona, the two sisters living and working here and we didn't have enough time to look after our father and he couldn't stay on his own. He was, well, he'd go off into a world of his own from time to time. He looked after himself but . . . him being alone was out of the question. So it was a question really of covering the hours when we couldn't be there and well . . . (female employer of immigrant carer, Pamplona 2004)

Employing an immigrant only takes place when other efforts to find a native to do the same job have failed. NGOs themselves informed families looking for carers that there were no native women willing to work in live-in care. So when faced with the impossibility of finding a native employee, the decision is then made to employ an immigrant.

> We took on a foreign person to look after my mother because I couldn't do it anymore in the daytime. They told me that there weren't any Spanish women willing to do this work. I have a bookshop and I'm out all day long. You know a bookshop really takes up your time because you have to open every day of the week, Saturdays and Sundays. My husband works too and so do my children, each of them has a job. When my mother got worse and I brought her home it was like everything got on top of me. I couldn't do all the work. Finally I decided to take someone on and the only people willing to do the work were immigrants. (female employer of an immigrant carer, La Coruña, 2003)

The people interviewed working in NGOs and institutions with employment agencies for foreign carers agreed that care work is normally taken by recently arrived foreign women whose residential situation has not been legalized. Most of the jobs on offer are for 'live-in' carers, and the circumstances of women without papers who have just arrived in the country adapt well to this type of employment. Legal regulations and family regrouping are the conditioning factors that will move the live-in carer from her previous post to a new one, where she works as a live-out carer (changing from working on an hourly basis to a full-time contract). This means that caring for the elderly has become a working niche for women with nationalities that are less solidly rooted in Spain. In Navarre, Ecuadorian and Bolivian women were notably present, while in La Coruña the figure of the Brazilian female carer was beginning to make an impact.

Family preferences also determine the potential employee's nationality. There is a preference for 'maids' from Latin America. The language similarity has always been the variable that best explains this predilection along with the cultural similarities that people from this region are said to have. These linguistic and religious similarities are factors that have led to positive discrimination (when looking for workers in the domestic service sector) for Latin American women.

> Well, we asked for someone who was middle-aged, and who spoke Spanish, I mean, we wanted South Americans more than anything because of the Spanish, and that she mustn't be very black, because my father has a thing about blacks . . . So we said 'Well, a girl that's a bit more light-skinned'. Normal colour, not completely white, normal colour skin. (female employer of an immigrant carer, Pamplona, 2004)

> No, the thing is then, it's true they did say why not use someone from Romania who didn't speak the language very well. And, well no, I'm very sorry but my father needed someone who could speak to him at night. And not someone he would have to teach the language. And so we employed a South American woman. (female employer of an immigrant carer, La Coruña, 2003)

This preference for Latin American women has created the situation in which caring for the elderly is now a *work niche*, as defined by Martinez Veiga (2000, 82).

> When we speak of a niche we mean certain ethnic groups of immigrants form around certain jobs because of the group's cultural characteristics, skills, or opportunities that were there for them at the beginning. The niche is formed after being occupied by a sizeable number of people from the ethnic group. The belief then arises soon after that people from that group are the best suited to the job and its requirements. (Martinez Veiga, 2000)

So the work niche is formed, and, in this particular case, by a demand that existed before the female carers arrived and settled in Spain. This is backed up by the fact that only two of the 30 women interviewed had worked in this occupation in their country of origin, and were the only women to have thought of working in the same occupation when they considered making the move to another country. Caring for the elderly is a job imposed by circumstances and times that do not allow the person to gain access to other work.

> If you've worked in a bank, they're not going to give you that kind of job either. Here you work as a cook, or you look after kids or old people, that's the work for us [. . .] No, the thing is, what you have from Ecuador is worth nothing here, nothing. Here, looking after old people, looking after kids. You don't have papers . . . (Ecuadorian female carer, La Coruña, 2003)

10.5   A COMPLEMENTARY WELFARE STATE AND MIGRATORY MODEL

Although few families have privately contracted female carers, the impact of this labour market on immigrant women has been notable. The in-depth interviews carried out with workers from different organizations, institutions and associations that have an employment agency for foreigners affirm that 90 per cent of the domestic service work on offer is for the personal care of dependents. According to a survey by the Colectivo IOE (IMSERSO 2004d) on domestic workers in the community of Madrid, 27 per cent of the people interviewed said that 'looking after sick or elderly people' was a habitual part of the job.

In all these cases, care for elderly people is regarded as a domestic service. Consequently the working conditions for this type of job are regulated by the Real Decreto 1424/1985 (Royal Decree), which regulates the conditions for Servicio del Hogar Familiar (Service in the Family Home). This law states that labour relations of this nature are

> those that are arranged by the holder of the title of head of the family home, as employer, with persons who as dependents or under contract, provide paid services within the family home, carrying out domestic tasks, such as the management or care of the home, care of members of the family or others who live in the home. Other tasks may include gardening, driving vehicles or other similar activities, with the proviso that these activities form part of the domestic service as a whole. (R.D. 1424/1985, 1 August (BOE) 13-8-85)

Care for the elderly in the home, therefore, is regarded as a domestic service and regulations concerning salary and taxation for this type

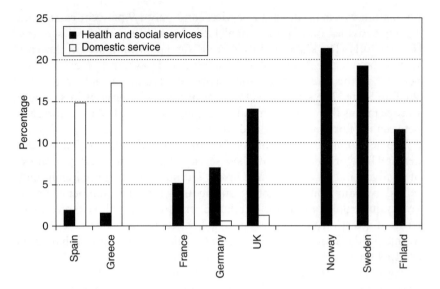

Source: OCDE (2004): Tendances des migrations internationels: rapport annuel, 2003, pp. 59.

Figure 10.1 *Foreign population employed in 'domestic service' and 'health and social services' activities, mean 2001–02*

of work are treated under the same legislative conditions for domestic work.

The 1985 regulation is contained in the Régimen Especial de Empleados de Hogar (Special Regulation for Home Workers) and was a major legal breakthrough in domestic service legislation due to the fact that domestic work was recognized for the first time as a 'job' that deserved payment. However, the Régimen Especial de Empleados de Hogar still maintains several discriminatory working conditions in comparison with other types of work included in the Régimen General (General Regulation). It also divides the workforce into two sectors according to their type of employment (live-in or live-out). The Real Decreto 1424/1985 contains some abusive working practices. Where live-in workers are concerned (previously named 'domestics') the salary may be paid in kind by providing the worker with food and lodging. The maximum deduction that can be made for payment in kind is up to 45 per cent of the total salary.

The working conditions that are offered to immigrant women working in care in Spain are not the same as those offered in northern and western Europe to personal care workers. In Spain, 14.8 per cent of the foreign population works in 'domestic services' and only 1.9 per cent carries out similar activities on a professional basis in 'health and social services' (Figure 10.1). The situation in Greece is similar, with figures in this case varying between 17.2 per cent and 1.6 per cent. However, in Norway, 21.3 per cent of the foreign population works in care and forms part of the Welfare State. The scarce development of the social services in southern Europe means that 'private' means of coping with these tasks are arranged between the family employer and employee.

The development of the job market for care of the elderly with a great demand for workers to provide these services has occurred within a context of relatively intense migration in Spain. During 2000–05 more immigrants settled in Spain than at any other time in its history. The number of immigrants quadrupled in Spain. In relative terms this growth is expressed in terms of growth from 2.3 per cent to 8.4 per cent according to the Padrón Municipal de Habitantes a 1 de Enero (Municipal Register of Inhabitants as of 1 January).

In general terms, all of the countries of Southern Europe have developed a similar migratory model. The basic characteristic is one of change from emigration to immigration with a high number of female immigrants. The latter characteristic is a new phenomenon in international migration. Up until the 1970s, migration was associated with the 'male head of the family'. Castles and Miller (1993, 8–9) identify the feminizing of international migration as the key tendency in 'the new era of migration'. King and Zontini (2000) point to a series of geographical, economic and sociodemographic factors that led southern Europe to have its own migratory model. This model has characteristics that are vastly different from the one that took shape shortly after World War II and continued up to the 1970s. This earlier model consisted of a flow of masculine labour directed towards industrial activity in the formal economy.

They point out that southern Europe occupies a strategic location for the movement of peoples. Economic and sociodemographic factors are regarded as even more important. The southern European economy has several principal sectors (tourism, maritime traffic, fishing and general service sector activities) that involve a group of nexuses with the outside world that ease immigration flow. Development and modernization of the region between the 1960s and 1980s has also been fundamental. An important sociodemographic factor is the ageing of its population, which is a phenomenon common to all European countries. Another important consideration is the growing participation of women in the workplace along with changes in family habits and customs. These two factors have given rise to women in their own country no longer being at home, and the commercialization of the space and work created by their absence.

In Spain another 'political' factor needs to be considered. After the events of El Ejido in 2001 and the great need that the Government appeared to have developed for Moroccan labour, efforts were made within the legislature to set in motion an arduous selection process for migrants. The aim was to 'choose other nationalities' regarded as less 'conflictive' for Spanish civil society. The chosen people were Latin Americans, who, because of their links with Hispanic culture, were believed to have 'fewer problems' in terms of the integration process. With this end in mind, the Government set in motion two regularization processes (in 2000 and 2001, known as Documentación por arraigo ['Documentation resulting from establishment']) from which people from Latin and South America benefited enormously. Previous regularization processes showed a majority of people from North Africa (1985, 1991 and 1996), but in the new millennium legalization of papers was becoming a predominantly Latin American phenomenon (for more details on this issue, see Izquierdo *et al.* 2003, Martinez 2003). Consequently what is known as a Latin-Americanization of the population took place, and in the naturalization process of 2005, 39.0 per cent of the applications presented came from only four Latin American nationalities (Ecuador, Colombia, Bolivia and Argentina).

This 'Latin-Americanization' has been accompanied by a feminizing of immigration, and Latin American emigration is characterized by a majority female presence, which is linked to the need for female labour to work in the hidden economy and the service sectors, such as care for the elderly. The Government is aware that foreigners are being employed (often without papers) to work as carers. On some occasions, the tendency towards privatization of home help services, which is often encouraged by local government bodies, has encouraged a process whereby female immigrants play an increasing role in domestic care.

The Comunidad Autonoma de Navarra (Regional Government of Navarre) is a good example of this. Since the mid-1990s economic assistance has been available for families that have had to take responsibility for the care of an elderly person who had difficulties looking after him/herself. The family is offered a quantity of money according to the level of dependence that must be used for employing a worker who will look after the elderly person. This quantity includes all social security payments. However, the paying body, in this case the Gobierno de Navarra (Government of Navarre), has not taken any measures to follow up or evaluate the assistance, which has led to some families receiving the money without externalizing the care costs. In other cases, families have preferred to employ an external carer, usually a foreigner, due to the difficulties inherent in finding a native worker willing to take on the work and the expense of employing a care professional.

The boosting of financial assistance schemes along with tax deductions (rebates on income tax and acceptance of debts) is a measure that has been taken with ever increasing enthusiasm by Spanish Regional Governments in the last few years as part of their formulae for social service spending, but it has functioned to the detriment of social service investment. Direct economic assistance is easier to spend and use and is also a more profitable practice for local governments that no longer have to directly employ workers or outsource social service management to other companies.

> These two options are on the increase (referring to economic help and fiscal incentives), they are definitely more flexible and simpler, and enable the use of free choice by making payment by users and families easier (co-payment). They make it possible to extend the services market and help to create jobs. However, they also have their limitations (for example they make it difficult to demand social treatment for certain needs) and can even have perverse side effects (such as the creation of parallel networks that depend on purely economic needs) (Vila 2001, 45).

This is what has happened in Navarre, with the generation of a labour market within the hidden economy and casual labour. Consequently it is not only the absence of public provision of social services that induces families to externalize care work: current tendencies in social policy towards privatization can also promote the employment of immigrants without papers.

10.6 CHANGES IN THE DOMESTIC SERVICE SECTOR

Although caring for the elderly forms part of the domestic service sector and is not considered as a job in its own right, it has brought about some changes in the nature of domestic work. These changes are linked to the intensity of the tasks involved, the training required of the worker and the employer/employee relationship. These changes are separately described below.

Changes in the Intensity of the Tasks

The care of elderly people is almost always combined with tasks such as cleaning the house and other jobs traditionally associated with housekeeping. Caring for the elderly is a domestic job, and the women runs the risk of not only working as a carer but also turning into a 'Girl Friday'. This situation occurs with greater frequency when the person works as a live-in carer, which is the case of the immense majority of foreign women. Of the women interviewed in the IMSERSO survey (2004c), 89.4 per cent emphasized that besides the job of personal care, they also had other domestic tasks (cleaning, ironing, cooking, and so forth). This has repercussions on their work by making it invisible, by creating low esteem for the work they do and by developing the belief that the act of caring is just another domestic task. Cleaning the floors and making personal contact with the elderly person are all done at the same time. Giving the elderly person a bath, controlling medication, accompanying him/her to the doctor and taking him/her out for a walk to help him/her recover some degree of mobility are amongst the simpler tasks for a carer. Incontinence of and late night vigils to the elderly person are other, tougher jobs.

> In Colombia you work as a nurse and all you have to do is take care of the person. You just look after the patient. If you have to give injections, if you have to put in a saline drip, if you have to keep an eye on the medication, only the patient. A girl comes here, a woman takes care of her personal hygiene, but I have to get her up at 9.00 every morning, I take a deep breath, then I make her an orange juice, then she gets up, I dress her, she walks a bit now, but she's in a bad way. (Colombian carer, La Coruña, 2003)

> You've got to have a lot of humanity. Today I didn't get any sleep because there are nights when she wants to go to the bathroom and doesn't want the bedpan, she wanted to go to the bathroom and in the bathroom she kept me waiting there for half an hour, half an hour. And other people say, that's terrible, she doesn't sleep, that's awful. But I say this is my job and what else can I do. (Ecuadorian carer, La Coruña, 2003)

> We moved the bed close to the wardrobe, and we slept, for example, on the floor. We slept by her side to see . . . if she tosses and turns, and if she falls she'll fall on top of us but at least we know it's happened. Sometimes, she wants to get up and I'm there and I say 'go to sleep, sleep, don't worry'. That way we sleep without worrying, although she gets up sometimes and calls us . . . (Ecuadorian carer, La Coruña, 2003)

Caring for the elderly differs from other domestic tasks such as cleaning, and even looking after children is not as similar to caring for the elderly as it might seem. 'Looking after old people' has created diversification in the activities that were seen as forming part of the 'maid's' job. It is no longer just a question of housekeeping, but also caring for and keeping watch over the elderly person. These tasks involve a responsibility for a person's life that goes beyond the purely physical. Care involves sympathy, affection and company. Besides the difficult tasks of personal care such as bathing, mobility, medication, night watches, housekeeping, cooking and cleaning, there is also the need for activities that can help to improve the elderly person's emotional state. Caring for children is regarded as less demanding psychologically because they are livelier and have more vitality than the elderly.

> Working with children is more gratifying. It's much more fun. You live each day with them. With old people you need to be so patient. You need to be incredibly patient. You can see how every day they go a little bit more downhill. A kid goes up. Because they learn and they take everything in and they want to know. So that's a stimulus for you and I taught them this and that and so on . . . But, the old person goes downhill, every day a little more downhill, you have to help him a little bit more every day, you can see him losing his faculties, you can see how much he needs you. (Ecuadorian carer, La Coruña, 2003)

The carer has to maintain a sympathetic and encouraging attitude with people who might soon die. The carers interviewed commented that one of the biggest problems amongst people receiving care was the tremendous depression they suffered from. This was not only a result of their health problems, but also for a number of personal reasons, and because of the side effects of certain types of medication they were taking. Sadness is something many old people feel precisely because of the dependent state they are in.

The physical effort and emotional cost involved in the constant care of the elderly has its consequences for the emotional state of the carer. More skills are required than a basic knowledge of medicine. Illnesses, irreversible pathologies, medication, all of these affect the old person's mood. It must be understood that many of these old people are going through a phase in which they know the illness they have is terminal. Others are no longer aware of what they are doing; they become disoriented and can no longer control their behaviour. Other elderly people without severe illnesses also suffer because they feel they are no longer valued by society. Boredom and bad temper are very common amongst old people because they no longer have a life plan that can give them an objective, an aim. There is nothing to motivate them because they are separated from the things they did all their lives, and so they fall into severe depressions that are aggravated by physical deterioration, which also affects their physical mobility. There is a phase when the elderly person goes through depersonalization, where they lose their sense of identity. The lack of effort in the elderly is often expressed through laziness. Old age is their excuse. All their difficulties and bad behaviour are justifiable because they are old (Beauvoir 1983). These attitudes do not always make it easy to get on with the elderly person.

> But when someone is really ill, that's got a lot to do with that, although they get finicky, you know that really it's the illness or their things because sick people

always get bored. There are days when they're really happy, but there are days when . . . well, there are moments when they're ill, but you think, what a pain . . . when they're ill they don't want you to touch them or talk to them, or tell them anything, but . . . (carer from Dominican Republic, La Coruña, 2003)

This type of situation can cause psychological exhaustion in the carer, especially if she works as a live-in carer. Female domestic workers make constant reference to the phenomenon of mental burnout, which has also been borne out by evidence from other studies (Oso 1998). However, psychological burnout can be even more marked amongst carers of the elderly, because of the greater effort and dedication necessary for effective care.

I tell you, sometimes when she gets like that with me . . . Every night for example, she calls for you. And she calls, and she calls, all the time. And she doesn't want anything, she just wants to see you. She doesn't sleep in the daytime either. You're tired because you didn't sleep last night, and another day looking after her, because she gets difficult . . . (Ecuadorian carer, La Coruña, October 2000)

And the other one, well let me tell you, he almost looked after himself, but this one you had to give him more attention and . . . you had to talk to him . . . Obviously, you're tired, you get up without feeling like doing anything, and I had to be asking him all the time 'and how are you, and how I don't know what else'. And sometimes I didn't feel like talking at all and I felt bad and 'What's wrong? Why are you like that? Why don't you speak to me? (Ecuadorian carer, Pamplona, 2004)

This part of the 'emotional work' of caring for the elderly is the hardest to do (the carers themselves say so), as well as being the least visible and least valued part of the job. 'The work of caring includes feelings and efforts, activities that are aimed towards giving answers to individual needs' (Cancian 2000). 'Care' is divided into a double sphere made up of 'work' and 'affection', and the latter cannot be given a price on the market. This is why 'care work' is not easily grouped into the accepted definitions of formal productive work.[1]

New Training Requirements for Female Domestic Workers

Caring for the elderly involves new tasks that do not form part of domestic service and which require specific training in two areas. First, the tasks that require some type of physical effort (lifting the elderly person, cleaning him/her, giving injections, and so forth) form part of what would be basic knowledge of medicine or nursing. At the same time, 'care work' requires establishing a personal relationship with the elderly person and the provision of wellbeing and support; and to do so a number of emotional skills are necessary. The second group of skills are much more difficult to quantify professionally and are often linked to personal abilities and approaches.

None of the families interviewed demanded qualified professional carers. The only characteristics that were valued in the future worker were 'patience' and 'affection'. Immigrants are attracted to a job where no experience is necessary other than some experience of life and where the immigrant only needs to utilize the training she received in her own country with her own family.

> I'd never been in a house doing what I do now either. It's not difficult for me because I had my home and my experiences. (Colombian carer, La Coruña, 2003)

Care of the elderly is not considered to be an occupation that requires professional training since employers take on workers to look after their elderly who have no special training in the job. This is so even when employers have elderly members of the family that need specific care treatment such as injections, resuscitation or monitoring of medication.

> No, I don't ask for someone with specific training or skills to look after the elderly. One of my customers told me about this girl she knew. And that was enough for me. No, because there are people around, the doctor's nearby . . . She doesn't need it. I don't need someone with nursing skills, because anyone can put on some morphine patches, can't they . . . (female employer of immigrant carer, La Coruña, 2003)

However, despite this type of discourse that maintains that a person with specific skills in looking after the elderly is not necessary, we are talking about people with reduced mobility, who on certain occasions need carers with specific knowledge about their illness. The immigrants themselves highlight the fact that they were not prepared for the job of caring for an elderly person and that at times they do not know what to do.

> I'd never done it before, but off I go and I look after them with all the love in the world. We'll see how it goes. (Colombian carer, La Coruña, 2003)

The market for care of the elderly has a number of features that require certain qualities from the people working in it. The people themselves define those qualities necessary in a good carer. What is intriguing is that they refer more than anything to personal qualities, adjectives of person-ality, rather than practical caring skills. The people themselves recognize that 'patience and affection' are the two most important things for looking after the elderly. Some of the carers interviewed said that although they had never worked in care of the elderly before, they felt they had some kind of special qualification, an innate sensitivity that made them the right people for the job. It seems that to be successful at caring for the elderly, it is more important for the employer to see how the carer personally relates to the elderly person and what the carer's nationality is than her quali-fications. A number of personal qualities are demanded that the carers themselves identify with.

> I don't ask her to know anything specific. She'll learn to look after my mother in much the same way as I did. (female employer of immigrant carer, La Coruña, 2003)

This means that what most families look for and require, and what most female immigrant carers identify with, are the emotional qualities required for the job. However, these 'skills' have always been undervalued, invis-ible and poorly paid, precisely because it is so difficult to give them an economic value.

The lack of demand for tacit or formal skills is greatly linked to care being a domestic occupation. Care is thought to form part of the woman's work. Second, it is believed that any training required for the job only develops what a woman 'innately' has, and so formal abilities are not recognized. 'Care is defined as women's work and that is why it is deval-ued. To sum up, good salaries are justified as a reward for the specialized application of skills and qualifications. Care is seen as an innate ability in women that needs no special skills or training' (Cancian 2000, 140. Author's translation).

An evaluation of this nature is applied more to the emotional side of care work than to the technical aspects. The physical skills necessary for personal care are easily converted into economic value. However, emo-tional work is not specified as a 'specialized skill' but is regarded as part of the carer's personality. Hothschild (1983) was one of the first authors to recognize the existence of 'emotional work' in service sector jobs where people are involved. James (1989) has fought for the recognition of emo-tional care as a 'job' in his research. Emotions such as affection, sympathy and love exist in privatized 'care'.

> From the moment that women become qualified in the management of emo-tions as part of their domestic work, they use them as tools for paid labour. The dichotomy between domestic work and other paid work is made plain

[. . .] Although emotional work is based on the maintenance and continuity of power and social relationships of production in the workplace and the domestic domain, it still remains invisible as a job (James 1989, 39. Author's translation).

When families demand 'emotional work' from their future employees they are not aware of the training necessary to do such a job. Analyses of the in-depth interviews of female carers and the women that contracted them highlight that both groups are unaware that the work of 'affection', 'love' and 'sympathy' might involve a set of aptitudes and acquired skills.

A New Employer/Employee Relationship

The demand for 'emotional work' by families has an important underlying meaning. Families do not want nurses for their nearest and dearest. They do not demand professional carers with medical training to do the job of caring. Families, and most notably the person whose job it is to select the employees, want someone who can look after grandfather/mother the same way as they themselves would. This is why affection, sympathy and love are given so much importance in the potential employee. These qualities appear to be a notable characteristic amongst Latin American women.

The employer/employee relationship in this case is therefore different from relationships in domestic service or in childcare. When domestic service consists only of cleaning and housekeeping, the absence of a personal relationship means that the emotional part of the job is not focused on one particular person. The emotional labour in this case consists of keeping a 'smiling face' in all circumstances, being polite to the employers and accepting a possible relationship of dominance/subservience with them. Childcare involves different aspects of emotional care and also implies a different employer/employee relationship. The emotional part of the job in this case involves links of affection with the children but with support from the parents with whom care is shared on a daily basis. The mother is the provider of 'love' and 'affection' while the employee is a support, a back-up that under no circumstances would attempt to act as replacement for 'mother's love' and Ulloa Oso (2001, 107) very astutely pointed out that:

sometimes the close contact in the privileged private social space of the home leads to jealousy on the mother's part, who sees the girl as a competitor that might supplant her role as wife and mother. They fear that the domestic employee might win over their husbands and monopolize the affections of their children. [. . .] Some female employers do not want the substitution of roles to include the affective part of wife and mother. So they feel their emotional territory is being invaded when the maid gains the affection of their children and makes friends with their husband or partner. The most unpleasant and dirty tasks traditionally associated with a housewife's work are reserved for the maid, while the domain that produces personal satisfaction, the property that is the affection and love of the other members of the family must be jealously guarded by the wife.

However, I found nothing of this in my fieldwork on carers for the elderly. The families even seem to prefer to commercialize this affective part, and actively look for 'affectionate' and 'patient' employees. On many occasions, the elderly live alone and depend solely on the skills and aptitudes of the carer. This enables the employee to have more direct control over the work process and greater responsibility in 'running the house' (shopping, receiving the bills, opening mail, and so forth) (Parreñas 2001). Decision-making depends much more on the employee's personal criteria, which can create a greater autonomy on her part and a more equal relationship with the family employing her.

Other factors are also at play to explain the greater degree of equilibrium between employer and employee in the area of care for the elderly. At some time or other the employer may have had to do the same job. This means that she is aware of the intense nature of the work and this awareness can help her to give a positive evaluation of the employee and greater understanding of her situation. One of the people responsible for an association employment agency for foreign carers commented on the depressed and anguished state of many of the women who came to the agency looking for a carer. They know how hard the job is, how difficult it is to find someone they can trust and how important the carer is for the emotional stability of the elderly person. This may explain why efforts are made to keep the 'girl' 'happy' at home. The absence of the carer would mean a sudden reorganization of care work within the family.

> More than the physical time I spent on caring for him it was the psychological strain. I'd go every morning to see him. The entire weekend. And at night I had to go as well. About eight hours a day. Just like a normal job and I was working outside home. And then this feeling that it was getting me down. It was getting on top of me. Because I wasn't used to dealing with my father, we never had this feeling of trust like father and daughter. When my mother was alive the relationship was more normal but after her death I realised my father was a stranger to me. (employer of immigrant carer, Pamplona, 2004)

> And I felt a sense of relief and relaxation when I took the girl on, tremendous. Now when I'm on night duty I feel relaxed because I know there's someone looking after my mother. (Employer of immigrant carer, Pamplona, 2004)

A second factor is that the decision to employ a carer for the elderly is not always unilateral, as may be the case in domestic service or childcare. Normally, it is the parents alone that decide when to externalize the care of their children. But where employing a carer for an elderly member of the family is concerned the decision is made by various parties (except when the dependent him/herself takes this decision). The normal process is that of a consensus reached within the family, with the final responsibility being in the hands of the person who has had to bear the greater part of the care work. This is another reason why it is so important for the employers to know how difficult the job can be and to understand the employee's needs.

The fact that a greater number of people are involved in the decision-making process of employment has led to another phenomenon in which the figure of the carer now forms part of the experience of other social classes. The opportunity to divide salary costs amongst several members of the family means that the use of immigrant carers has 'extended' to the working classes. This in turn has led to changes in the traditional relationship of dominance and subservience that previously existed in domestic service.

> We've always been normal people, we've never had someone working for us in domestic service, never. That happened when my mother started to get really ill and we tried to do it ourselves but we couldn't. My sister and I paid the girl along with some money from my mother's pension. That covered all the costs. (female employer of immigrant carer, Pamplona, 2004)

10.7   CONCLUSIONS

The main way to privatize assistance to the elderly is domestic service. The maid establishes herself as the main actor in providing mercantilized care. The advantages that this resource provides in terms of working conditions and availability of working hours are two aspects that affect its demand, as well as the deficiencies in social care and the native women's incorporation to work.

The internationalization process that the Spanish labour market is experiencing has made of this job a true work niche for immigrants. Considered as domestic workers, most of them without legal stability, the care needs of the employer families become invisible in the absence of a proper social service network. At the same time, these workers' vulnerability becomes hidden behind the border that marks home privacy. The preference for hiring Latin American carers is rooted in a symbolic cultural component, considered similar to the Spanish one, and in the creation of stereotypes related to personality attributes essential to carry out this work, such as 'patience' and 'affection'. Professional requirements are ignored, while those traditionally associated with female character become prioritized. Thus, the immigrant worker performs the physical (house cleaning) and emotional (care providing) work that some time ago was covered by the native women's reproductive work.

NOTE

1. In the case of Pamplona, if the work is found through an association or NGO with an attached employment agency, the salary is agreed using a salary scale. Sometimes the salary set by the organization will depend on the level of dependence and the work load this implies for the carer. This means that some organizations distinguish between purely domestice service and care work, which is seen as involving a number of tasks that are harder in the domestic service context.

REFERENCES

Beauvoir, S. (1983), *La vejez*, Barcelona: Edhasa.
Cabrero, G.R. (2005), 'La protección social de las personas dependientes como desarrollo del estado del bienestar en España', *Panorama Social*, 2, 21–33.
Castles, S. and M. Miller (1993), *The Age of Migration*, New York: The Guilford Press.
Cancian, F. (2000), 'Paid emotional care', in M. Harrington Meyer, (ed.), *Care, Work, Gender, Labour and the Welfare State*, New York: Routledge.
CES (2003), *Segundo informe sobre la situación de las mujeres en la realidad sociolaboral española*, Madrid: CES.
Colectivo IOÉ (2001), *Mujer, inmigración y trabajo*, Madrid: Ministerio de Trabajo y Asuntos Sociales.
Colectivo IOÉ (2005), 'El cuidado de personas mayores dependientes realizado por ciudadanos inmigrantes en la Comunidad de Madrid', in IMSERSO (ed.), *Cuidado a la dependencia e inmigración*, Madrid: IMSERSO, pp. 233–370.
Consejo de Europa (1998), 'Recomendación Nº R (98) 9 del Comité de Ministros a los estados miembros relativa a la dependencia', accessed September 2005 at www.imsersomayores.csic.es/documentos/documentos/consejoeuropa–rec989. 01.pdf. EDDES (1999).
Ehreinreich, B. and A.R. Hochschild (2004), *Global Woman. Nannies, Maids and Sex Workers in the New Economy*, New York: Henry Holt and Company.
Graham, H. (1991), 'The concept of caring in feminist research: the case of domestic service', *Sociology*, **25** (1), 61–78.
Hochschild, A. (1983), *The Managed Heart: Commercialization of Human Feelings*, Berkeley, CA: University of California.
Hochschild, A. (2000), 'Global care and chains and emotional surplus value', in

W. Hutton and A. Giddens (eds), *On the Edge: Living with Global Capitalism*, London: Jonathan Cape.

Huber, M. (2005), *Data on Long-term Care: Services, Eligibility and Recipients*, París: OECD.

IMSERSO (2002), *Las personas mayores en España. Informe 2002*, Madrid: Ministerio de Trabajo y Asuntos Sociales.

IMSERSO (2004a), *Atención a las personas mayores en situación de dependencia en España. Libro Blanco*, Madrid : Ministerio de Trabajo y Asuntos Sociales.

IMSERSO/Gfk–Emer (2004b), 'Encuesta de Apoyo Informal a las personas mayores en España', accessed September 2005 at www.imsersomayores.csic.es/estadisticas/encuestas.

IMSERSO (2004c), 'Empleados de Hogar. Apoyo a Mayores', accessed September 2005 at www.imsersomayores.csic.es/estadisticas/encuestas.

IMSERSO (2004d), *Inserción y dinámicas laborales de los trabajadores inmigrantes*, Madrid: Ministerio de Trabajo y Asuntos Sociales.

IMSERSO (2005a), *Cuidado a la dependencia e inmigración*, Madrid: Ministerio de Trabajo y Asuntos Sociales.

IMSERSO (2005b), *Cuidados a las personas mayores en los hogares españoles*, Madrid: Ministerio de Trabajo y Asuntos Sociales.

IMSERSO (2007), *Informe 2006. Las personas mayores en España*, Madrid: Ministerio de Trabajo y Asuntos Sociales.

INE (2000), *Encuesta sobre discapacidades, deficiencias y estados de salud*, Madrid: INE.

INSERSO (1993), *Plan Gerontológico*, Madrid: INSERSO.

Izquierdo, A. (1992), *La Immigración inesperada*, Madrid: Trotta.

Izquierdo, A., *et al.* (2003), 'The favourites of the twenty-first century: Latin American immigration in Spain', *Studi Emigrazione*, 149, 98–124.

James, N. (1989), 'Emotional labour: skill and work in the social regulation of feelings', *Sociological Review*, 37, 1542.

King, R. and E. Zontini (2000), 'The role of gender in the south European immigration model', *Papers*, 60, 35–52.

Martínez Buján, R. (2005), 'El cuidado de ancianos: un vínculo entre la inmigración y el envejecimiento', *Panorama Social*, 2, 86–97.

Martińez, R. (2003), *La reciente immigratión latinoamericana en España*, Śerie Problación y Desarrollo, Santiazo de Chile: CEPAL-OVU.

Martínez Veiga, U. (2000), 'Evolución y clasificación del trabajo doméstico inmigrante', *Ofrim/Suplementos*, 6, 76–96.

Martínez Veiga, U. (2004), *Trabajadores invisibles: precariedad, rotación y pobreza*, Madrid: La Catarata.

Moreno, L. (2001), 'La vía media española del modelo de bienestar mediterráneo', *Papers*, 63/64, 67–82.

OECD (2004), *Tendances des Migrations Internationales: Rapport Annuel, 2003*, Paris : OECD.

ONU (2001), *Replacement Migration. Is it a Solution to Declining and Ageing Populations?*, New York: United Nations Publications.

Oso, L. (1998), *La migración hacia España de mujeres jefas de hogar*, Madrid: Instituto de la Mujer.

Oso, L. and M. Ulloa (2001), 'Tráfico e inmigración femenina desde la voz de las mujeres inmigrantes', in E. Bonelli and M. Ulloa (eds), *Tráfico e inmigración de mujeres en España*, Madrid: ACSUR–Las Segovias, pp. 65–118.

Parreñas, R. (2001), *Servants of Globalization: Woman, Migration and Domestic Work*, Stanford, CA: Stanford University Press.

Vila, A. (2001), 'Normativa autonómica para personas mayores', in A. Martinez (ed.), *Gerontologia y derecho: aspectos jurídicos y personas mayores*, Madrid: Editorial Médica Panamericana.

PART III

Problems of return and migrant integration

11. Turkish minorities in Europe: towards societal integration or the rise of 'parallel societies'

Olga Kutsenko

11.1 INTRODUCTION

Ethnic-based conflicts intensifying in different European regions reaffirm the point argued by Anthony H. Richmond about the increasing activity of minor communicative social networks, which is forming under the influence of heightened migration (Richmond 1987, 3–18). Such networks contribute to the strengthening of peripheral ethnic and language nationalism as a claim of ethnic and language-based minorities on their exceptionality as well as on territorial and political independence. Revival of a peripheral nationalism provokes a nationalism of a 'big society' (Serbian, Moldovan, Russian, French, German and so forth). The powerful and obvious ethnicization of politics and the politicization of ethnicity has made its comeback in Europe and confronted researchers and politicians alike with challenges that seem to be revivals of issues which were suppressed after World War II. Such issues have new features in the contemporary context, which has resulted in the topics of ethnicity and interethnic relations gaining new momentum in both practical politics and social science discourse.

This chapter will look at the way theories on ethnicity and interethnic relations apply to some Turkish and related minorities who have more or less successfully integrated into the receiving society. The chapter draws its research from the database and outcomes of the special research project 'Comparing societal integration of Turkish and related minorities in INTAS and NIS' which was supported by funds from the European Union. The INTAS Research Project 04-79-7018 (2005-2007) is coordinated by Prof. Nikolai Genov (Free University, Berlin) and involves national teams from Bulgaria, Germany, Moldova, Russia and Ukraine. The author is the leader of the Ukrainian team and the person responsible for the international monitoring data collection and analysis. The initial outcomes of the project are presented in a special edition of the Free University's (Berlin) working papers collection (Genov 2007a).

11.2   THE PROJECT DESIGN

Five Specific Constellations of Turkish Minorities in Europe

The major aim of this project was to determine the similarities and differences between ethnic migrants' integration strategies under different conditions. The task is to compare these particular cases with the intention of identifying a common typology and those unique to the ethnic group. Five specific samples of Turkish migrants were selected to provide primary information for comparative analysis and conclusions.

- In Bulgaria, the Turkish ethnic group is a traditional minority. Given the interethnic tensions during the 1980s and the complicated social differentiation thereafter, one notices relatively positive developments of mutual understanding between the two major ethnic groups in the country (the Bulgarians and Turks). The political arrangements concerning the representation of the Turkish ethnic group in state institutions seem to be quite successful. However, recent events involving the development of nationalist movements and parties are indicative of latent interethnic tensions in Bulgarian society.
- Turks constitute a new (allochtonous) ethnic group in Germany. Because of this status, the group is not constitutionally recognized as an ethnic minority. But, the massive Turkish (and Kurdish) ethnic presence in the country put the receiving German society under pressure to achieve the integration of the Turkish ethnic group.
- In Moldova, the Autonomous Gagaouz Republic is still another special case of the ethnicization of politics after the collapse of the former Soviet Union. In order to avoid additional interethnic tensions after the bloody conflict in Transdnistria, the government in Chisinau agreed to include the political autonomy of the Gagaouz people (who are Turkish-speaking Christians) in the Constitution of the Republic of Moldova. But, the situation in the Gagaouz Autonomous Republic still very much depends on the further political process both inside and outside.
- The Autonomous Republic of Tatarstan in the framework of the Russian Federation has experienced a complicated, but basically peaceful and successful, process of mutual understanding and

cooperation between the local Tatar ethnic majority and the local Russian ethnic minority in the Republic and with the Russian ethnic majority in the Federation.

• The achievement of a relatively stable situation cannot yet be claimed concerning the Autonomous Republic of the Crimea in Ukraine. Crimea is currently predominantly populated by Russians and Ukrainians. However, the Crimean Tatars who were forcibly deported from the Crimea to the Central Asian Republics of the former USSR (Uzbekistan and Kazakhstan) and Siberia in 1944 have been returning to the Crimean peninsula since the late 1980s and at the turn of the century this ethnic group had increased up to about 14 per cent taking the third rank based on its size among the Crimean population. The mass and irregular repatriation of the Crimean Tatars sparked a burst of complex social, economic, political and civic issues dealing essentially with their societal integration.

Research Methods and Database

The fieldwork was conducted between October 2005 and December 2006. In order to systematically describe and explain the state of, and changes in, interethnic integration. In the following study, triangular methods and corresponding tools were elaborated and applied (Genov 2007b, Golovin 2007, Kutsenko 2007):

Events relevant to the study of interethnic relations and of reactions to these events
About 18 published national and regional sources were selected in each country, The sampling of the published media sources was made on the basis of the following status criteria of the published media sources: (1) national/regional/local status, (2) official/oppositional status, and (3) a mass-media tribune of the ethnic group under scrutiny/other published source which does not concern this ethnic group. The articles for further systematical analysis were selected in each published source according to their relevance in covering interethnic relations. The total number of selected articles amounted to 981 cases (see Table 11.1).

The analytical scheme for the description and interpretation of events, and of reactions to them includes three key parameters for the event under scrutiny. The first parameter concerns the identification and characterization of the actor or actors involved in the event (individual or collective actors and their position in the social structure and in the chain of events). The second parameter is the spatial and temporal location of the event (its relevance at a local, regional or national level in a society; its nature as a

Table 11.1   *The number of articles analysed regarding Turkish and related*
                minorities

National cases:	First wave 1 October 2005–31 March 2006	Second wave 1 October 2006–31 December 2006	Total
Bulgaria (Turkish minority)	93	35	128
Germany (Turkish-speaking minority in Berlin)	9	45	54
Moldova (Gagauz minority)	266	121	387
Russia (Tatars in Tatarstan)	90	101	191
Ukraine (Crimean Tatars in the Crimea)	158	63	221
Total cases:	616	365	981

Source: INTAS Research Project 04-79-7018 (2005–2007).

one-time event or repeated event; and whether it is a short-term or long-term event). Given the specific aims of the comparative research project, the third analytical parameter of monitoring the events and the reactions to them includes a description and interpretation of the events in terms of the presence of conflict (no conflict, low intensity conflict, high intensity conflict). The combined analysis of events on the basis of these three parameters makes it possible to broadly identify, interpret and generalize the impact of events in the locality under scrutiny.

Content analysis of leading newspapers representing the official point of view in the relevant political space

This research tool is intended to collect the information needed for the comparative study by focusing on the point of view of the state institutions in the locality under scrutiny. This point of view might belong to the nation-state or to the government of an autonomous part of the nation-state. The following newspapers were selected for further content-analysis: the most popular newspaper in Bulgaria – *Trud*; in Germany, the *Berliner Zeitung* as an official newspaper, which is popular among the educated middle classes of the German capital; the national newspaper *Moldovan* and regional newspaper *Vesti Gagauzii* published in Russian in Moldova; the official newspaper *Respublika Tatarstan* published in Russian in Russia; in Ukraine, the official national newspaper *Golos Ukraini* and the regional official newspaper of the Crimean Parliament *Krimskie Izvestija* with its weekly appendix *Krimskij Dialog*. In just the first wave of the data collection 624 articles were analysed.

The tool of content-analysis is structured to capture selected parameters of the interethnic situations. The first parameter for the comparison of information items on interethnic issues concerns the form of the item published in the newspaper (brief article about a fact, editorial article, a report on the issue, an analytical article, interview, and so forth). The second line of the content analysis concerns the aim or aims of the publication of the item (neutral information, attempt to form or change public opinion on the issue or suggestion for resolving the issue). Other parameters of the content analysis refer to the type of policies covered in the newspaper (national or regional, economic, social or cultural, and so forth); the presentation and interpretation of interethnic conflicts in the published item; and whether there were any intentions of political manipulation through the publication and its language style.[1]

In-depth interviews with successful members (elites) of the ethnic minority under scrutiny
There are members of ethnic minority communities who manage to attain higher positions in economic, political and cultural life under varying local conditions. Such successful individuals of the minority group might serve as the best qualified experts for assessing the situation and prospects of the societal integration of the ethnic group under scrutiny. In each country, in-depth interviews were carried out with 30 successful members of the studied minority group from the fields of business, politics and culture (arts, media and education). The interviews are structured around three key points. At the beginning, the respondents are questioned about their own biography. Then the current situation of their ethnic group is discussed. The third part of the interview is focused on prospective questions presented as vignettes about the desirable ethnic characteristics of collaborators of the respondent, the official status of the mother tongue of the respondent and the desirable political status of his/her ethnic group of origin.

Theoretical Framework

The study was conducted within a general conceptual framework of social integration as a process involving persons, social groups and society. According to David Lockwood (Lockwood 1964), integration can be distinguished between system integration, which refers to relationships between different parts of the social system, economy and political system, and their internal cohesion; and social integration, which refers to individual and social group systems, and mutual penetration of their norms and values. Lockwood points out that social integration can exist without system integration, however, both of these processes are able to complement each other. Following these ideas, we understand social integration as the inclusionary process of the development and application of equal opportunities and rights for all human beings in any given society. By becoming better socially integrated, individual and collective actors improve their opportunities in life, create or strengthen their identities and develop conditions for further cooperation. By using the concept in this way, it has assumed a closeness to concepts of social justice, equality, material well-being and democratic freedom.

Given this interpretation, social integration is characterized as a co-engaging process of development and application of equal opportunities and rights for all human beings and their groups in a given society. From the sociological and social psychology points of view, integration, its preconditions, state and aftermath are to be considered as one of some different strategies (or variations in attitudes and behaviours) of minorities'/migrants' acculturation in new sociocultural surroundings which migrants choose meaningfully and freely, or under circumstances which force them to follow one of these strategies.

According to J.W. Berry, these variations in strategy may be termed assimilation, integration, separation and marginalization (Berry 2005). If assimilation is related to the loss of the original culture by migrants along with development of intercultural (interethnic) contacts, marginalization means the loss of the original culture with the lack of well-established intercultural contacts. Separation means migrants cleave to the original culture with a rejection of developed contacts with other cultures and ethnic groups, and, finally, integration would be the preservation of the original culture by all the interacting groups along with the creation of new intercultural forms of mutual social coexistence. These strategies were considered in our study as the stochastic models of interethnic relationships between the ethnic groups under scrutiny and the corresponding 'dominant' societies as well as the stochastic models of interethnic strategies initiated and realized by the successful representatives of the ethnic communities in the certain societies.

As a result of human intention and action, social integration is attainable at the individual, societal and institutional level; this might be supported by system integration processes (and vice versa) but is not directly related to it. The understanding of a set of issues accompanying social integration at any level is impossible without taking into account their historical and cultural background and the particularities of social relations. Following Allardt's theory regarding the preconditions of solidarity (Allardt 1993, 2006), we may assume that one dimension of satisfying basic human needs is 'having' resources and attaining a certain standard of living (as well as prerequisites for its maintenance, such as employment and income).

Another dimension might be identified as 'loving' (in the sense of social networks and emotional support, family, children, friends, and so forth). The third dimension elaborated by Allardt is 'being' (general recognition and participation).

Allardt's conclusions were elaborated upon in the 'Quality of Life in Europe' research project by Petra Bohnke (Bohnke 2004). She interpreted that having designates resources, such as jobs, dwellings or quality education, as factors facilitating social integration and a high quality of life in all European countries. The rankings for loving, despite a relatively lower average percentage of this factor in the EU states, are basically the same. Family life (living with a partner and having children) is reported to be very important in the new member states, while the citizens of the EU member states also place a strong emphasis on social integration outside of the family (leisure time and seeing friends) as well as on participation and recognition (on the feeling of being recognized by society, together with participation in associations). Overall recognition (being) is not important to citizens who are likely to face economic problems, either in the new or old member states of the EU (Bohnke 2004, 57).

Following Allardt's conception of the preconditions of social solidarity and the further testing of this conception one can suppose that discontent with the important individual and societal needs ('having', 'loving', 'being' in Allardt's terms) determines essentially a type of societal integration. Meanwhile, the institutional quality of a society or its 'vital environment', which is able to satisfy the requirements as well as the prevailing social interests and conflicts within a society and its particular ethnic groups are the principal preconditions of the way that social integration develops.

11.3   MAIN RESULTS

Macro-micro Interplay

The outcomes of the InterEthno project point to trends that establish important differences in the strategies for institutional integration prevailing among ethnic groups and their elites and in the corresponding countries under scrutiny. It was confirmed that the social integration of migrants/ethnic minorities depends essentially on both the national quality of life and the content of social interests and conflicts. The countries involved in the InterEthno project are marked by great differences with respect to the indicators of their quality of life:

For example, according to research data verified by interviews with the ethnic group's elite, the most painful problems that the repatriated

Table 11.2 Population and indicators on national quality of life

Selected indicators:	Bulgaria	Germany	Moldova	Russia	Ukraine
Population (millions), 2006*	7.7	82.5	4.2	143.0	47.1
Portion of Turkish related group under scrutiny, 2006*	9.4% (Turks)	2% (Turkish-speaking group)	less 5% (Gagauz)	3.8 % (Tatars)	0.5 % (Cr.Tatars)
Life Expectancy, 2006*	72	79	68	66	68
Life Expect. Change (1989–2002)*	0.31 years/0.44%	no statistics	−0.55 year/−0.81%	−3.57 year/−5.16%	−0.59 year/−0.86%
Income Category, 2006 (the World Bank' ranges)**	lower middle	high income	low income	upper middle	lower middle
GNI per capita, 2006 (in US$)**	2130	25270	590	2610	970
Informal economy (% GNP), 2005**	36.9	16.3	45.1	46.1	52.2
Political stability and violence index 2006 (PV), −2.5 is the worst record, +2.5 is the best record****	0.29	0.83	−0.48	−0.74	−0.27
Governance effectiveness index (GE) 2006, −2.5 is the worst record, +2.5 is the best record	0.14	1.52	−0.85	−0.43	−0.57
Civil liberties, 2007 (1 is the most free country, 7 is the least free)****	2	1	4	5	2
Political rights, 2007 (1 is the widest rights, 7 is the most restricted rights in a country)****	1	1	3	6	3
Transparency international index, 2007 (1 is the most corrupted, 10 is the least corrupted country)*****	4.1	7.8	2.8	2.3	2.7

Sources: * Europe in figures / Eurostat yearbook 2006.** Doing Business, 2006.*** Freedom in the World 2008. **** Kaufmann, D., A.Kraay and M. Mastruzzi, 2007.***** Report on the Transparency International, 2006.

Crimean Tatars experience in the Ukraine are unemployment and poverty, a low quality of basic living conditions, a lack of an allotment of land for more than 80% of the Crimean Tatars who had lived in villages, and the loss of professional and social status on the part of most repatriates (Chubarov 2005). Unlike the Crimean Tatars, these problems are not so significant for the Tatars in Tatarstan/Russia. They are the dominant ethnic group in that region where the intensification of oil production has been accompanied by an increase in world prices. Successful regional policy has contributed to the significant economic and social development of Tatarstan and its population.

The interplay of institutions, individual and group interests and actions that have brought about social integration do not imply a causal relation. An individual is relatively free to make personal choices within the framework of structural and cultural restriction and opportunity. If social institutions are not able to serve personal interests and needs, people find ways to create new means to indemnify themselves against institutional failures in everyday life. Formal institutional and informal practices co-exist and are reproduced in everyday life thus leading to the development of 'parallel societies' with their own regulatory and supporting mechanisms. This social reality cannot remain stable consistently, but in some periods, they may make it possible to satisfy various interests and needs more efficiently in the face of a formal institutional deficit in a society. And, what is particularly important, such reality is able to form a specific societal aftermath leading to separatism and forming a 'parallel society'.

Actor-centred Description of the Migrant Networks Strategies

The research project on institutional strategies for ethnic-based social integration was focused on the relationship between actors, actions and institutions in an attempt to explain their performance from both the input and output side. The changing institutional arrangements in society are to be considered as a filter, through which the relevant actors deal with challenges and problems. An event becomes a spatially and temporarily located point in the dialogue between the actors and institutions. Thus, the event might be a clash between the actors' interests and the ensuing actions undertaken within the formal and/or informal rules. The perception of events through the prism of the actors involved leads to a revelation of the structure of the dominating social interests. The comparison of various national cases helps to elaborate the particularities of the groups examined and the context of the actor-institution interaction.

The data analysis (see Table 11.3) shows marked differences between the societies under scrutiny and allows them to be separated into three groups:

Table 11.3   *Major participants in ethnic-based events, October*
2005–December 2006 (multiple alternatives, in %)

Major participants:	Bulgaria	Germany	Moldova	Russia	Ukraine
Ordinary individuals from the Turkish/Tatar minority	9.4	15.4	36.4	21.1	28.9
Leaders, successful representatives of the ethnic minority	32.8	17.3	33.8	35.1	24.4
The Turkish / Tatar ethnic group(s)	1.6	9.6	12.6	0	4.9
Other ethnic groups	3.1	36.5	2.3	1.8	8.4
Ethnic-based parties, movements	8.6	7.7	2.6	7.6	9.8
Other political parties, social movements, etc.	12.5	1.9	1.8	5.3	8.4
Religious organizations, movements	12.5	3.8	0.5	10.5	4.0
Firms, enterprises, etc.	0.8	3.8	11.0	7.0	7.6
Local authorities	3.1	7.7	49.7	38.6	29.3
National or regional public institution(s)	14.1	17.3	16.9	36.8	39.1
International actors.	5.5	15.4	10.0	19.9	11.6
	$N=128$	$N=54$	$N=387$	$N=191$	$N=221$

Source: INTAS Research Project 04-79-7018 (2005–2007).

Germany, post-Soviet societies and Bulgaria. The sharp distinction of the German case on some indicators studied can probably be explained by the small sample size of cases. Despite the growing interest in the Turkish-speaking ethnic group on the part of the German media, the research found that this interest has not yet materialized into a large number of publications, at least during the period of monitoring.

In Moldova, Russia and the Ukraine, the major participants in the ethnic-related events can be tentatively split into two types. They are either 'public institutional actors' (the local, regional/national authority and public institutes) or 'individual actors' (successful representatives, as well as ordinary individuals related to the Tatar/Gagauz minority). According to the publications, all mediators between the state or the public authorities and individual representatives of the minority group are rather peripheral to the interethnic relations. This pattern applies to the ethnic minority group as a whole, to other ethnic groups, as well as to political organizations, religious organizations, to firms and enterprises. Despite the fact that a number of historical and cultural events were represented in the national samples studied, the voice of the cultural elite is not influential in the publications analysed.

In comparing the national cases, the case of Bulgaria is of particular interest. The public authorities and institutions at the national, regional and local level rarely play a dominant role in the ethnic-related events in the country. Successful representatives of minority groups take a more active role in the cultivation of interethnic relationships. An active position, but perhaps one of lesser significance, is also played by the political parties and religious organizations.

The analysis highlights a principle question concerning the degree of correlation between the events and their representation in the published discourse, particularly for the cases of the Crimean Tatars in the Ukraine and the Turkish minority in Bulgaria. Their ethnic based non-governmental and political organizations have strong institutional traditions of intermediation between the state and the respective ethnic group. This assumption was verified by the in-depth interviews with experts and by the analysis of events. In this respect, the Ukrainian case turns out to be rather indicative: there are no publications about the activities of the Kurultai and Mejlis as the authoritative bodies of self-government of the Crimean Tatar's regional and local community, despite the fact that they were elected by a vote amongst all adult Crimean Tatars in the Autonomous Republic of Crimea. The analysis of events in Bulgaria offers a rather different picture: the bulk of publications concerns the activities of the Turkish Democratic Party and the 'Millet-Trakia' movement with their demands for Turkish to be adopted as the second official language in Bulgaria. Together, both cases highlight two varying strategies in the printed media discourse. One of them aims at ignoring certain public figures who can be 'inconvenient' to the dominant public discourse. The second aims at revealing scandals rather than at discussing in depth the issues of interethnic relations and the real challenges of societal integration of the Turkish and related minorities.

Non-Conflict Events or Discourse Concealment Principle?

It is apparent from the data that when a conflict is reported (except the Ukrainian case), it is typically a conflict of low intensity. At the same time, the conflict intensity represented by the publications tends to differ among the national cases. So after the 1990s which were characterized by strong ethnic-based conflicts in Tatarstan (Russia), Moldova and parts of Bulgaria, in recent years, ethnic-related events have assumed a peaceful character.

Table 11.4   Nature of conflict in events: national media discourse, October 2005–December 2006, in % and index

Type of the event:	Bulgaria	Germany	Moldova	Russia	Ukraine	Total
Non-conflict	75.8	62.3	91.5	83.0	49.6	76.9
Low-intensity conflict	24.2	32.1	5.4	5.9	29.8	15.0
High-intensity conflict	0	5.7	3.1	11.2	20.6	8.1
Total	100.0	100.0	100.0	100.0	100.0	100.0
Index of conflict, $0 < I < 1$	0.121	0.218	0.058	0.142	0.355	0.156

Source: INTAS Research Project 04-79-7018 (2005–2007).

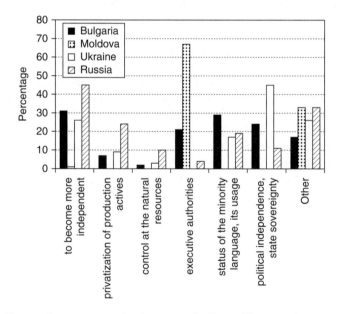

Note: Germany is not represented owing to non-significant differences of percentages.

Figure 11.1   Major kinds of issues provoking the conflict ethnic-based events*, October 2005–December 2006

Against the background of these three cases the highest conflict potential can be seen in the integration of the Crimean Tatars' in the Ukraine and the Turkish-speaking ethnic group in Germany. More than a half of registered events in the Crimea are described as conflict; among which 21 per cent of such events had very intensive features. In Germany about 38 per cent of the events were apprised as conflict. Both cases are related to migration effects (repatriation and immigration accordingly), which are largely absent in the cases of Tatarstan, Moldova and Bulgaria.

Each national case appears as a visible peculiarity concerning the conflict interests. Thus the very strong interests provoking interethnic conflicts in Moldova concern both the aspiration by the Gagaouz people to be more independent in a political and cultural sense and to restrict institutional control over their own issues from the side of the public authority.

Unlike the Moldovan case, in Tatarstan one may detect tension and even conflict in interethnic relationships: (1) aspiration of the Tatars to more political independent and state sovereignty, (2) interests connected with privatization of the production assets as well as acquisition of a control over natural resources, (3) interests of reviling of the ethnic culture (particularly concerns the issue of a status of the Tatarian language in the Tatarstan). On one side, these interests feed political tension in the society; on the other they are evidence of the intensive process of societal integration involving the Tatars and taking place under relatively favourable institutional conditions within the Tatarstan Republic in Russia.

The Bulgarian case displaces a complex of conflict interests in political and cultural areas relating to the Turkish minority. It means the widespread aspiration within this group to restrict the excessive intrusion from the side of the executive authority into a private sphere, the issues of a status of the ethnic language as well as participation in privatization (mainly of the state and municipal land with the further aim of building mosques).

In Germany the societal risks connected with integration of the Turkish-speaking community have appreciably penetrated into all levels of social interaction: international, national and local as well as into this ethnic group per se. The risks of conflicts concern not only the cultural aspects of societal integration which are particularly based on quickly widespread negative ethnic stereotypes (which occurred in 79 per cent of the analysed cases). Risks of conflicts arise from the geopolitical sphere, economic living conditions as well as quality of the home policy in Germany reflecting directly on social integration. Such risks (as it will be also seen in the Ukrainian case) may appear to be a 'time bomb'.

The most complex interests threatening to social integration of the Crimean Tatars in Ukraine are hidden in the core of the conflict events, viz. aspiration of the Crimean Tatars to political independent and national sovereignty. This kind of interest is connected directly to other strong economic (especially possession of land) and cultural (particularly religious and language) interests. All these interests are rooted deeply both in the ancient and new history of this ethnic group and are strengthened by outside (in relation to the Ukraine) interest groups. What is more, the study reveals that the Crimean-Tatars factor has been used during the study period more and more frequently like a mask shading a conflict of interests concerning geopolitical control over the Crimean peninsula. In this case the matter turns to the interests of (1) Ukraine as the state, (2) Russian interests (of the state and business), (3) Turkey (having the numerous Crimean-Tatars community), (4) Islam in general and in a concrete sense connected with forming new areas of its strong influence, (5) the USA (also having a well-organized Crimean Tatars diaspora which supports financially, organizationally and symbolically the Crimean-Tatars movement in the Crimea), and finally, (6) the EU. The research data collected give some evidence of increasing involvement of the international organizations based in these countries and regions into the Crimean-Tatars situation. These organized interests have their mediators among the successful representatives of the Crimean Tatars. Political instability in Ukraine promotes penetration of such outside interests. Taking into account the participation of the outside interests in such a delicate sphere of interethnic relationships, it may be seen that such interests are able to escalate uncontrolled interethnic and international conflict.

11.4   CONCLUDING REMARKS

Taking into account the national cases under scrutiny, it is possible to single out the following empirical types of social interaction strategies by certain ethnic groups.

(1) assimilation coupled with preservation of the strong social networks with the native community. This strategy presupposes the presence of a wide international context of the ethnic issues arising within the country. Such a strategy is inconsistent: on one hand, this strategy may promote an integration process between an ethnic group and 'dominant' society; on the other hand, the use of the strategy may be a source of strong latent tension concentrated in a cultural sphere of interaction. The experience of realizing such a strategy can be seen in the case of the Turkish-speaking minority in Germany;

(2) assimilation supplemented by either of the acculturative strategies, that is, accepting the norms and values of the 'dominant' society

conserving some ethnic originality, or the marginalization of the ethnic group. Implementation of this strategy as well as its integrative aftermath is determined essentially by two main factors. The first one is an adaptive potential of an ethnic group coupled to a strong willingness to keep the ethnic identity; the other is connected with a readiness of a 'dominant' society to accept specific ethnic interests. Such a strategy seems to be applied by the Turkish group in Bulgaria;

(3) localization combined with either integration or separation strategies (the cases of the Gagauz people in Moldova and the Crimean Tatars in Ukraine accordingly). The first version of such a strategy may favour the more or less successful integration of a society coupled with maintenance of the originality of the interacting ethnic groups. The second version of the strategy may lead to escalation of interethnic conflicts as well as to intensifying a threat to social integration in a society;

(4) societal integration coupled with the strategy of ethnic domination at all levels of interaction between an ethnic group and a 'big' society (the case of the Tatars in Tatarstan/the Russian Federation). Such integration strategy can be successful and may contribute to joint integrative process. The possible aftermath of a combination of a tendency towards societal integration by an ethnic group and its aspiration to be more independent in a cultural as well as a political sense, remains uncertain. German society and the corresponding Turkish-speaking group is facing such a dilemma.

Proceeding from Lockwood's idea, one can assume that in a case with a lower rank of system integration and institutional efficiency, a process of social integration turns towards the strengthening of an intra-group feature as opposed to inter-group cohesion and as a reaction to the insufficiency of the institutional system. The interplay of institutional, individual and group interests and actions that have brought about social integration do not imply a causal relation. The development of 'parallel societies' (Rieck 2004) with their own regulative and supporting mechanisms may appear as a specific kind of integration outcome. This outcome seems to be the one taken among many of the Turkish-speaking minority in Germany. This is indeed the case with the Crimean Tatars' community in Ukraine where a strong self-government and ethnic-based system (the Crimean Tatars ethnic movement) mediates between the Crimean Tatar community and the Crimean and Ukrainian power centres.

How is it possible to combine the strong tendency towards societal integration based on growing interdependency at different levels of social interaction and the aspiration to be more independent in a cultural as well as political sense? The very different cases of Tatarstan and the Crimea, where the aspiration of the Tatars and Crimean Tatars for national political independence remains quite significant, and of Moldova and Bulgaria, where the relevance of independence in a cultural and linguistic sense is more important, make it clear that a simple solution to such a core problem is impossible. It seems that the blending of issues will cause a constant societal tension.

Social integration is a multidimensional process which is predominantly based on historical and cultural interconnections, as well as on economic and social situations. The unresolved economic and cultural issues of minorities can provoke interethnic and intraethnic conflicts. Moreover, the integration process cannot be free from the influence of power relationships, personal and group ambitions and the aspiration to dominate or to achieve independence. These aspirations penetrate all areas of ethnic interaction.

NOTE

1. See the detailed description of the tool and the indicators in Golovin (2007, 134–47).

REFERENCES

Allardt, E. (1993), 'Having, loving, being: an alternative to the Swedish model of welfare research', in A. Sen and M. Nussbaum (eds), *The Quality of Life*, Oxford: Clarendon Press, pp. 89–94.

Allardt, E. (2006), 'Fruitful contradictions Alapuro', *Acta Sociologica*, **49** (2), 139–47.

Berry, J.W. (2005), 'Acculturation: living successfully in two cultures', *International Journal of Intercultural Relations*, 29, 697–712.

Bohnke, P. (2004), 'Perception of social integration and exclusion in an enlarged Europe', *Quality of Life in Europe*, EFILWC, 57–8.

Chubarov, R. (2005), 'Interview', *Zerkalo nedely* [*Mirror of the Week*], 22 February, Kyiv, 2.

Europe in figures Eurostat yearbook (2006), *European Commission, THEME General and Regional Statistics*, Luxembourg, accessed at www.europa.eu.int/comm/eurostat/.

Freedom House (2008), 'Freedom in the world 2008',. selected data from *Freedom House's Annual Global Survey of Political Rights and Civil Liberties*, Freedom House country report, accessed at www.freedomhouse.org/.

Genov, N. (2007a), 'Comparing patterns of interethnic integration', in N. Genov (ed.), *Patterns of Interethnic Integration*, Arbeitspapiere des Osteuropa-Instituts der Freien Universität Berlin, Berlin: Osteuropa-Institut, pp. 7–15.

Genov, N. (eds) (2007b), *Comparative Research in the Social Sciences*, Paris and Sofia: ISSC, REGLO.

Golovin, N. (2007), 'A press in the interethnic interactions: international comparative content-analysis', in N. Genov (ed.), *Comparative Research in the Social Sciences*, Paris and Sofia: ISSC, REGLO, pp. 134–47.

Kaufmann, D., A. Kraay and M. Mastruzzi (2007), 'Governance Matters VI: Aggregate and Individual Governance Indicators 1996–2006', World Bank policy research working paper 4280, Washington, DC: The World Bank Group, accessed at www.govindicators.org, July http://papers.ssrn.com/sol3/papers. cfm?abstract_id=999979#PaperDownload/.

Kutsenko O. (2007), 'Monitoring of events in InterEthno INTAS project', in N. Genov (eds), *Comparative Research in the Social Sciences*, Paris and Sofia: ISSC, REGLO. pp. 121–33.

Lockwood, D. (1964), 'Social integration and system integration', in G.K. Zollschan and W. Hirsh (eds), *Social Change: Explorations, Diagnoses and Conjectures*, New York: John Wiley, pp. 370–83.

Park, R.E. and E.W. Burges (1924), *Introduction of the Science of Sociology*, Chicago, IL: The University of Chicago Press.

Richmond, A.H. (1987), 'Ethnic nationalism: social science paradigms, *International Social Science Journal*, **39** (1), 3–18.

Richmond, A.H. (2002), 'Social exclusion: belonging and not belonging in the world system', *Refuge*, **21** (1), 40–8.

Rieck, C.E. (2004), 'Lead culture versus parallel societies. Germany and its Turkish minority', accessed at www.politikwissen.de/expertenforum/exp_down-loads/rieckdez04.pdf/.

Samar, V. (2006), 'Freedom of speech as political engineering?' *Zerkalo Niedeli* [*The Weekly Mirror*], 7 (586), accessed 25 February at www.zn.kiev.ua/nn/show/586/52710.

Social Integration: Approaches and Issues (1994), 'World Summit for Social Development', UNRISD briefing paper 1.

Transparency International 2006, 'Report on the Global Corruption Barometer', Berlin, http://www.transparency.org/#barometer.

The World Group (2006), *Doing Business*, Washington DC: The World Bank Group.

12. Employment rates of return migrants: the Finnish case

Jan Saarela and Fjalar Finnäs

12.1 GENERAL BACKGROUND

In recent decades, return migration has emerged as a critical element of many a government's migration policy (IOM 2006). Return migrants also constitute a large fraction of all people in the labour market. Approximate numbers for the USA state that at least 20 per cent of all legal immigrants subsequently return migrate, and for many European countries the proportion is even larger (Dustmann 1996, Constant and Massey 2003). A comprehensive picture of the employment situation of return migrants is still missing, however, because most countries have no population registers that allow researchers to distinguish people who have lived abroad.

Data from Finland provides an exception in this context. The country has a register that covers the total population, in which each person can be observed in concurrent censuses. These population files can be linked to other existing registers, such as those containing labour force statistics. The present chapter makes use of this in order to identify return migrants and study their employment levels in relation to non-migrants.

Similar to the way of treating employed immigrants in a host country as successfully integrated (Arowolo 2000, OECD 2001), we here regard persons who are employed in the home country subsequent to return migration as successfully reintegrated. Of specific interest is the question of how the employment rates interrelate with migration duration and duration subsequent to return migration.

Finland is a country that has experienced large migration flows, but also large rates of return migration (Institute of Migration 2006, Statistics Finland 2006a). Over 50 per cent of the more than half a million Finns who moved abroad during the latter half of the twentieth century, predominantly in the direction of Sweden, also returned to Finland (Figure 12.1). At least every twentieth person in the country's current population has consequently lived abroad, and over three-quarters of these return

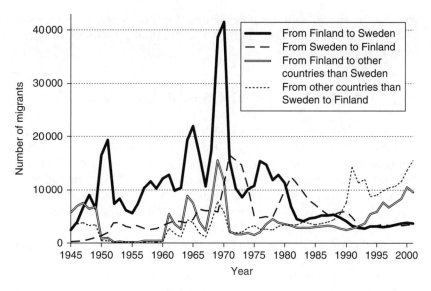

Source: Institute of Migration (2006).

Figure 12.1 Migration from and to Finland 1945–2001

migrants had been in Sweden. Sweden attracted Finnish migrants primarily due to the need for labour in industry.

There are strong reasons to expect that return migrants in the Finnish labour market have lower employment rates than non-migrants. Migration rates from Finland, and return migration rates from Sweden, have been found to be higher among non-employed than among employed persons (Finnäs 2003, Saarela and Finnäs 2006). This may partly be due to inadequate skills, as Finnish migrants in general have relatively low educational levels (Finnäs 2003, Rooth and Saarela 2007). A central issue here is therefore whether any employment difficulties of return migrants interrelate with structural confounders, such as education. Unobservable factors might still also be important, as the migrants' employment propensities tend to correlate heavily across countries and time (Saarela and Finnäs 2008).

Besides census data, which cover the total population in certain birth cohorts at the end of every fifth year from 1970 until 1995, we also use complementary data that contain annual information for the period 1987–99. Both data sets are based on population registers, but the latter is, due to confidentiality reasons, in the form of a random sample. Data from the censuses will give a comprehensive picture for long periods, whereas the annual data facilitate analyses for shorter periods, with more detailed focus on migration duration and duration subsequent to return migration.

12.2   DATA AND SETTINGS FOR ANALYSIS

The census data come from the Finnish longitudinal census data file compiled by Statistics Finland. They consist of linked individual information from the censuses at the end of the years 1970, 1975, 1980, 1985, 1990 and 1995 (Statistics Finland 2006b). At our disposal we have a multidimensional matrix that includes all individuals and information about their year of birth, sex, educational level, mother tongue, region of residence and employment status. The data quality is very high, which implies that persons who were missing in one census, but observed again in any subsequent census, can be categorized as having resided abroad.

The Lexis diagram in Figure 12.2 illustrates the observation plan for the return migrants. Under analysis are people born 1951–70, subject to that they were living in Finland at ages 15–19 years. These are the youngest persons who can be assumed to make an autonomous decision to migrate. To also include somewhat higher ages into the analysis, we additionally studied people who were aged 20–34 years in 1970 (i.e. born 1936–50) and lived in Finland at that time. Some of them may have been abroad before that census, but they were born in Finland. Given these conditions, we define return migrants as people who lived abroad at one or more of the subsequent censuses, and had returned to Finland by the 1995 census at the latest. Consider for instance people born 1951–55, i.e. those who were aged 15–19 years in 1970 and lived in Finland at that time. In this birth cohort, a person defined as a return migrant migrated abroad by the 1975, 1980, 1985 or 1990 census, and stayed abroad for any number of subsequent censuses until being observed again in Finland (in the 1995 census at the latest).

For all birth cohorts under study, the number of return migrants is given in Table 12.1 according to which censuses they were abroad and the censuses thereafter when they are observed in the home country. The illustration is for men and women separately. For simplicity's sake, we consistently focus on the first return migration. Repeated migrants and people who died are treated as right-censored observations at the time they cannot be observed in a census, which is the reason why the number of return migrants, for any given census abroad, diminishes over censuses subsequent to return migration. The large number of return migrants who were abroad at the time of the 1980 census (approximately three times

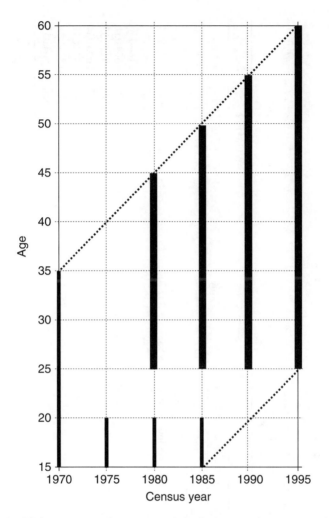

Notes: The thin bars represent the target population in the sense that persons under study were living in Finland at these ages and points of time. The thick bars represent the period and age in which each person may be analysed with regard to employment.

Figure 12.2 Lexis diagram of the observation plan for the census data

as many as at the time of any of the other three censuses) is due to the large migration flows from Finland to Sweden in the late 1970s and from Sweden to Finland in the early 1980s (cf. Figure 12.1).

The comparable groups of non-migrants are defined as persons in the same cohorts who were living in Finland at the time of all of the censuses.

Table 12.1   Number of return migrants by the census(es) they were abroad and the census(es) they were observed in Finland subsequent to return migration, and the number of non-migrants in the same birth cohorts

Census abroad				MEN					WOMEN				
				Census after return migration				Non-migrants	Census after return migration				Non-migrants
1975	1980	1985	1990	1980	1985	1990	1995		1980	1985	1990	1995	
1975				2788	2594	2441	2317	667 247	1886	1766	1709	1671	664 031
1975	1980				8560	7943	7563	852 704		6443	6055	5913	841 953
1975	1980	1985				2872	2626	1 038 618			2309	2126	1 020 064
1975	1980	1985	1990				2817	1 209 725				1884	1 184 456
	1980				1536	1391	1336	667 247		1392	1301	1284	664 031
	1980	1985				2168	1963	852 704			2006	1848	841 953
	1980	1985	1990				544	1 038 618				531	1 020 064
		1985				495	453	667 247			493	463	664 031
		1985	1990				640	852 704				605	841 953
			1990				151	667 247				184	664 031

The right-most column for each sex refers to the number of non-migrants. In total, we observed 40 304 return migrants and 2 394 181 non-migrants.

Return migration rates to Finland tend to be very high during the first few years after migration. Almost every second migrant returns within three years (Finnäs 2003). The taxonomy of the data used imply that all persons categorized as return migrants with certainty had lived abroad, but some of the migrants who stayed less than five years abroad could not be observed. On the basis of previous findings, we approximate that persons classified as return migrants in the census data amount to one-quarter of all return migrants. Analyses of the census data are therefore, by definition, concerned with return migrants with relatively long stays abroad.

Within the group of people categorized as non-migrants there are consequently persons who had lived abroad. These have both migrated and return migrated between two consecutive censuses, and had thus stayed abroad for a maximum of five years. They amount to approximately 5 per cent of all persons categorized as non-migrants. If return migrants as a group have lower employment rates than non-migrants, observed differences in the data will therefore, to some extent, underestimate the true difference.

The annual complementary data consist of an extract from Statistics Finland's longitudinal population register file *Työssäkäyntitilasto* (Statistics Finland 2006c). It is very similar in nature to, and partly based on, the census file described above. In contrast to the census data, it gives all information on a yearly basis for the years 1987 to 1999 and therefore facilitates detailed analyses for shorter periods, albeit for fewer individuals. The extract consists of a random sample, comprising 5 per cent of all Finnish speakers and 20 per cent of all Swedish speakers. People in each group are weighted by their sample proportion in the analyses. These data focus on the southern and western parts of Finland, which cover a quarter of the total population of the country. For each individual and year, there is information about whether the person lived in the country, lived abroad or had died. In addition to year of birth, sex and mother tongue, variables that measure each person's level and field of education, municipality of residence and employment status at the end of each year are also available. Since the data are annual we observed all return migrants who had stayed abroad over the turn of the year, and could thus measure time abroad and time in the home country with reasonably good accuracy.

The observation plan for these annual data corresponds highly with that used for analysing the census data. Under study are people born 1973–82, subject to that they lived in Finland at 15 years of age. Also included are persons born 1940–72 (i.e. aged 16–48 years in 1987), if they lived in

Finland at the end of 1987. Return migrants are defined as persons who lived abroad at one or more of the years subsequent to being observed in Finland, and had returned to Finland by the end of 1999 at the latest. They amount to 1238 individuals. Non-migrants are defined as persons in the same birth cohorts, who were living in Finland at the end of all of the years 1987 to 1999. They amount to 88 564 individuals.

12.3 RESULTS

Relative Employment of Return Migrants

We begin by reporting employment rates of return migrants in groups that differ by time of return and number of censuses abroad. These are, together with corresponding rates of non-migrants, found in Table 12.2.

In spite of employment rates varying considerably across censuses due to changes in the macroeconomic environment, it is very evident that people categorized as return migrants have consistently lower employment rates than non-migrants.

Those who have return migrated during economic recessions are found to have poorer relative performance than those who return migrated during economic upswings, probably because job competition is stronger then and contacts with the home country labour market more important. Between 1976 and 1978, unemployment rates in Finland tripled from 2.5 to over 7 per cent, but by the end of 1980 they had fallen back to just below 5 per cent. Return migrants were obviously more vulnerable than non-migrants to these circumstances. Men who return migrated during the second part of the 1970s had an employment rate in 1980 that was only 65 per cent, as compared with an employment rate of almost 90 per cent for male non-migrants in 1980. A similar pattern can be observed for women and for people who return migrated in the early 1990s when unemployment rates in Finland increased dramatically from under 7 to over 15 per cent. The best relative performance is found for people who return migrated when unemployment rates were low in the 1980s.

The large variation in absolute levels makes it somewhat difficult to compare groups. The employment rates have therefore been transformed into relative differences in terms of odds ratios (Table 12.3). In 1980, for instance, male return migrants had an employment rate of 65.2 per cent, whereas the corresponding number for non-migrants was 88.6 per cent. This corresponds to an odds ratio of 0.24 ((0.652/(1-0.652)]/[0.886/(1-0.886)), which indicates that return migrants had 76 per cent lower odds of being employed than non-migrants. In this group the odds ratio increased with

Table 12.2   Employment rate of return migrants by the census(es) they were abroad and the census(es) they were observed in Finland subsequent to return migration, and of non-migrants in the same birth cohorts (%)

MEN

Census abroad				Return migrants — Census after return				Non-migrants — Census of observation			
				1980	1985	1990	1995	1980	1985	1990	1995
1975				65.2	73.8	71.5	52.8	88.6	90.5	86.6	68.8
1975	1980				73.4	75.8	59.2		89.0	86.9	70.6
1975	1980	1985				68.5	51.3			86.2	71.4
1975	1980	1985	1990				46.5				70.6
1975	1980				76.2	78.9	60.6		90.5	86.6	68.8
1975	1980	1985				69.2	57.5			86.9	70.6
1975	1980	1985	1990				35.5				71.4
1975	1980	1985				69.3	53.9			86.6	68.8
1975	1980	1985	1990				35.5				70.6
1975	1980	1985	1990				24.5				68.8

Table 12.2 (continued)

Census abroad		WOMEN							
		Return migrants				Non-migrants			
		Census after return				Census of observation			
		1980	1985	1990	1995	1980	1985	1990	1995
1975		54.0	70.3	76.1	65.0	76.8	84.8	85.2	70.7
1980	1985		66.6	75.9	66.9		83.0	84.3	71.3
	1990			66.5	56.3			82.9	70.6
					43.5				68.8
1975			67.5	79.4	66.4		84.8	85.2	70.7
1980	1985			68.0	60.5			84.3	71.3
1980	1985				33.1				70.6
	1990								
1975				63.1	56.2			85.2	70.7
1980	1985				34.5				71.3
1980	1985								
	1990								
1975					38.0				70.7
1980	1985								
	1990								

duration subsequent to return migration (0.30 in 1985, 0.38 in 1990, and 0.49 in 1995). Thus, relative outcomes improve with time, but the employment rates do not reach parity with those of non-migrants. A similar pattern applies to people who lived abroad at other censuses, and to women.

There is also some evidence in support of an inverse relationship between time spent abroad and the relative employment rates. As compared with male non-migrants in 1995, the odds for employment of men who return migrated during the early 1990s was 0.36 for those with one census abroad, 0.22 for those with two censuses abroad, 0.23 for those with three censuses abroad, and 0.15 for those with four censuses abroad. A similar negative correlation cannot be observed in the other censuses, however. For women there is a quite clear level difference, specifically when return migrants who spent one census abroad are compared with those who spent more than one census abroad.

The Role of Structural Factors

To account for characteristic differences between return migrants and non-migrants, we estimated logistic regression models that include age, educational level, mother tongue and region of residence. Finnish speakers and Swedish speakers are known to differ with regard to migration and employment rates (Finnäs 1986, 2003, Saarela and Finnäs 2003, 2006). Within each language group, however, we found that the employment differential between return migrants and non-migrants was roughly similar. Mother tongue is therefore included to account simply for a level difference in employment rates.

Results of the estimations are included as odds ratios within the parentheses in Table 12.3 (unadjusted odds ratios are outside the parentheses). The impact of covariates on the employment differential between return migrants and non-migrants is marginal. The above conclusions therefore largely remain. In many instances the employment differential even becomes more pronounced when the structural factors are accounted for.

The variables still play a large role for the overall model fits. Male non-migrants with basic education had an employment rate of 59.7 per cent in 1995, those with vocational education 73.5 per cent, and those with undergraduate or higher education 87.2 per cent. Corresponding numbers for male return migrants who had been abroad only for the 1990 census, for instance, were 27.4, 48.9 and 81.8 per cent, respectively (not shown). Hence, employment rates of higher-educated return migrants were substantially better than those of lower-educated ones, but still much worse than those of higher-educated non-migrants.

To see if there is variation in the rate of improvement over time across

Table 12.3   *Odds for employment of return migrants in relation to odds for employment of non-migrants*

| Census abroad | | | | MEN | | | |
| | | | | Census after return migration | | | |
1975	1980	1985	1990	1980	1985	1990	1995
1975				0.24 (0.27)			
1975	1980				0.30 (0.32)	0.38 (0.38)	0.49 (0.44)
	1980	1985			0.34 (0.36)	0.47 (0.42)	0.59 (0.47)
		1985	1990			0.35 (0.30)	0.42 (0.33)
			1990				0.36 (0.30)
1975	1980				0.34 (0.41)	0.58 (0.64)	0.69 (0.63)
	1980	1985				0.34 (0.31)	0.56 (0.47)
		1985	1990				0.22 (0.19)
1975	1980	1985				0.35 (0.40)	0.53 (0.51)
	1980	1985	1990				0.23 (0.20)
	1980	1985	1990				0.15 (0.15)

WOMEN

Census abroad	Census after return migration			
	1980	1985	1990	1995
1975	0.35 (0.40)	0.43 (0.45)	0.55 (0.50)	0.76 (0.54)
1980		0.41 (0.47)	0.59 (0.58)	0.80 (0.60)
1985			0.41 (0.40)	0.54 (0.42)
1990				0.35 (0.31)
1975		0.373 (0.45)	0.67 (0.72)	0.80 (0.65)
1980			0.40 (0.41)	0.62 (0.50)
1985				0.21 (0.16)
1975			0.30 (0.32)	0.53 (0.43)
1980				0.21 (0.17)
1985				0.26 (0.21)

Notes:
Numbers outside parentheses refer to unadjusted odds ratios.
Numbers within parentheses refer to odds ratios adjusted for age, educational level, mother tongue and region of residence.
Age is measured in five-year intervals.
Educational level consists of the categories (1) basic, (2) lower vocational, lower level, (3) lower vocational, upper level, (4) upper vocational, (5) undergraduate and (6) graduate.
Mother tongue is Finnish or Swedish.
Region of residence has 13 categories with one separate for the Helsinki metropolitan area.

people with different levels of education, we estimated separate regressions for people with (1) basic education, (2) vocational education, and (3) undergraduate or higher education. Heterogeneity in the return-migrant group was reduced by focusing on people who had been abroad for only one census. The results, which are summarized in Table 12.4, show that not even highly educated return migrants over time manage to come close to the employment levels of non-migrants.

Migration Duration and Duration Subsequent to Return Migration

The census data revealed that the return migrants' relative employment rates improve with duration subsequent to return migration, whereas the interrelation with migration duration appears to be more ambiguous. To use more precise duration measures, we proceed with analyses of the annual data. We now categorize return migrants into subgroups according to the number of years they had spent abroad and the number of years they had spent in the home country subsequent to return migration, respectively. Results of logistic regression models that estimate adjusted odds ratios for employment of return migrants in relation to non-migrants are summarized in Figures 12.3 and 12.4. The two former depict the situation by duration subsequent to return migration and the two latter by migration duration. The nature of the data implies that observations are relatively few for longer durations. In the figures we therefore illustrate the situation only up to seven years in the home country and six years abroad. Confidence intervals are outlined to give some insight on the statistical power of the estimated parameters.

Relative employment rates of return migrants tend to increase with time spent in the home country. During the first year subsequent to return migration, migrants have particularly low odds of employment. Thereafter, there is slight progress towards a catching-up effect for men, as the gap in relation to non-migrants decreases with time spent at home. Not even after five or six years in the home country, however, have return migrants reached parity with non-migrants, as the odds of employment still are about 30 per cent lower. For female return migrants there is no progress in relative rates at all after the second year in the home country, which places them at approximately 50 per cent lower odds of employment than non-migrants. Considering that women are more likely to be tied movers and not equally attached to the labour market (Mincer 1978; Boyle *et al.* 2001), the variation across sexes should still be considered small.

Figure 12.3 and 12.4 indicate that the relative employment rates tend to correlate negatively with migration duration. Male migrants who had been abroad only one year have odds ratios of employment that are 35 per

Table 12.4   Odds for employment of return migrants in relation to odds for employment of non-migrants, by educational level

Census abroad	Educ. level	MEN Census after return migration				WOMEN Census after return migration			
		1980	1985	1990	1995	1980	1985	1990	1995
1975	low	0.23	0.33	0.37	0.42	0.37	0.41	0.44	0.52
	semi	0.32	0.27	0.35	0.41	0.42	0.51	0.53	0.58
	high	0.45	0.55	0.62	0.64	0.41	0.35	0.75	0.49
1980	low		0.31	0.41	0.45		0.43	0.51	0.54
	semi		0.38	0.41	0.47		0.49	0.64	0.66
	high		0.53	0.47	0.48		0.52	0.52	0.56
1985	low			0.26	0.26			0.34	0.33
	semi			0.31	0.35			0.44	0.48
	high			0.42	0.51			0.50	0.51
1990	low				0.23				0.25
	semi				0.30				0.32
	high				0.57				0.38

Note:
The odds ratios are adjusted for age, mother tongue and region of residence.
Data on return migrants are restricted to those who had been one census abroad.
The results are based on regressions estimated separately across sexes, censuses, and educational levels. Low refers to people with basic education only, semi to those with vocational education and high to those with undergraduate or higher education.

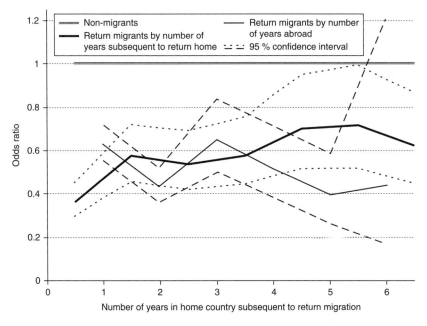

Notes:
The logistic regression models used adjust for age (in five-year intervals), educational level (six categories), educational field (nine categories), mother tongue (Finnish or Swedish), area of residence (seven categories) and observation year (a dummy for each calendar year).

The mean employment rate of return migrants with one year in Finland subsequent to return migration is 55.4 per cent and of non-migrants 71.1 per cent. This corresponds to an odds ratio of 0.505. It decreases to 0.364 when account is taken for the structural variables.

Figure 12.3   Odds for employment of return migrants in relation to odds for employment of non-migrants, by duration subsequent to return migration, men

cent lower than those of non-migrants, whereas those of return migrants who had been abroad for six years, for instance, are as much as 55 per cent lower. The corresponding numbers in women are 45 and 60 per cent. Thus, the employment disadvantage of return migrants decreases by almost 5 per cent per additional year the return migrant had been abroad.

12.4   CONCLUSIONS

Previous analyses that have used census data for similar purposes as ours are very scarce. The contribution that comes closest to ours in spirit was

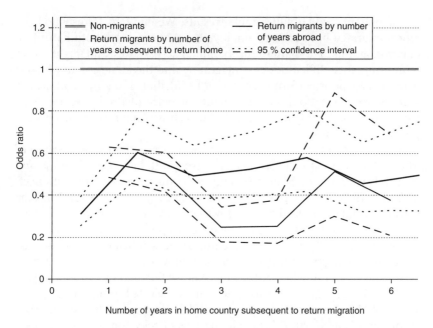

Number of years in home country subsequent to return migration

Note:
The logistic regression models used adjust for age (in five-year intervals), educational level (six categories), educational field (nine categories), mother tongue (Finnish or Swedish), area of residence (seven categories) and observation year (a dummy for each calendar year).

The mean employment rate of return migrants with one year in Finland subsequent to return migration is 46.3 per cent and of non-migrants 70.0 per cent. This corresponds to an odds ratio of 0.370. It decreases to 0.311 when account is taken for the structural variables.

Figure 12.4   Odds for employment of return migrants in relation to odds for employment of non-migrants, by duration subsequent to return migration, women

based on data from the 1970 and 1980 population censuses of Puerto Rico (Muschkin 1993). Unlike our data, those censuses were not linked, so it was not possible to observe the same individuals over time. The sample sizes were also small. Muschkin found that Puerto Ricans who had returned to their home country from the USA had notably lower adjusted employment rates than non-migrants. The results were explained by the changing context in which the return migrants were seeking employment, which was argued to override any potential gain that may accrue through the migration process, that is any premium due to human capital of foreign work experience and other practices gained abroad. Lost contact with the home country labour market consequently seemed to have made the return migrants particularly vulnerable to discontinuities in employment.

The present study obtains similar results. We find that Finns who have return migrated have odds of employment that are only about half those of non-migrants. This pattern is very similar across sexes, and might reflect return migrants' difficulties in reintegrating into the home country labour market. This poor performance cannot be attributed to structural factors such as age, education, mother tongue, or place of residence, and even within the group of highly educated Finns, return migrants are in a poorer position than non-migrants.

If the low relative employment rates of return migrants are because of lost contact, they should correlate negatively with migration duration and positively with time in the home country subsequent to return migration (cf. Chiswick 1978, Lichter 1983, Maxwell 1988, Borjas *et al.* 1992). To some extent, we find this to be the case. However, also return migrants with short stays abroad and long periods at home are in a poor relative position.

It is consequently obvious that the employment difficulties are associated with some latent personal characteristics that we cannot observe explicitly. Our results therefore highlight the well-known fact that migrants, and particularly return migrants, constitute a highly selected group of the population of the source country (Ramos 1992, Borjas and Bratsberg 1996, Rooth and Saarela 2007). Explicit analyses of selection processes, which are beyond the scope of this chapter, are essential for a more detailed understanding of the labour market situation of return migrants.

Future research in this area might, tentatively, attempt to make use of even more informative population register data than those we have had access to here. Present findings also illustrate the complexity involved when studying migrant populations, and that there are obvious reasons for attempting to implement policies that facilitate the labour market situation of people who had lived abroad.

REFERENCES

Arowolo, O.O. (2000), 'Return migration and the problem of reintegration', *International Migration*, 38, 59–82.

Barrett, A. and P.J. O'Connell (2001), 'Is there a wage premium for returning Irish migrants?', *Economic and Social Review*, 32, 1–21.

Borjas, G.J. and B. Bratsberg (1996), 'Who leaves? The outmigration of the foreign–born', *Review of Economics and Statistics*, 78, 165–76.

Borjas, G.J., S.G. Bronars and S.J. Trejo (1992), 'Self–selection and internal migration in the United States', *Journal of Urban Economics*, 32, 159–185.

Boyle, P., T.J. Cooke, K. Halfacree and D. Smith (2001), 'A cross-national comparison of the impact of family migration on women's employment status', *Demography*, 38, 201–13.

Chiswick, B. (1978), 'The effect of Americanization on the earnings of foreign-born men', *Journal of Political Economy*, 86, 897–921.

Constant, A. and D. Massey (2003), 'Self-selection, earnings, and out-migration: a longitudinal study of immigrants to Germany', *Journal of Population Economics*, 16, 631–53.

Dustmann, C. (1996), 'Return migration: the European experience', *Economic Policy*, 22, 213–50.

Finnäs, F. (1986), 'Den finlandssvenska befolkningsutvecklingen 1950–1980. En analys av en språkgrupps demografiska utveckling och effekten av blandäktenskap', PhD dissertation, Finland: Åbo Akademi University.

Finnäs, F. (2003), 'Migration and return–migration among Swedish–speaking Finns' in R. Höglund, M. Jäntti and G. Rosenqvist (eds), *Statistics, Econometrics and Society: Essays in Honour of Leif Nordberg*, research report 238, Helsinki: Statistics Finland, pp. 41–54.

Institute of Migration (eds) (2006), 'Tilastot', accessed at www.migrationinstitute. fi/db/stat/fin/

IOM (eds) (2006), *Return Migration: Policies and Practices in Europe*, Geneva: International Organization for Migration.

Lichter, D.T. (1983), 'Socioeconomic returns to migration among married women', *Social Forces*, 62, 487–503.

Maxwell, N.L. (1988), 'Economic returns to migration: marital status and gender differences', *Social Science Quarterly*, 69, 108–21.

Mincer, J. (1978), 'Family migration decisions', *Journal of Political Economy*, 86, 749–73.

Muschkin, C.G. (1993), 'Consequences of return migrant status for employment in Puerto Rico', *International Migration Review*, 27, 79–102.

OECD (eds) (2001), 'The employment of foreigners: outlook and issues in OECD countries' in OECD (eds), *Employment Outlook 2001*, Paris: OECD, pp. 167–206.

Ramos, F. (1992), 'Out-migration and return migration of Puerto Ricans', in G. Borjas and R. Freeman (eds), *Immigration and the WorkForce: Economic Consequences for the United States and Source Areas*, Chicago, IL: University of Chicago Press, pp. 49–66.

Rooth, D.O. and J. Saarela (2007), 'Selection in migration and return migration: evidence from micro data', *Economics Letters*, 94, 90–95.

Saarela, J. and F. Finnäs (2003), 'Unemployment and native language: the Finnish case', *Journal of Socio-Economics*, 32, 59–80.

Saarela, J. and F. Finnäs, F (2006), 'Adjustment failures in an immigrant population: Finns in Sweden', *Social Indicators Research*, 82, 545–63.

Saarela, J. and F. Finnäs (2007), 'Cross-country employment propensity of Finnish migrants: evidence from linked register data', *Migration Letters*, **5** (1), 63–77.

Statistics Finland (2006a), 'Taulukot aihealueella Muuttoliike', accessed at http:// pxweb2.stat.fi/database/V%E4est%F6/Muuttoliike/Muuttoliike.asp/.

Statistics Finland (2006b), 'Rekisteriseloste: Väestölaskentojen pitkittäistiedosto 1970–1995', accessed at www.stat.fi/meta/rekisteriselosteet/rekisteriseloste_ vaestolaskenta70–95.html/.

Statistics Finland (2006c), 'Työssäkäynti', accessed at www.stat.fi/til/tyokay/index. html/.

PART IV

State control and citizen rights

13. The future of border control: risk management of migration in the UK

James Hampshire

13.1 INTRODUCTION: RISK AND THE MIGRATION STATE

Like most other advanced capitalist economies, the UK has developed into what James F. Hollifield calls a 'migration state' (Hollifield 2004). Migration states seek competitive advantage by opening their economies and societies to international migration, but at the same time they must also accommodate powerful political forces that drive them towards closure. Faced with these conflicting dynamics, migration states seek to manage migration in their interests by encouraging or 'soliciting' some flows, while preventing or 'stemming' others (Joppke 2002).

As migration states increasingly seek to discriminate between migration flows, and also balance the costs and benefits of migration, new policy instruments and organizational forms are emerging. In the UK, an important recent development is the reconceptualization of migration in terms of risk, and the reorganization of migration management as a form of risk management. This reconceptualization is multi-faceted. On the one hand, across migration states, immigration is often portrayed as posing negative risks. This is risk as threat – threat of terrorism, crime, social disorder, cultural anxiety, public health and so on. While the intensity of these associations may have increased – especially the security and terrorism associations since 9/11 – the fears and antipathies that underlie them are hardly new.

Indeed, the history of migration is replete with claims about the 'immigrant threat' (Lucassen 2005). If it were just a case of redescribing these threats using the language of risk then one might be forgiven for doubting whether the idea of 'migration risks' amounts to very much. And the implications for migration policy would also hardly be new: the appropriate response would be simply to institute more draconian control measures, to build up the walls of the fortress. For migration states, however, imposing excessive controls on migration poses its own risks, and it is here that the reframing of migration management as risk management becomes important.

To see why, consider the impact of migration on two of the state's functional imperatives: accumulation of wealth and provision of security. As Christina Boswell (2007) argues, migration actualizes a tension between these core functions. On the one hand, migration feeds the accumulation of wealth, contributing to economic growth by meeting skills and labour shortages; on the other hand, it presents real and perceived security risks, in the form of terrorism or organized crime, as well as more nebulous societal insecurities and their associated fears. To some extent the trade-offs between these two goals have always been present. But they have been exacerbated in recent years as the importance of migration to *both* functions has increased: migration is increasingly important to economic growth in an era of globalization *and* it is increasingly associated with counter-terrorism and the security agenda, especially since 9/11 (Hampshire *in press*, Huysmans 2006).

If both imperatives are to be met, migration management must strike a difficult balance: inadequate migration controls leave a state open to potential security threats (and the perception of inadequate controls stokes fear of perceived threats); blanket control instruments designed to protect from security threats create the risk of deterring 'wanted' migrants who make important contributions to economic growth. Manageing migration becomes a matter of risk management, both in terms of addressing first-order risks posed by certain kinds of migration, but also second-order risks brought about by the (unintended) effects of control-oriented policies.[1] The paramount second-order risk is that control measures deter wanted migration, but there are also other second-order risks associated with displacement effects, such as when increases in security at major ports displace migration to smaller, less well policed ports; or when a contraction of legal entry channels pushes migrants towards illicit modes of entry, thereby fuelling illegal migration and the criminal organizations that run the booming people smuggling business.

This balancing act becomes especially apparent at the border. Border controls are intended to prevent the entry of people and goods that present a security threat, but they must also facilitate the flow of legitimate travellers and trade. Stringent control measures that discourage or slow movements of people and goods in the name of security impose transaction costs on cross-border movement and therefore risk limiting the economic benefits of migration. The borders of migration states must therefore simultaneously facilitate beneficial flows and prevent threatening ones.

For the migration state then, managing migration is about identifying the 'risky migrant' (Gammeltoft-Hansen 2006) – or more precisely identifying higher and lower-risk passenger categories and routes – and calibrating policy interventions accordingly. High-risk migration is targeted for particular attention, while low-risk migration is subjected to lighter-touch controls and increasingly channelled through specially designed entry programmes. If it is to be more than merely symbolic (though the political symbolism should not be overlooked) then the risk management of migration, as with any risk management, rests upon surveillance and gathering of accurate data, analysis and risk assessment of this data, and a reorganization of institutions, policies and operational processes so as to utilize this information.

A shift to risk-based migration management implies that migration controls are not simply intensified, but reconfigured. As we shall see, the attempt to reconcile accumulation and security imperatives motivates increasingly *differentiated* control instruments and interventions. It is here that risk management plays a crucial role, in the determination of which flows to target for more stringent checks, and which to target for facilitated entry and exit. While security imperatives motivate biometric visas, improved watchlists, juxtaposed controls, and many other policy initiatives, the need to facilitate non-risky flows underpins the creation of 'trusted traveller' and 'smart trade' schemes.

13.2 THE RISK MANAGEMENT OF MIGRATION: UK BORDER STRATEGY

Since the Labour government came to power in 1997, and especially during its second and third terms in office (2001–present), UK migration policy has been in a state of near permanent revolution. The British government has passed no fewer than five major parliamentary acts on immigration and asylum, issued countless strategy documents, overhauled the immigration rules and engaged in major reform of the immigration system (see Somerville 2007). It is striking that the language of risk and risk management is largely absent from policy discourse for most of this period.

In the last couple of years, however, this has rapidly changed. Starting in 2006, the government began a major overhaul of migration policies, including the introduction of a new points-based economic migration system, organizational changes to the immigration and border agencies, and a raft of initiatives on border security. It is through these reforms, reasonably described by the Minister for Borders and Immigration, Liam Byrne, as the 'biggest shake-up of Britain's border security for 40 years,'[2] that the language of risk and risk management has become pervasive. In the recent Strategy Unit report that sets out the government's strategic objectives on migration and border controls, the word risk is used no fewer than 168 times: the report proposes that 'a single overarching border and risk management strategy is required that takes account of the full range of border objectives' (COSU 2007, 9); the border agency must provide 'security from the range of risks' (10); it must sort 'low risk' from 'high risk movements', targeting interventions at the latter (17); and so on.

Beyond the penetration of risk vocabulary into migration policy discourse, an emergent risk-based approach to migration in the UK can be seen on four levels: redefinition of the strategic objectives of migration and border control; reforms to the institutional architecture and organizational structures of the migration regime; specific policies and programmes; and lastly, changes to the operational processes of migration control at the frontline.

Strategic Objectives

The strategic objectives of migration policy, especially border controls, are now explicitly framed in terms of risk. According to the new objectives, the 'risks being addressed' include providing effective and robust immigration controls, protection of the UK tax base, and protection against organized crime, terrorism and prohibited goods. 'A border crossing represents a risk' and 'the border provides an opportunity to track high risk individuals or freight, identify suspicious movements, and monitor travel patterns' (COSU 2007, 20). This way of discussing migration risks is clearly negative and broadly consistent with the idea that risk-based management represents a securitization of migration (see for example Huysmans 2006). Official statements, especially those intended for public consumption, also tend to emphasize the control and protection objectives of the new policy. For example, the Home Secretary, Jacqui Smith, has promised that the reforms will ensure 'ours is one of the toughest borders in the world'.[3] While a news release on the Border and Immigration Agency (BIA) website reports that the three-tier approach to migration control (remote controls, territorial border and in-country controls) creates 'a triple ring of steel to control illegal immigration and crime'.[4] But such robust imagery is tempered by the equal importance attached to facilitating wanted migration.

Despite the emphasis on security in its title, the recent strategy paper focuses as much on the facilitation of cross-border flows deemed legitimate and desirable as it does on the prevention of those flows seen to present a threat. Indeed, migration is defined as essential to the UK: 'if we are to maintain our prosperity and our way of life, the UK cannot afford to damage is attractiveness as a global hub' (COSU 2007, 24). With trade accounting for 60 per cent of GDP or GBP735 billion in 2006 (up from 25 per cent in 1970), tourism worth more than £15 billion to the economy, and international students contributing an estimated £5 billion per year, not to mention the contribution to economic growth made by migrants who fill skills and labour shortages and facilitate international trade and investment, the impact of excessive controls in the name of security weigh heavily indeed. In the report, some of the costs are even quantified: the cost of delays in transiting goods through customs are estimated to be possibly as high as 2 per cent of the value of the goods; while a ten minute increase in the transit time for passengers clearing UK border controls has an opportunity cost of almost £400 million per annum based on current flows (COSU 2007, 26, 27).

Here, the risks are not conceptualized in terms of the threat or danger posed by migration; on the contrary, they are risks posed by migration *controls*. Consistent with the discussion of migration states above, the second-order risks of migration controls are central to the strategy: 'Measures that discourage, or slow, movements of people or goods risk limiting the opportunities presented by trade and travel and will therefore incur a cost. However, the two objectives of security and prosperity in a global hub are not necessarily in conflict. There is significant potential for general wins through improved targeting . . . which can lead to minimising contact and burdens on the legitimate traveller or trader while focusing impact on the illegitimate' (COSU 2007, 28). 'The goal,' the report states, 'is to find the optimal relationship between an appropriate degree of security, and the free flow of people and goods.' This balancing objective is elaborated into 'five key principles', which are worth reproducing at some length:

1. Act early. The most effective – and efficient way of addressing risks to the UK is to identify those movements which present a threat and to stop or control them before they reach the UK. Equally, low risk movements can be identified early to facilitate movement of legitimate goods and passengers,

2. Target effort. Border controls need to target activity to achieve both their control and facilitation objectives and minimize tension between the two. Control activity should be direct at those movements and in those locations that pose the greatest risk, while legitimate movements should be facilitated,

3. Manage bottlenecks. High volumes of goods and people converge at the main points of entry to the UK . . . Striking the right balance is crucial. Getting it right enables the smooth flow of legitimate goods

and people and the effective identification of threats; getting it wrong results in delays, inefficiency, duplication and the risk of overlooking threats,

4. Maximize depth and breadth of protection . . . border controls should be arranged so as to be able to recognize as many risks as possible and deploy the full range of powers necessary to address them, and

5. Reassure and deter . . . the UK border . . . need[s] to project a clear, identifiable and professional presence. This is important in deterring those who wish to do harm as well as providing reassurance for the general public and business (COSU 2007, 8–9).

The idea of balancing 'control' and 'facilitation' objectives is evidently pivotal to the new strategy, with risk-based interventions envisaged as the way to meet them. As I argue below, this shapes the institutional, policy and operational dimensions of the new migration regime.

Institutional Architecture

From ministerial level down to frontline service delivery, the institutions that comprise the UK's migration regime are undergoing a process of reform shaped by the new strategic objectives discussed above. The two most important institutional reforms are departmental diversification in policymaking and organizational integration in policy delivery.

Throughout the twentieth century, immigration policy was under the remit of the Home Office. This remains the case, but as migration is increasingly recognized to have cross-departmental impacts a wider range of actors is being incorporated into the policymaking structure. For example, two of the recent strategy papers – on border security and foreign policy dimensions of migration control – were co-published by the Home Office and Foreign and Commonwealth Office (HO/FCO 2007a, HO/FCO 2007b). Readmission agreements are increasingly important to bilateral relationships and Lord Triesman, Parliamentary Under-Secretary of State at the FCO, was appointed as the Prime Minister's Special Envoy for Returns in 2007.

This provides one illustration of the widening range of departmental interests involved in migration management. More important still from the point of view of the new risk-based strategy is the growing influence of the Treasury. Historically, the Treasury has acted as an expansionist actor within government – often supporting more liberal immigration policies on the grounds of economic benefits – whereas the Home Office has tended to take a more restrictionist view (Hampshire 2005, 105–6). Given the dual control and facilitation objectives of the new border strategy, it is striking that the Treasury is being given a more powerful role in policy-making under the reforms. As the strategy report puts it: 'while there are a range of departmental interests in border work, the two most significant are those of the Home Office and HM Treasury. Because the submersion of either security concerns or economic and fiscal concerns would not be acceptable, work to develop this strategy should be jointly led' (COSU 2007, 62).

Given the past dominance of the Home Office, it is difficult not to read this as an implicit criticism of its restrictionist bias which, though comprehensible in terms of its security mandate, public opinion management and high profile media coverage of asylum and illegal migration, has sometimes led to unbalanced policy. Whatever its implication at Whitehall, this argument is used to justify the recommendation for a single minister, appointed to both the Home Office and Treasury. This innovation is reinforced by a new governance structure 'that properly reflects the full range of wider interests' and which addresses what are frankly described as 'competing objectives'. To this end, a revised Cabinet Sub-committee on Border and Migration (DA(BM)) was set up in early 2008, chaired by the Home Secretary but including Treasury Ministers as well as others 'who have a strong interest in the full range of the organisation's new work, including prohibitions and restrictions and facilitation.' (COSU 2007, 62) This includes ministerial representation from the FCO, the Department for Business, Enterprise and Regulatory Reform (BERR), the Department for Culture, Media and Sport (DCMS), the Department for Environment, Food and Rural Affairs (Defra), the Department for Transport (DfT), and the Department of Health (DoH).

At the same time as diversification of departmental interests is underway at the policymaking level, at the level of policy implementation organizational integration is taking place. In the wake of a series of political scandals, notably the foreign prisoners' debacle, a wide-ranging review of the immigration system was conducted in 2006. This concluded that 'urgent organisational reform' of the Immigration and Nationality Directorate (IND) was needed to 'de-clutter' processes and improve performance (HO 2006a, 14). IND was portrayed as a failing organization, mired in a culture of reaction. As the Home Office review put it: 'IND still reacts to events rather than manageing risks and anticipating and pre-empting new problems' (ibid). A programme of change was announced which included, *inter alia*, simplification of the legal framework, establishment of a Migration Advisory Committee, and the re-establishment of IND as an executive agency with greater operational freedom. In April 2007, IND was established as a 'shadow' agency, the Borders and Immigration Agency (BIA). At the same time, inter-agency cooperation between BIA, Her Majesty's

Revenue and Customs (HMRC), the Serious Organised Crime Agency
(SOCA) and UKvisas was developed through the Border Management
Programme.

In July 2007, the new Prime Minister, Gordon Brown announced
that the reforms would be taken further by integrating the immigration,
customs and visa agencies to create a unified border force. According
to the subsequent strategy report, while previous reforms and operational innovations such as the Border Management Programme had
made 'important strides . . . more radical change is necessary to realise
the greater potential for improvement' (COSU 2007, 63). The new UK
Border Agency launched in 2008, incorporating BIA, UKvisas, and the
border work of HMRC. The Agency has a remit to 'improve the UK's
security through strong border controls, while welcoming, facilitating and
encouraging legitimate travellers and trade' (COSU 2007, 64). Indeed, its
organizational structure is designed to prevent either security or facilitation imperatives from predominating: for example, although an agency of
the Home Office, the new organization will have a 'dual and symmetrical'
reporting line to the Chancellor and Home Secretary; its executive board
will report to both the Home Office and Treasury; and the board will
include an HMRC Commissioner, a senior police officer, and a senior
FCO official among its members.

Policies and Programmes

In order to achieve the objective of balancing 'security' and 'prosperity',
migration policies are increasingly differentiated according to risk. On the
one hand, controls and interventions are targeted at high-risk migrants;
on the other, special facilitation programmes are developed for low-risk
migrants. Given the impracticality and second-order risks associated with
stringent universal controls, the intention is that a risk-based approach
will be both more efficient and efficacious: filtering out risky migrants and
thereby protecting from threats, while making cross-border movement
easier for certain categories of travellers. This gives rise to what might be
called the *differentiated* border.

Of course, differentiated border controls are not entirely new – states
have long concentrated their immigration control efforts at major ports
of entry or policed those territorial borders associated with illegal entry.
And to some extent migration controls were risk-based for much of the
twentieth century, as in the case of visa regimes which have a twofold risk
management structure: first, visa regimes are typically based on a country-
by-country risk assessment, with visa requirements imposed on those
countries deemed high-risk (i.e. number of asylum seekers, incidence of

illegal migration, overstaying, terrorism, etc.); second, in order to qualify for a visa, a citizen of a high-risk country is individually risk-assessed by an immigration official, often using profiling techniques in her/his decision to grant entry clearance. In the UK, risk assessment is currently being formalized at both levels of the visa regime. The UK Visa Waiver Test is under review, to assess 'the risk posed by all non-EEA countries to ensure the control provided by a visa regime is targeted to those nationals posing the greatest threat' (COSU 2007, 57); and Risk Assessment Units are now embedded in all 'high-volume, high-risk posts'. In Ghana, for example, this has resulted in a decline of 75 per cent of visa applications containing forged documents (COSU 2007, 40).

The recent policy changes go well beyond a formalization of implicit risk-based controls, however. A new set of policies designed to focus control interventions on specific migration flows are in development. This builds on the use of 'remote controls' (Zolberg 1999), such as pre-embarkation screening and carrier sanctions (see Guiraudon and Lahav 2000, 185), which characterized policy development in the late twentieth century. Increasingly, remote controls are seen as an 'upstream' intervention in an end-to-end flow management of passengers and goods which targets resources according to risk. Remote border controls are intended to gather information that is then risk assessed for further action at ports of entry.

For example, the UK's network of Airline Liaison Officers (ALOs) based at 'nexus points for illegal movements', has remote control functions of pre-screening passengers and ensuring that carriers meet their obligations under the Carrier Liability Regulations, but it is also increasingly used for risk management functions, such as gathering advanced passenger information (API) and regional intelligence to inform risk-based interventions 'downstream', that is, upon arrival in the UK. Travellers accepted for boarding may still find themselves targeted for special attention or even refused entry on arrival if their API reveals anomalies or fits risk-profiles used during analysis at the Joint Borders Operation Centre (J-BOC) in the UK.

At the moment, these policies are in their infancy, but they will be significantly expanded through the forthcoming e-Borders programme. The programme has already been tested through a 'proof of concept' trial, Project Semaphore, which analyses API on key routes in and out of the UK. Project Semaphore currently processes 27 million passengers per annum, has issued 16000 alerts to date, and resulted in 1300 arrests (COSU 2007, 41). When it is fully operational, e-Borders will use biometric and information systems technologies to capture electronic API direct from carriers on all passenger movements in and out of the UK. API data will then be risk-assessed and analysed against watchlists[5] by the e-Borders

Operations Centre (eBOC) while travel is in progress, 'allowing for early risk-profiling against immigration, customs, serious organised crime and counter-terrorism risks before traveller reach the UK' (COSU 2007, 41). Immigration officers at UK ports will then target higher risk passengers and facilitate the movement through controls of others. Passengers will also be counted out of the UK, which will provide immigration compliance data to inform future decision-making, and from April 2008, all visa applicants will have to submit biometric data, making it easier to track overstayers. Thus data collected through the operational risk management of e-Borders will feed into future risk-based policy such as visa regimes, expansion of the ALO network, and so on.

The inverse of increasingly targeted interventions on high-risk migrants is the advent of policies to facilitate the flow of people and goods deemed low-risk. Along with a number of other countries, including the Netherlands whose Privium scheme has operated at Schiphol airport since 2001, the UK has recently developed a biometrics-based 'trusted traveller' scheme named Project IRIS (Iris Recognition Immigration System), which provides an automated entry system for pre-registered travellers. Travellers who register their biometric profiles can proceed through automated gates at selected airports which use biometric scanners to confirm identity. So far 143000 people have registered for the scheme. These schemes are seen as the future of border management for regular, low-risk travellers. As the government puts it, Project IRIS, as well as the miSense Plus trial which ran from December 2006 to March 2007, 'provides a basis for the further development of automated entry clearance using biometrics' (COSU 2007, 42). It is important to note that both sides of the risk management coin – targeted controls and facilitated entry programmes – rest upon secure identity management, hence the zeal with which the UK government is pursuing biometric documentation for visas, passports, and possibly identity cards.

The facilitation objective applies equally to the movement of goods as people, which is the basis of so-called 'smart trade' initiatives. These initiatives allow registered businesses to benefit from simplified customs controls, reducing time and administrative burdens of trading with the UK. As of January 2008, HMRC has been operating an Authorised Economic Operator (AEO) process, which allows businesses that have been vetted for customs compliance to ship goods using facilitated or simplified customs controls. The UK has also cooperated on a 'smart trade' pilot project with the Netherlands and China. This project is intended to test, refine and agree principles for the development of 'end-to-end supply chains' between Asia and Europe. In addition, a Freight Targeting System (FTS) has been established to track suspicious movements.

Operational Procedures

Lastly, a risk-based approach to migration management can be seen at the level of operational procedures, both existing and planned. As discussed in preceding sections, risk assessment and profiling are used by officials across the migration system – from Entry Clearance and Air Liaison Officers to customs officials, staff at ports of entry, and staff at the Joint/ e-Borders Operations Centre. At the frontline, immigration and customs officials are already trained in using profiling systems to identify a 'suspicious pattern of behaviour' (COSU 2007, 50), including travel patterns and visual signals. Notwithstanding this, one of the major operational challenges for the new Border Agency will be to train staff 'to identify and respond to a wider range of risks . . . so that wherever an officer is deployed, there is some coverage of the full range of risks' (COSU 2007, 81). Cross-agency training has already been implemented, with the aim that, for example, a customs operation on drug trafficking could yield risk-profiles that although of no interest from a customs perspective might alert suspicion from an immigration perspective (COSU 2007, 50). This kind of inter-operability is a key aspiration for the new Agency.

Another dimension of operational change informed by risk management considerations is the re-branding and increased visibility of border controls. Here, the risks involved are not only actual but also, and perhaps especially, *perceived* risks. Recall that the government's fifth key principle of an effective control system is to 'reassure and deter'. In addition to tangible activity – often behind the scenes – the new border arrangements are intended to project a more 'visible and dynamic' image of control to all passengers, both so as to 'deter potential wrongdoers' and, perhaps more importantly, to 'reassure public and business' (COSU 2007, 28, 58). While the deterrence function relates primarily to first-order migration risks (i.e. deterring entry of individuals who pose a threat) visible border controls should also perform a second-order risk function related to UK citizens and visitors.

Visible controls are intended to allay fears about migration risks and promote public confidence in the government's management of migration. As the strategy report makes clear, public perception of risk may well differ from actual risk, but the former must be addressed if the government's management is to be seen as competent and, more fundamentally still, if the state's migration regime is to retain legitimacy. With regard to visitors, the reassurance consists of making it feel safe to visit the UK, for 'if the threat of a terrorist attack is perceived to be high or the government response perceived as inadequate, then business and tourists abroad may avoid the UK' (COSU 2007, 28). As with other areas of risk management,

the risk management of migration is as much about public perception as
actual risk.

13.3   EXPLAINING THE RISK MANAGEMENT OF MIGRATION

What explains the recent penetration of risk discourse into the migration
policy domain and the development of a risk-based approach to migration
and border control? Five factors are driving change.

The Functional Need to Control and Facilitate Migration

The major factor driving the risk management of migration is the functional need for migration states simultaneously to control and facilitate
migration. Both security and accumulation imperatives inform the new
strategy, institutional reforms, policy developments and changes to operational procedure at the frontline. As the government puts it: 'the objectives are clear: the facilitation of legitimate travel and trade; security from
the threats and pressures of crime, whether illegal migration, terrorism or
attacks on the tax base; and protection of the border itself' (COSU 2007,
5).

In the burgeoning literature on the securitization of migration, security imperatives are often seen as the main driver towards biometrically
enabled, risk-managed borders (for example Bigo 2000). Certainly in the
USA, the move to 'smart borders' and the creation of the US-VISIT programme was a direct response to 9/11 (Koslowski 2005, 5–6). But as the
earlier discussion of migration states illustrates, the influence of accumulation imperatives should not be underestimated. My argument is that risk
management – as discourse and practice – furnishes the organizational
logic for a balancing of these conflicting imperatives. All migration is put
under greater surveillance and those migrants believed to pose a risk are
targeted for interventions, while those who do not are not. Differentiated
border controls are the concrete expression of this logic. The risk management approach also highlights second-order risks, which are invisible in a
purely securitized framing, that is, the risk that policy interventions can
have a deterrent effect on wanted migration.

Risk management also helps politicians navigate the conflicting currents
of contemporary migration politics, which have become more acute since
9/11 and the July 7 bombings in London. On the one hand, the political
debate about migration policy has indeed been increasingly 'securitized',
with pressures to drive some aspects of policy (for example on illegal

migration, asylum, and immigrant integration) in a more restrictionist direction (Hampshire *in press*, Huysmans 2006); at the same time, economic and demographic pressures are driving a more liberal approach to labour migration (Favell and Hansen 2002).

These trends – concurrent securitization *and* liberalization – converge on risk. The concept of risk is certainly associated with security logics, but it is also being pressed into use for more expansive aims. By emphasizing the second-order risks of deterring beneficial migration through excessive controls, the language of risk helps policymakers to present policy in a balanced way, while the practice of risk-based migration control holds out the possibility of better controlling migration threats while harnessing migration benefits. Caught between the Scylla of excessive securitization (which jeopardizes accumulation) and the Charybdis of liberalization (which undermines security), the risk management of migration has considerable rhetorical and instrumental appeal for policymakers.

The Impracticability of Blanket Controls in a Period of Mass Migration

The second reason for the turn to risk in British migration policy is the sheer impracticability of intensifying blanket controls in a period of mass migration. The scale of migration is not only considerable, it is also growing. There are over 218 million passenger journeys and 440 million tonnes of freight crossing the UK border every year. The government forecasts that by 2030 the number of international passenger journeys will increase to 450 million (COSU 2007, 5, 25). Not only is it undesirable to intensify blanket controls to this scale of traffic, it is simply infeasible. The cost and logistical implications of increasing scrutiny across all passenger and goods flows at all ports of entry, let alone the extent of the territorial border, means that universal controls are not a viable option. In theory, risk-based interventions promise control where control is needed, and are therefore both more effective and efficient.

Technological Developments in Biometrics and Information Systems

The third reason for the rise of risk-based migration management relates to technological capabilities. New information and biometric technologies are a necessary, if not sufficient, condition for the risk management of migration. Risk management of any kind rests on data collection, storage and analysis. Without the technical capacity to gather and analyse data, risk management amounts to little more than impressionistic guess-work. In the context of migration management, the collection and transmission of API, real-time risk analysis, fingerprint and iris-scanners, and other instruments have only become possible with the development of information and biometric technologies in recent years.

Unsurprisingly, the producers of these technologies trumpet their transformative potential. Raytheon Systems, the lead partner of the Trusted Borders consortium which won the contract to design and implement the e-Borders programme, emphasizes the importance of technological capacity: 'by harnessing passenger information, performing risk assessments on passengers planning to enter or leave the UK and utilising new developments in technology which allow the swift and secure transfer of data, e-Borders will, in effect, export the border and provide more effective levels of border control and deliver faster processing and greater flexibility in control operations.' (Trusted Borders Press release 27 November 2007)

In a 2005 speech to the RUSI, a spokesman for Raytheon Systems argued that new technologies made a step-change in migration policy, based on a unified 'systems' approach, possible. Citing the cases of the 9/11 terrorists and Kamel Bourgass, the failed asylum seeker who murdered DC Stephen Oake during a 2003 raid in Manchester, Ian Leath claimed that 'what was lacking was a joined up system of technology able to process the massive amount of information that was available, and to accurately identify in real time where the threat lay. In military parlance, an application of network centric warfare.' To date, many 'tactical point solutions, such as lorry scanning systems at ports, biometrics, recognition systems' have been deployed, but 'what is required for the evolution of trusted borders are strategic solutions'. Migration management has 'more parallels . . . with defence developed mission critical systems rather than civilianised call centre solutions'.[6] A technologically enabled 'total systems approach' should be developed.

Interestingly enough, even within this militarized vision of migration control, the functional imperative to facilitate migration is not omitted. All stakeholders, including passengers, carriers and port operators, as well as government and security services should be consulted. And the decision to brand the bid as 'trusted' rather than 'secure' borders was based on a recognition of the facilitation objective: 'the demands on borders are clearly about security . . . but not just about security – the issue is also about trust and facilitation of travel and trade.'

Notwithstanding the enthusiastic claims of industry advocates, the relative significance of technology as a causal factor in the rise of risk-based migration management is difficult to unpick. It could be argued that technology (and the interests of the producers of technologies) is the underlying driver of the new risk-based approach. Paraphrasing Marx, while the paper passport gives you society with visual inspection at the territorial border, information systems and biometric passports give you society with advanced passenger screening, risk assessment, trusted traveller schemes, and so on (see Marx 2000 [1846], 219–20). However, such technological determinism is open to familiar objections and it is probably better to view information and biometric technologies are a necessary although not sufficient factor.

The Influence of the Wider Risk Management Orthodoxy in British Government

A fourth, contextual factor behind the rise of risk-based migration management is the influence of the wider risk management orthodoxy in British government. Risk management has become a core idea across government, being advocated by the current and previous Prime Minister and elaborated at length in major strategy documents from the Cabinet Office (COSU 2002) and Treasury (Hampton 2005). Within the wider context of changes to British governance, the arrival of risk management in the migration policy domain may be viewed as a somewhat inevitable development.

It is interesting to note in this regard that the recent reforms have been driven more from the core executive – Number 10, the Cabinet Office, and the Treasury – where the risk orthodoxy is arguably stronger than in the Home Office or IND/BIA. The 2007 strategic report on migration was written by the Cabinet Office, from where risk management has been promoted and applied across government, and it contains direct references to the Hampton Review's recommendation that risk assessment be embedded across government, for example: 'maximum control activity should be directed at that which poses the greatest risk . . . this risk based approach has been adopted elsewhere as a result of the Hampton Report, which proposed that intervention be carried out in a risk based and targeted manner' (COSU 2007, 56–7).

Although it is tempting to view the risk management of migration as an inexorable development in the current climate, such an interpretation obscures more than it enlightens. No doubt, the risk orthodoxy provides a ready made policy paradigm, and the specific dynamics do seem to support the idea that risk-thinking has come from strategic reviews at the centre of government. But the specific way in which risk management is being embedded – as well as the fact that it *is* being embedded rather than just used as a new discourse to mask business as usual – requires attention to how and why risk resonates in a migration context. As I have suggested, its appeal as an organizational logic for migration management is shaped by migration-specific factors, notably the conflicting objectives of migration control.

Blame Management, Reactions to Crises and Public fears

Lastly, the risk management of migration is being driven by political considerations which are independent of the instrumental role that risk can play in reconciling accumulation and security imperatives. This has two, interrelated dimensions. First, as with other areas of reforms to the 'British regulatory state' (Moran 2003) the development of risk-based migration controls are marked as much by crisis and fiasco as incremental, rational reform. Changes to the immigration system have been driven by reactions to a series of media-fuelled scandals, which include *inter alia*: inaccurate estimates given by the Home Office of the number of citizens who would migrate to the UK after the government decided to open the labour market following EU enlargement in 2004; a scandal surrounding the failure to deport foreign national prisoners after their sentences had finished; allegations that the government had no reliable estimates of the number of illegal migrants living in the UK; and most recently, a row about how many new jobs have gone to migrant workers as opposed to British citizens. In the febrile climate of contemporary migration politics, the language of risk and the structures of risk management can be viewed as an attempt to reassert authority and competence, by presenting an image of carefully managed and realistic government.

But risk management is not only about political symbolism and 'impression management' (Schlenker 1980). The institutional reforms to the migration regime can also be viewed as a political strategy for blame avoidance. As Christopher Hood has argued, where there is risk there is blame, and where there is blame there is blame avoidance (Hood 2002). It does not take a cynic to view the new institutional architecture of the UK migration regime as an exercise in anticipated blame-shifting. There is a governmental need to deflect blame in the context of antagonistic media, sceptical public opinion, and migration scandals; and the new institutional architecture closely fits the delegation strategies familiar to students of 'blame games' (see Weaver 1986, 1988). Hood (2002) identifies three typical delegation strategies adopted in risk regulatory regimes: managerialization, privatization and expertization. All three can be seen in the UK migration regime: the creation of a Border Agency with managerial autonomy; use of non-state actors for migration functions (for example carriers, outsourcing of visa application processing); and expert input to policymaking from the MAC and MIF. All three strategies can be (and are) justified in terms of improved policymaking and delivery; but all can be (and are) used to shift blame by elected politicians. By transferring liability for operational failures onto managers or private actors, or holding experts responsible for technical judgements, politicians create the space to blame others when policymaking or delivery goes wrong.

13.4 CONCLUSION: THE RISKS OF RISK-BASED MIGRATION MANAGEMENT

A risk-based approach to migration control, especially at the border, is emerging in the UK. To the extent that risk management offers a way of reconciling functional imperatives that are inherent to migration states, we should expect this to be more than a passing fad and also expect that risk-based migration policy will become a feature of many such states. 'Hyper-innovation' in the contemporary British state (Moran 2003) may mean that risk discourse finds especially fertile ground there, but other states already are and many will yet adopt the language and structures of risk management in their migration policymaking. These developments beg at least two questions: *can* migration risks really be managed? And are there risks associated with the risk management of migration?

First, there are considerable logistical and technical obstacles to be over-come. The efficacy of risk-based migration management turns on accurate and interoperable data, robust information systems, and considerable organizational coordination. None of these can be assumed, especially given the track record of the immigration agency to date. Moreover, the risk management of migration rests on a belief that a process as complex and indeterminate as international migration can be made essentially know-able or at least sufficiently understood to allow for accurate risk-profiling. This is not to say that risk-based interventions are impossible, but rather that the actual ability to risk manage is unlikely to match the ambitions of recent proposals. As Rey Koslowski points out with regard to US-VISIT, there are 'real challenges for virtual borders' (Koslowski 2005).

This leads to the second consideration, namely that there are also political risks associated with the risk management of migration. As discussed, migration policymaking and delivery takes place in an often febrile political climate, in which expert knowledge may conflict with public and media opinion. The management of blame through delegation – managerialization, privatization, and expertization – does not always work, as delegatees will sometimes successfully push blame back onto politicians, what Hood (2002) calls 'blame boomerangs'. It is far from guaranteed that the new institutional architecture will insulate politicians from blame for policy failures.

Lastly, risk management regimes often result in behavioural adjustments such as 'risk compensation' (Adams 2007) and 'secondary risk management'

(Power 2004). These are arguably pathologies of risk management as such, insofar as any attempt to intervene to regulate risks caused and experienced by reflexive agents will likely have effects on the behaviour of those agents. Thus compulsory car seat-belts, mandated in the name of road safety, cause *more* fatalities because a heightened sense of security among drivers results in less cautious driving, and effectively redistributes risk from drivers to pedestrians and cyclists (Adams 2007). In the context of migration management, interventions to manage first-order risks, such as terrorism and illegal entry, will almost certainly cause behavioural adjustments in potential terrorists or illegal migrants, for example by displacing entry to smaller ports.[7] This does not mean that risk management cannot work; only that it rarely works without unintended and even perverse consequences.

A risk-based migration regime will not of course function perfectly. The question is how prone to crisis it will be, and how it will manage the inevitable policy failures. To paraphrase James C. Scott (1998), analysis of the recent reforms helps us to see like a migration state, but it does not reveal how sharp that state's vision will be in practice. Even a passing acquaintance with the history of migration policy – strewn with policy failures, unintended consequences, crises and fiascos – suggests that a healthy scepticism is warranted.

NOTES

1. On the distinction between first and second-order risks see Luhmann 1993.
2. http://www.bia.homeoffice.gov.uk/sitecontent/newsarticles/immigrationandcustomsunite accessed on 20 February 2008.
3. http://www.ukba.homeoffice.gov.uk/sitecontent/newsarticles/primeministerlaunchescontract accessed on 20 May 2008.
4. http://www.bia.homeoffice.gov.uk/sitecontent/newsarticles/immigrationandcustomsunite accessed on 20 February 2008.
5. By December 2008, it is intended that these will link to the Interpol Lost and Stolen Passport Database to 'enhance the ability of border officers to target intervention on high-risk individuals' (COSU 2007: 84).
6. Ian Leath, Presentation to RUSI on 'The Need for Trusted Borders', 29/6/05, available at http://www.raytheon.co.uk/news_room/files/TheNeedforTrustedBorders.doc
7. This is one behavioural adjustment that *is* discussed in the recent reforms, which emphasize the need to improve security at smaller ports of entry (COSU 2007, 69–71). There are likely to be others not thought of however.

REFERENCES

Adam, B., U. Beck and J. van Loon (2000), *The Risk Society and Beyond: Critical Issues for Social Theory*, London: Sage.

Adams, J. (2007), 'Seat belt laws – repeal them?', *Significance*, **4** (2), 86–9, accessed at http://john–adams.co.uk/wp–content/uploads/2006/12/Seat%20belts%20for%20significance.pdf/.

Beck, U. (1992), *Risk Society: Towards a New Modernity*, London: Sage.

Bigo, D. (2000), 'When two becomes one: internal and external securitisations in Europe' in M. Kestrup and M.C. Williams (eds), *International Relations and the Politics of European Integration*, London: Routledge.

Boswell, C. (2007), 'Theorizing migration policy: is there a third way?', *International Migration Review*, **41** (1), 75–100.

COSU (Cabinet Office Strategy Unit) (2002), *Risk: Improving Government's Capability to Handle Risk and Uncertainty*, London: Cabinet Office.

COSU (2007), *Security in a Global Hub: Establishing the UK's New Border Arrangements*, London: Cabinet Office.

Douglas, M. (1994), *Risk and Blame: Essays in Cultural Theory*, London: Routledge.

Durodié, B. (2005), 'The concept of risk', Nuffield Trust Global Programme on Health, Foreign Policy and Security, accessed at www.durodie.net/pdf/HEALTH.pdf/.

Gammeltoft–Hansen, T. (2006), 'Filtering Out the Risky Migrant: Migration Control, Risk Theory and the EU', AMID working paper 52.

Giddens, A. (1990), *Towards a New Modernity*, Cambridge: Polity.

Giddens, A. (1999), 'Risk and responsibility', *The Modern Law Review*, **62** (1), 1–10.

Guiraudon, V. and G. Lahav (2000), 'A reappraisal of the state sovereignty debate: the case of migration control', *Comparative Political Studies*, **33** (2), 163–95.

Favell, A. and R. Hansen (2002), 'Markets against politics: migration, EU enlargement and the idea of Europe', *Journal of Ethnic and Migration Studies*, **28** (4), 581–601.

Hampshire, J. (2005), *Citizenship and Belonging: Immigration and the Politics of Demographic Governance in Postwar Britain*, Basingstoke: Palgrave.

Hampshire, J. (forthcoming), 'Disembedding liberalism?' in G. Freeman, T. Givens and D. Leal (eds), *Migration Control since 9/11*, Boulder, CO: Lynne Rienner.

Hampton, P. (2005), *Reducing Administrative Burdens: Effective Inspection and Enforcement*, London: HM Treasury.

Hansen, R. (2000), *Citizenship and Immigration in Postwar Britain*, Oxford: Oxford University Press.

Hollifield, J.F. (2004), 'The emerging migration state', *International Migration Review*, **38** (3), 885–912.

HO (Home Office) (2006a), *Fair Effective, Transparent and Trusted: Rebuilding Confidence in Our Immigration System*, London: Home Office.

HO (2006b), *Borders, Immigration and Identity Action Plan*, London: Home Office.

HO (2007), *Enforcing the Rules: A Strategy to Ensure and Enforce Compliance with our Immigration Laws*, London: Home Office.

HO/FCO (Home Office/Foreign and Commonwealth Office) (2007a), *Securing the UK Border: Our Vision and Strategy for the Future*, London: Home Office/Foreign and Commonwealth Office.

HO/FCO (2007b), *Manageing Global Migration: A Strategy to Build Stronger International Alliances to Manage Migration*, London: Home Office/Foreign and Commonwealth Office.

Hood, C., H. Rothstein and R. Baldwin (2001), *The Government of Risk: Understanding Risk Regulation Regimes*, Oxford: Oxford University Press.

Hood, C. (2002), 'The risk game and the blame game', *Government and Opposition*, **37** (1), 15–37.

Huysmans, J. (2006), *The Politics of Insecurity: Fear, Migration and Asylum in the EU*, London: Routledge.

Joppke, C. (2002), 'European immigration policies at the crossroads' in P. Heywood, E. Jones and M. Rhodes (eds), *Developments in West European Politics 2*, Basingstoke: Palgrave.

Koslowski, R. (2005), *Real Challenges for Virtual Borders: The Implementation of US–VISIT*, Washington, DC: Migration Policy Institute.

Lucassen, L. (2005), *The Immigrant Threat: The Integration of Old and New Migrants in Western Europe since 1850*, Urbana, IL: University of Illinois Press.

Luhmann, N. (1993), *Risk: A Sociological Theory*, Berlin: De Gruyter.

Marx, K. (2000 [1846]), *Karl Marx: Selected Writings*, D. McLellan (ed.), Oxford: Oxford University Press.

Moran, M. (2003), *The British Regulatory State: High Modernism and Hyper-Innovation*, Oxford: Oxford University Press.

Power, M. (1997), *The Audit Society: Rituals of Verification*, Oxford: Oxford University Press.

Power, M. (2004), *The Risk Management of Everything*, London: DEMOS.

Royal Society (1992), *Risk: Analysis, Perception, Management*, London: Royal Society.

Schlenker, B. (1980), *Impression Management*, Monterey, CA: Brooks/Cole.

Scott, J.C. (1998), *Seeing Like a State: How Certain Schemes to Improve the Human Condition Have Failed*, New Haven, CT: Yale University Press.

Somerville, W. (2007), *Immigration under New Labour*, Bristol: The Policy Press.

Weaver, R.K. (1986), 'The politics of blame avoidance', *Journal of Public Policy*, **6** (4), 371–98.

Weaver, R.K. (1988), *Automatic Government*, Washington, DC: Brookings.

Zolberg, A.R. (1999), 'The archaeology of 'remote control'' in A. Fahrmeir, O. Faron and P. Weil (eds), *Migration Control in the North Atlantic World*, Oxford: Barghahn, pp. 195–222.

14. Tracing, identifying and sorting: the role of EU migration databases in the internal control on irregular migrants

Dennis Broeders

14.1 INTRODUCTION

In recent years irregular migration has reached the top of the western European policy agenda. Much has been invested in the various images of the borders of the European Union and its member states. The view of a 'Fortress Europe' emerged to describe the development of policies aimed at keeping out (bogus) asylum seekers, irregular migrants and 'unwanted' immigrants in general. The external borders of the EU (including sea- and airports) have been transformed into formidable boundaries. Borders have been strengthened with guards, watchtowers, concrete and fences. They have also been equipped with state-of-the-art technology, such as infrared scanning devices, motion detectors and video surveillance. Moreover, visa requirements have been stepped up, and the visas themselves have been modernized and are increasingly difficult to forge. And yet, despite funding and political backing for the 'fight against illegal immigration' and the strengthening of borders and border control, the presence of irregular migrants remains a fact of life for most EU countries. The gradual realization that borders alone cannot halt irregular migration has led to a widening of the scope of immigration policy. Border control is 'moving away from the border and outside the state' (Lahav and Guiraudon 2000), or is becoming 'remote control' (Zolberg 2002) or is moving 'upwards, downwards and outwards' (Guiraudon 2001).

Within these many transformations of the European border this chapter focuses on two developments. The first is the development of internal migration control, that is the control on those irregular migrants that scaled the walls of the Fortress Europe or gained entry through legal loopholes and have settled in one of its member states. The second is the development by the EU of large-scale electronic surveillance systems, such as the Schengen Information System (SIS), Eurodac and Visa Information System (VIS), that can be used for border control as well as for internal migration control. The use of these systems for purposes of internal migration control is primarily at stake here. Many European states have defined the exclusion of irregular migrants an explicit policy goal, and are searching for means and methods at both the national and the international level to effectuate that exclusion. The active surveillance and exclusion of irregular migrants by the state depends heavily on information and knowledge production. In other words, control depends on information to make society, in the words of James Scott (1998), 'legible' so that the state can act and implement policy. In the current information age where filing cabinets are being rapidly replaced with searchable databases and technology simplifies interconnectivity and (remote) accessibility, computerization and technological innovations play a lead role in matters of in- and exclusion. The use of the SIS, Eurodac and the VIS for (internal) migration policy is, however, still in its infancy and some of the systems analysed in this chapter are not even in operation (SIS II and VIS). The question is, therefore, how this emerging trend of electronic surveillance develops and what will be its significance for the internal control on irregular migrants.

14.2 THE EXCLUSION OF IRREGULAR MIGRANTS BY DIGITAL MEANS

Irregular migration comes in many shapes and sizes. Many of those we call irregular migrants started their journey perfectly legally, for example travelling on a tourist visa, and became 'illegal' or 'irregular' when they stayed on after its validity expired. Most typologies of 'irregular' migration are therefore set up around three variables. There is legal and illegal entry, legal and illegal residence and legal and illegal employment. These variables can combine in many ways and produce many forms and 'degrees' of irregularity (see for example Tapinos 2000, 18 or Van der Leun 2003, 19). As legal entry does not preclude the possibility of later 'irregularization', border policy alone cannot be the sole policy response to 'irregular migration'. In recent years policies to counter irregular immigration have increasingly turned inwards. Border controls remain important, but in light of their 'structural flaws' have to be supplemented with policies of discouragement of those unwanted aliens that passed the border. This shift towards internal migration control comprises a wide array of policy measures such as employer sanctions, exclusion from public services and surveillance by the police (Van der Leun 2003, Cornelius *et al.* 2004).

Engbersen (2001, 242) suggests that the Fortress Europe may be turning into a panopticon Europe in which governments shield off their public institutions and labour markets by means of advanced identification and control systems. The metaphor of the panopticon comes from the work of Foucault (1977), who in turn borrowed the term from Bentham's design for a prison in which individual prisoners could be seen at all times by a centrally located guard who was invisible to them. The panopticon has become a central metaphor in the literature on surveillance. In Foucault's writing there is an intimate connection between power and knowledge. According to his theory the panoptic power of vision and the constant surveillance are meant to go beyond mere control of the inmates. The final aim is to discipline the individual under surveillance. The idea is that the prisoners under the 'perpetual eye' will experience a process of discipline in which they lose the opportunity, capacity and will to deviate.

The panopticon Europe that is built to control irregular immigration however, differs from the prison and correction system that inspired its name. First the panopticon Europe, unlike most of the surveillance systems the state has created, is not primarily aimed at citizens or even subjects of the state. The system of immigration databases under construction is meant to gain knowledge on the actions and movements of non-citizens. Second, the element of correction, of the 'internalization of the gaze', is not a central element of the panopticon that the member states of the EU are constructing. Engbersen (2001), borrowing from Bauman's (1998) analysis of modern American prisons, claims that the aim is not correction, but exclusion. 'Panopticon Europe is not a "factory of correction". Its aim is not disciplining and correcting undesirable migrants. Panopticon Europe is designed as a *factory of exclusion* and of people habituated to their status of the *excluded*' (Engbersen 2001, 242).

The practical organization of this exclusion is a labour- and information-intensive process. Torpey (1998, 2000) – writing about the state's control on mobility – has argued that the modern state's capacity to penetrate more deeply and effectively into society depends on its ability to embrace those societies. As states grow larger and more administratively adept they can only penetrate society effectively if they embrace society first. This means that 'individuals who remain beyond the embrace of the state necessarily represent a limit on its penetration' (Torpey 1998, 244). Irregular migrants are of course both likely – they are after all 'irregular' because they do not fit into any legal administrative category – and eager to stay beyond the embrace of the state. Internal migration control is therefore aimed at embracing them and the institutions and circles in which they move, in order to exclude them.

The link between the exclusion of illegal immigrants and policies of surveillance can follow two separate, and essentially contradictory, logics.

The first may be captured under the notion of 'exclusion from documentation' and the second under the notion of 'exclusion through – or by means of – documentation and registration'. Policies operating under the first logic block irregular migrants' access to documentation and registration in order to exclude them, while policies operating the second logic aim to register and document the individual irregular migrant himself in order to exclude him.

Exclusion from Documentation and Registration

First, surveillance may be deployed to exclude illegal immigrants from key institutions of society, such as the labour market and the housing market and even from informal networks of fellow countrymen and family. This is the panopticon Europe as described by Engbersen (2001) in which the state raises a protective wall of legal and documentary requirements around the key institutions of the welfare state and 'patrols' it with advanced identification and control systems. The first logic of exclusion reads as follows: Irregular migrants are (formally) excluded from legal documentation and registration, and are thus excluded from the institutions themselves while it is exactly these documents and registrations that allow access to the institutions. One might say that the state's embrace in this perspective is aimed at the institutions and networks illegal immigrants use and need for their daily lives. It is a strategy of exclusion through the delegitimization and criminalization of all those who may be employing, housing and aiding illegal immigrants. Seen from this perspective the panopticon does contain some elements of correction and discipline as it aims to discipline first of all public and semi-public institutions, and second, the social networks and institutional surroundings of irregular migrants. These strategies are prominent in both the Netherlands and Germany where registration is routinely used to exclude irregular migrants from (semi-) public institutions and the labour market.

Exclusion through Documentation and Registration

In the second type of logic, the state aims to embrace illegal immigrants themselves. The state follows the strategy of developing detection and identification tools aimed at exclusion. Embrace of illegal aliens is necessary for detection, but especially for expulsion, as states have gradually found out that 'unidentifiable immigrants are constitutionally rather invulnerable to expulsion' (Van der Leun 2003: 108). The expulsion of illegal aliens can only function when identity, nationality and (preferably) migration history can be established. If not, expulsion is likely to be resisted from within (lawyers and judges) and from abroad (countries of transit and origin) in addition to personal resistance from illegal aliens themselves. It is therefore vital for the state to be able to connect illegal aliens with their 'true' identities. The second logic of exclusion then reads as follows: Documentation and registration are aimed at the irregular migrant himself, in his capacity *as* an irregular migrant. Documentation and registration have to establish (1) the illegal status of the migrant and (2) establish and (re)connect the irregular migrant with his legal identity. In other words, registration is used to identify or even re-identify irregular migrants (see Broeders 2007). This is in turn needed in order to facilitate exclusion in the ultimate sense: expulsion from the state. This strategy is dominant in the advanced welfare states of northern Europe (Engbersen 2004, Levinson 2005). Since the 1990s Germany and the Netherlands have, for example, been increasing their detention capacity for irregular migrants and rejected asylum seekers with the aim of facilitating expulsion (Jesuit Refugee Service 2005, Welch and Schuster 2005). Both countries have also been investing heavily in database systems that are able to register, track and identify the resident migrant population and are leading advocates of organizing and equipping data exchange at the European level in matters of migration management (see for example Aus 2003, 2006).

In the computer age surveillance and registration are loosening their historical bonds with writing and paper. Filing cabinets and card indexes are rapidly being transformed into searchable digital databanks. Information and communication technology has made it possible to link various databases and to create networks between them. Communication technology has 'liberated' registrations and administrations from fixed places and locations through remote accessibility. This interconnectivity and accessibility of information makes cross-referencing potentially a matter of seconds. From a purely technological perspective the limit may indeed be approaching the sky. Whether or not governments connect and combine different bodies of information will increasingly become a matter of political choices and legal constraints, as the technological constraints are losing their relevance quickly. Technological possibilities often underlie 'function' or 'surveillance creep', meaning that systems originally intended to perform narrowly specified functions are expanded as a reaction to new (political) circumstances, often sidestepping or pushing the limits of the original legal framework and safeguards. European integration offers new challenges and possibilities for member states in the field of (illegal) migration control. Dropping internal borders makes irregular (transit) migration easier, but the joint efforts in the field of Justice and Home Affairs seek to close off old and new pathways into the European Union for irregular migrants (and some categories of regular migrants). Domestic surveillance on irregular migrants also makes use of some of the policy innovations and 'tools' that are constructed at the EU-level, and some EU Justice and Home Affairs policies are even primarily meant for 'domestic use' (Broeders 2009).

14.3 IRREGULAR MIGRANTS AND EU COOPERATION: CREATING DIGITAL BORDERS

Since the treaty of Amsterdam, which entered into force in 1999, political attention for irregular migration at the EU level became more structural and gradually took on a grim tone: policy on irregular migration became the 'fight against illegal immigration'. This was in part a 'heritage' of the Schengen cooperation. The Schengen agreement, and the later convention, were originally negotiated outside the normal EU institutions. The Schengen agreement (1985) aimed to give real meaning to the long-standing European goal of free movement of people by abolishing the internal borders among the signatory states. However, it was the later Schengen Convention (1990) – that was basically an inventory of 'flanking measures' – that associated 'Schengen' with securitization and the image of the Fortress Europe. The convention is the starting point for a wide range of instruments for the registration and surveillance of large population groups in the countries concerned (Mathiessen 2001). The Schengen agreements – including the Schengen Information System (SIS), its 'database-flagship' – were integrated into the European Union through the Treaty of Amsterdam.

Measures taken in the post-Amsterdam period include strengthening of borders and carrier sanctions, the adoption of a regulation for determining the member state that is responsible for an asylum application (known as the Dublin II regulation, as it replaced the original Dublin Convention). Dublin II is linked with the Eurodac central database that contains the fingerprints of all asylum claimants over the age of 14. A database that has gradually taken on the secondary aim of preventing irregular migration (Cholewinski 2004).

Visa policy was stepped up for those countries considered to be the major sources of irregular migration. In order to create an effective common visa policy the member states are working on a Visa Information System (VIS), a database that will register issued and refused visa, copies of travel documents and biometric identifiers. Furthermore, initiatives were taken to promote cooperation among member states in matters of expulsion policy and 'illegal immigration' became part and parcel of EU-development aid through the recording of readmission clauses in for example the Contonou Agreement between the EU and the ACP-countries. The fight against illegal immigration also targeted the traffickers and smugglers who facilitate illegal migration to the EU (Cholewinski 2004, Mitsilegas, Monar and Rees 2003, Samers 2004). At the top of the political agenda now is the comprehensive plan to combat illegal immigration and trafficking in human beings, which was adopted in 2002. The ambition of a comprehensive plan for all aspects of illegal immigration indicates that EU policy is 'moving away from the border': border management is just one of the issues on the list. The notion that erecting gates alone lacks effectiveness if migrants who pass the hurdle of border controls – legally or illegally – are able to live an unimpeded life in illegal residence has sunk in at the EU. This is most clearly expressed in the European Commission's Return Action Plan of 2002 which would have to ensure that 'the message gets across that immigration must take place within a clear legal procedural framework and that illegal entry and residence will not lead to the desired stable form of residence' (EC quoted in Samers 2004, 41).

Some member states were eager to speed up the Justice and Home Affairs agenda even further. In May 2005, seven member states of the EU signed a new treaty in the German city of Prüm. The Prüm treaty is also – unofficially – known as 'Schengen III' as there are some striking similarities: it was negotiated outside the EU legal order, among a limited number of member states and deals with 'Justice and Home affairs issues'. Furthermore, information exchange is the dominant theme of the treaty. The preamble states that the treaty seeks to establish 'the highest possible standard of cooperation especially by means of exchange of information, particularly in combating terrorism, cross-border crime and illegal migration' (in Balzacq *et al.* 2006, 1). The treaty outlines the role of (additional) 'document advisors' that are to assist and advise consulates, carriers and host country border control authorities in their task of separating real from false documents and also introduces new procedures for mutual assistance and cooperation among signatory states in matters of repatriation. The treaty seems to rest on the view that 'data exchange will bring greater security to all' and aims to facilitate the exchange of the following types of data: DNA profiles, finger prints, vehicle registration, non-personal and personal data' (Balzacq *et al.* 2006, 13). This adds to, and in many cases doubles with, all kinds of data exchange that are already in effect at the European level, especially the data collection and surveillance equipped by EU migration data systems, such as the SIS, Eurodac and VIS.

Schengen Information System (SIS), SIRENE and SIS II

'Schengen' operates two comprehensive registration and surveillance systems. The first is the Schengen Information System (SIS), a data-based registration and surveillance system. The SIS is in operation, but is also under renegotiation and redevelopment in light of its operability in an enlarged EU of 25. The need to design a SIS II also prompted member states to place new 'wish lists' on the table. The other system, SIRENE which stands for *Supplément d'Information Requis a l'Entrée Nationale*, is twinned with the SIS as an auxiliary or supplementary system.

The SIS is made up of a central database (called C-SIS) that is physically housed in a heavily guarded bunker in Strasbourg and of national SIS-bases (called N-SIS) in all of the Schengen states. Its purpose is to maintain 'public order and security, including State security, and to apply the provisions of this convention relating to the movement of persons, in the territories of the contracting parties, using information transmitted by the system' (article 93 of the Schengen Convention, quoted in Mathiesen 2001, 7). This broadly defined purpose provides the legal base for a large data system that stores information on persons and objects.

There are five categories of persons on whom information may be entered into the SIS. In light of internal surveillance on irregular migrants the entries under article 96, 'persons to be refused entry to the Schengen area as unwanted aliens', are the most important. Of the objects than can be entered into the SIS the most important category is that of lost and stolen 'identity papers', which already in 1998 constituted the largest number of entries. Information on persons that may be stored in the SIS consists of a rather basic and limited set of information: first and last name, known aliases, first letter of the second name, date and place of birth, distinctive physical features, sex and nationality, whether persons are considered to be armed and/or dangerous, reason for the report and action to be taken. Data are entered according to national standards and the national authorities are responsible for their accuracy. Not all authorities have overall access to the system; immigration authorities for example only have access to the data on irregular migrants.

The system is a so-called hit/no hit system: a person is fed into the computer and produces a 'hit' if he or she is listed in the database. Even in the case of a hit, not all information is readily accessible. Rather, the computer 'replies' with a command, such as 'apprehend this person' or 'stop this vehicle' (De Hert 2004, 40). According to the German Interior ministry there were more than 30 000 terminals in the Schengen area on which the SIS can be accessed in 2005.

All in all, the SIS is a rather basic system, with a limited range of options for the user, which is exactly why SIRENE was added. The SIS was not designed for detailed data exchange and in practice it serves as an index to the associated SIRENE system that facilitates the exchange of complementary information, including fingerprints and photographs. Although

SIRENE is often described as the operational core of Schengen, there is no reference to the system in the Schengen Convention (Justice 2002: 19). The factual data are stored on the SIS but the SIRENE system makes it possible to exchange 'softer' data such as criminal intelligence information. In order to make this a 'convenient' arrangement the National SIS and the SIRENE bureaux are in most countries entrusted to the same organization, usually a central police department responsible for international cooperation. It is obligatory to notify the state that made an entry when the SIS produces a hit. After all, this state is responsible for its accuracy and is able to double-check. When it comes to irregular migrants however, the rules are less strict. Hits are only reported in exceptional cases and the standard procedure is to refuse entry (at the border) or to arrest, interrogate and turn over to the authorities responsible for expulsion when detected inside the country (Colvin 2000, 22).

Though the SIS is an instrument intended to maintain 'order and security', its main preoccupation seems to be with illegal immigration (Guild 2001). In 1999, the overwhelming majority of the entries on persons were on 'unwanted aliens to be refused entry to the Schengen countries' (Colvin 2000, 8). The figures on the SIS since 1999 suggest that this still holds true. The total number of entries is increasing at a firm pace: in 2007 the SIS held about 17.6 million entries. Entries on persons in the SIS are not the main contributors to this increase as its yearly averages vary between 800 000 and 900 000 entries. But, as can be seen from the Table 14.1, the entries on irregular migrants (art. 96) in turn do take up the lion's share of the entries on persons.

The hits on irregular migrants are relatively low and recently even dropping. Over the years the hits represent about 3 to 5 per cent of the entries on irregular migrants. The last couple of years about 21 000 irregular migrants annually produce a 'hit' in the SIS, which means that they will be refused entry or a visa or, when they are inside a member state, there may be an information exchange (through SIRENE) to make expulsion possible. Whether or not this actually happens cannot be determined on the basis of these data, and it is unlikely that the authorities keep records of such a nature, or when they do, make them available to the public.

The SIS proved to be a popular instrument. Even the UK, which never acceded to Schengen and negotiated an opt-out for its Acquis when it was incorporated into the EU at Amsterdam, participates in the SIS through a selective opt-in. The rapid growth of the Schengen-group, outside of the EU through association agreements with Norway, Iceland and Switzerland, and the prospect of further enlargement of the EU led to the decision to develop a second generation of the system as early as December 1996. This so-called SIS II should accommodate the new members and facilitate new,

Table 14.1   Selected entries and 'hits' in the SIS, 1999–2007

Year	Entries	Entries on wanted persons	Entries on art 96	Hits on art 96
1999	8 687 950	795 044	703 688	21 711
2000	9 697 252	855 765	764 747	21 170
2001	9 856 732	788 927	701 414	26 363
2002	10 541 120	832 312	732 764	35 856
2003	12 274 875	874 032	775 868	32 856
2004	11 746 847	883 511	785 631	21 957
2005	13 185 566	818 673	714 078	21 090
2006	15 003 283	882 627	751 954	21 836
2007	17 615 495	894 776	752 338	n a

Sources: Bundesministerium des Inneren 2002–2005, House of Lords (2007, 22), CEU 2005 and 2007.

additional functions (de Hert 2004). The system should have been up and running by 2007, but various delays have pushed the date back a number of times. At the time of writing SIS II is still not in operation and recently the Commission announced that its latest scheduled 'end of the test phase' – which was set for September 2009 – will not be met (CEC 2009). In terms of options and functions of the new system the Justice and Home Affairs Council in 2003 made it very clear that SIS II would have to be a 'flexible tool that will be able to adapt to changed circumstances' (CEU 2003, 18).

The prospect of a new generation of the system prompted member states to put forward all kinds of suggestions to increase the possibilities and the use of the system. The Joint Supervisory Authority of Schengen (2004, 14) signalled two major trends. It noted repeated moves to add new categories of information, such as biometric data and a second trend to allow other (new) organizations, such as Europol, access to the data held in the SIS. Many of these proposals amount to a departure from the hit/no hit character of the SIS, making it more of an 'investigative' system. Suggestions to link the SIS II with other European systems are an even bigger step further in the architecture of the European network of databases and some documents even opted to integrate all systems into one European Information System (Brouwer 2004, 5). Uncertainties about the functionalities of the SIS II have been dealt with in a 'flexible manner'. In 2003 the Commission wrote in a communication that, pending the decision by the Council 'SIS II must be designed and prepared for biometric identification to be implemented easily at a later stage, once the legal basis, allowing for the activation of such potential functionalities, has been defined' (CEC 2003,

16). In other words, politics would only have to follow the path laid out by the technology. SIS II will not be a cheap system. Between 2001 and 2006 the European Commission spent about €26 million on the development of the central data base and infrastructure of SIS II. Between 2007 and 2012 the EU budget will be charged a further €114 million to get the system up and running (House of Lords 2007, 15).

Now that the definitive regulation on the establishment, operation and use of the SIS II (EP and CEU 2006) entered into force in January 2007 the additions to and expansions of its functions are clear. Most importantly, the new legislation provides for the inclusion of biometric information into SIS II, more specifically fingerprints and photographic data. In the future it might even be possible for the system to hold DNA profiles and retina scans, but this would require amendments to the legislation (House of Lords 2007, 20, 43). The addition of biometrics makes new searches possible. The data can be searched in two ways. First, in a 'one-to-one' search, using the data to confirm a 'known' person's identity, that is comparing Jim Jones' fingerprints with the fingerprints in the SIS II that are registered to Jim Jones. Second, a 'one-to-many' search, in which the fingerprints of a person are fed into the SIS II to compare them to all stored fingerprints. These broad searches (sweeps) on the basis of biometric data make the SIS a more investigative tool for law enforcers and immigration authorities. In particular, the 'one-to-many' searches cause concern among many observers as these ideally require a very high levels of accuracy of the biometric data (in order to prevent faulty hits). The European Data Protection Supervisor warned in 2006 against a tendency to overestimate the reliability of biometrics and their use as a unique means of identification (see in House of Lords 2007, 21).

The circle of organizations that will have access to new generation of the SIS database has also been significantly widened. Europol and Eurojust have been granted access and the list of national authorities that have access to (parts of) the database also grew longer. Some authorities are described in such general terms that there seems to be ample room for expanding the list of organizations that have access, and for a (wide) variation between member states. In short, moving from the first to the second generation of the system has been much more than a technological affair. The scope, functions and possibilities of the system have changed and with it, its character changed.

Eurodac

A second important European database is the Eurodac system, which is linked to the Dublin II regulation, and its predecessor, the Dublin

Convention. The objective of the Dublin Convention was to curtail the possibilities for 'asylum shopping' – that is, individuals entering into the asylum procedure in more than one country successively – and to determine which state is responsible for an asylum claim. In order to do this the member states devised a system that could determine whether or not an asylum claimant had already lodged an application in another member state. To this end they decided to create a community-wide system for the comparison of fingerprints of asylum claimants named Eurodac (an acronym that stands for *Euro*pean *Dac*tylographic system). The development of the system was a long and politically rocky ride (see Aus 2006 for a detailed analysis). The decision to set up the system may have been taken in 1991, but it would take until January 2003 for the system to become operational. By then, the scope of Eurodac had been significantly widened. Originally it was meant to contain just the prints of asylum seekers, but in 1998 Germany pushed for the inclusion of irregular migrants (Aus 2003, 12). Irregular migrants were already following in the footsteps of asylum seekers as the 'most problematic' group of immigrants. In 1997 the Schengen Executive Committee had concluded, 'that it could be necessary to take the fingerprints of every irregular migrant whose identity could not be established without doubt, and to store this information for the exchange with other member states' (quoted in Brouwer 2002, 235). As the SIS could not accommodate the registration of fingerprints the member states had to look elsewhere. Mathiesen (2001, 18) asserts that the 'history of the issue of fingerprinting "illegal immigrants" shows how Schengen and Eurodac concerns are intertwined'.

Eurodac became operational in January 2003 and started with an empty database. Since this date the database has been 'filled' with three categories of fingerprints. Category 1 comprises the prints of all individuals of 14 years and older who apply for asylum in one of the member states. These are the prints that are necessary to detect cases of 'asylum shopping' in light of the original goal of the Dublin Convention. Category 2 contains the fingerprints of irregular migrants apprehended in connection with the irregular crossing of an external border and who could not be turned back. Category 3 contains the fingerprints of aliens found illegally present in one of the member states. These last prints are checked against categories 1 and 2, but are not stored. Furthermore, the transmission of this category of data is optional, member states can decide for themselves if they want to use this option (CEC 2004). It is especially this category that is an indication for the development of internal control on irregular migrants by means of EU surveillance systems such as Eurodac.

Like the SIS, Eurodac is a hit/no hit system and the database contains only limited information. The data that are taken up in the central database

Table 14.2   Entries and 'hits' in Eurodac (2003–05)

Category	2003		2004		2005		2006	
	Entries	'Hits'	Entries	'Hits'	Entries	'Hits'	Entries	'Hits'
Asylum claimants (cat. 1)	246 902	19 247a	232 205	40 759a	187 223	31 636 a	165 958	27 014a
Aliens crossings the external border irregularly (cat. 2)	7 857	673b	16 183	2 846b	25 163	4 001 b	41 312	6 658b
Aliens found illegally present in a member state (cat. 3)	16 814	1 181c	39 550	7 674c	46 229	11 311 c	63 413	15 612c

Notes:
(a) fingerprints of an asylum seeker sent in by a member state matched against the stored fingerprints of an existing asylum applicant (cat. 1 against cat. 1).
(b) fingerprints of an asylum seeker sent in by a member state were matched against the stored fingerprints of an alien who illegally crossed the external border (cat. 1 against cat. 2).
(c) fingerprints sent in of an alien found illegally present within a member state were matched against the stored fingerprints of an existing asylum applicant (cat. 3 against cat. 1).

Source: CEC 2004, 2005, 2006, 2007.

are, again like the SIS, limited: the member state of origin, place and date of application for asylum, finger print data, sex, reference number used by the member state of origin, date on which the finger prints are taken, and date on which the data were transmitted to the central unit (Brouwer 2002, 237). Eurodac is a relatively cheap system; between 2000 and 2003 the commission spent about €7.5 million. Eurodac has been up and running for 4 years and the commission has published annual reports that provide insight into the growing use and 'effectiveness' of the database.

The Eurodac database filled up rather quickly in its first years of operation. Most of the entries are related to asylum claimants and most of the hits are 'detections' of double (or even multiple) asylum claims filed by one individual (its main function for the Dublin system). More significantly, the number of entries and 'hits' on irregular migrants apprehended inside a member state (cat. 3) are steadily rising as well. The Commission considers the entries in category 2 to be too low when compared with the expectations and calls upon the member states to 'carry out their legal obligations'. Aus (2006, 12), in a less diplomatic phrasing, calls this category 'a near complete failure'.

Some authors (Brouwer 2002, Aus 2003) point to the fact that fingerprinting individuals who were apprehended while crossing the border illegally, is hardly the logical 'thing to do' from the perspective of border states. As this fingerprinting can only have the result that the person concerned, who is later found in another member state, will be sent back to the former member state; one can reasonably doubt if the authorities of the first state will be very willing to execute the Eurodac Regulation' (Brouwer 2002, 244).[1]

Through the use of category 3 data, the Eurodac system is steadily becoming more important for the European 'fight against illegal immigration'. It is primarily northern members states (Germany, the Netherlands, the UK and the Czech Republic) that use this optional category. The number of hits for irregular migrants found inside member states went from 1181 in 2003 to 15612 in 2006. These are fast rising numbers considering that Eurodac contains only asylum data from 2003 onwards which means that only irregular migrants who have a recent asylum history will produce a hit in the system. Many of the irregular migrants currently present in the member states will have an older asylum history – if they have an asylum history at all – and do not show up in a Eurodac search. As the database fills up and holds information from a longer period of time, the number of hits is therefore likely to grow further. The main value of the system for the member states lies in its contribution to expulsion policy, as one of the big bottlenecks in expulsion policy is the lack of information on the identity and country of origin of irregular migrants, without which expulsion is practically impossible. A 'hit' in the Eurodac system can provide a link to a dossier on an asylum application made in another country that will contain information and perhaps documentation on the identity and the country of origin of an irregular migrant that is silent about his identity. In other words, it could 're-identify' him or her (Broeders 2007). Just as the SIS and SIRENE system are used to exchange supplementary information to help make expulsion possible, Eurodac can function in a similar way.

The 'popularity' of the category 3 data among certain member states did not go unnoticed. In June 2007, the Commission published an evaluation of the first three years that the Eurodac system was in operation (CEC 2007) which emphasized the future possibilities of this specific category of data. The high use of this category led the Commission to propose that the data on irregular migrants found in member states should in the future also be *stored* in the database, instead of just checked against the data stored under the categories 1 and 2. This takes Eurodac another step into the direction of being a database on irregular migrants in addition to an asylum related database. Furthermore, the Commission intends to explore the possibilities 'to extend the scope of Eurodac with a view to use its data for law enforcement purposes and as a means to contribute to the fight against illegal immigration' (CEC 2007, 11). In short, Eurodac's future is likely to become a textbook example of 'function creep'.

Visa Information System

From the perspective of 'the fight against illegal immigration', the Visa Information System (VIS) is the next logical step in the emergent network of databases. In general, irregular migrants have three possible 'migration histories'. They either crossed the border illegally (with or without help), they were asylum seekers and stayed after the claim was rejected or they came on a legal visa and stayed after its validity expired. The network of databases develops accordingly. Irregular immigration itself defies registration, but irregular migrants found in member states can be registered in the SIS II, and in the future perhaps also in Eurodac. Those who enter through asylum procedures will be registered in Eurodac and those who enter on a legal visa will, in the future, be registered by the VIS. Control over identity has taken a central place in much EU discussion on (illegal) immigration, terrorism and the (perceived) 'links' between them. According to Guild (2003) this emphasis on identity control has elevated visas to the prime, and in the eyes of the member states, most trustworthy method of identification of third country nationals: 'Documents issued by non-member states are no longer definitive for determining identity. [. . .]

The Union takes over the task of identifying all persons who seek to come to the Union and determines where they belong' (Guild 2003, 344). Under the heading of 'measures to combat illegal immigration' the European Council conclusions of Seville (June 2002) called for 'the introduction, as soon as possible, of a common identification system for visa data' (CEU 2002, 8). This new system became the Visa Information System that is currently being developed.

In December 2004, the Commission presented a proposal for a regulation on the VIS to the Council and the European Parliament (CEC 2004b) which was amended and finally adopted by the Council and the European Parliament in June 2007 (CEU 2007). With regard to the use of this latest database in 'the fight against illegal immigration' the phrasing has become more diplomatic, but the substance remains the same. In 2004 the VIS was 'to assist in the identification and return of illegal immigrants', while in 2007 it is to 'assist in the identification of any person who may not, or may no longer fulfil the conditions for entry, stay or residence of the territory of the member states'. The central importance of the system is for visa and immigration policy, but for the purpose of internal surveillance on irregular migrants the VIS can serve as an instrument to detect and identify them when found and apprehended on the territory of member states. It will make it possible to identify those irregular migrants that travelled into the EU legally at any border, and then 'overstayed'. Once identified, the system can facilitate the provision of travel documents for undocumented illegal residents, on the basis of the exchange of information through the VIS (Samers 2004). In this way the VIS will also function as a system of re-identification for illegal aliens that travelled legally into the EU, but try to hide their identity when apprehended.

The VIS is a very ambitious project and requires a technically powerful system. On the basis of its feasibility study on the VIS the Commission aimed for a system with a capacity to connect at least 27 member states, 12 000 VIS users and 3500 consular posts worldwide. This was based on the estimation that the member states would handle 20 million visa requests annually (CEC 2003, 26). In 2007, the press release accompanying the political agreement on the adoption of the VIS regulation stated that the VIS will store 'data on up to 70 million people'. The technical set-up of the system is an exact mirror of the SIS II. Just like the SIS, the new visa system will have a central database (C-VIS), an interface at the national level (N-VIS) and local access points (terminals) for the police, immigration authorities and consular posts. The magic words in the development of SIS II and the VIS are 'interoperability' and 'synergy'. The systems are 'sharing' in the development costs and more importantly they will 'share a common technological platform' so that the systems are compatible, interoperable and able to cross-reference, couple and maybe even exchange information. The database themselves will remain separate (containers), but at the functional level SIS users can (will? must?) have their entries and queries checked against the VIS database and vice versa.

The central systems of the VIS and the SIS will even be direct neighbours in a physical and geographical sense, as they are to be 'hosted in the same location', which means they will both be housed in the SIS bunker in Strasbourg. The political wish of an increased interoperability also includes the Eurodac system, as was clearly set out in the so-called 'The Hague Programme', which is the agenda for the next five years for EU-policies on Justice and Home Affairs the council agreed upon in 2005. Article 1.7.2 of this new agenda calls for maximization of the 'effectiveness and interoperability of EU information systems in tackling illegal immigration' and specifically names Eurodac alongside the SIS II and the VIS (CEU 2005, see also CEC 2005c). As with the SIS (II) the European Council already proposed to grant 'internal security authorities' access to the system. This new example of function creep caused the European Data Protection Supervisor (EDPS, 2006, 2) to remind the member states that the VIS was developed in 'view of the European visa policy, not as a law enforcement tool'.

As with Eurodac the member states agreed that the VIS should start with an empty database. The data to be stored in the VIS have a broad scope. In the first place there are the so-called alphanumeric data on the applicant (a digital version of the application form); data on visas requested, issued, refused, annulled revoked or extended. The alphanumeric information also includes the details of the person or company that issued an invitation or is liable for the cost of living during the stay. This means that the family members and companies that 'vouch for' the visa-recipient – and who may be held accountable should he or she overstay the visa – are also registered. For these groups registration by 'panopticon Europe' may well have a direct disciplining effect. Second, the system will include biometric data: each applicant will be fingerprinted for all ten fingers and will have their photo entered intro the VIS. This will make the VIS the largest ten fingerprint system in the world. The use of biometrics on such an unprecedented scale will bring the system, according to a 2003 feasibility study by the Commission, into a new and largely unknown dimension, both technically and financially (CEC 2003, 26). In the best scenario (optimal synergy with the SIS II) and including biometrics and supporting documents the development investment will amount to almost €157 million and the annual operating costs will be around €35 million CEC 2003, 29–30). The commission intends to make the VIS operational by the spring of 2009 (CEU 2007, 3).

14.4   CONCLUSIONS

The EU's 'fight against illegal immigration' is being equipped with state of the art database technology. The analysis of the SIS, Eurodac and the VIS shows that these systems (will) operate on an unprecedented scale that is likely to grow even further as a result of technological advancements and the political desire to increase the 'interoperability' of the systems. The analysis also shows that the mere existence of the data stored in these systems tempts policy makers to use them for goals other than for which they were originally constructed. This so-called 'function creep' or 'surveillance creep' is certainly not an imaginary fear. Steps towards linking the various databases have been taken and have not met with substantial resistance. Eurodac's goals have been significantly 'broadened' along the way. This system may be become just as important for the internal control on irregular migrants as it is for the prevention of 'asylum shopping' for which it was devised. The second generation of the SIS will include biometric identifiers and the VIS will even become the largest 'ten finger print' database in the world. Furthermore, all of the systems have been 'opened up' to new organizations that were originally kept out for a reason. In particular, law enforcement agencies and authorities dealing with the fight against terrorism have been added to the lists of organizations that can access (parts) of the databases.

If the domestic part of 'the fight against illegal immigration' is understood as a matter of tracing, identifying, sorting and, ultimately, the exclusion and expulsion of irregular migrants, then the network of databases is an impressive tool indeed. The amount of data stored on potential irregular migrants is enormous and is set to grow at great speed as the Eurodac database fills up and the VIS and the SIS II will go online. Torpey's notion that the state first has to embrace society if it aims to penetrate and control it effectively has most certainly been adhered to. If anything it is a massive effort to embrace. These European databases seek to register as many immigrants from 'suspect' legal categories (asylum) and 'suspect' countries of origin (visa) as possible, in order to get at the percentage of immigrants that crosses the line into irregularity at a later stage. These systems can be used to re-identify irregular migrants that try to conceal their identity in order to avoid expulsion. In this way the 'identity routes' of asylum and visa may get cut off which might in turn provoke the side effect of an increasing dependence of irregular migrants on smuggling and trafficking organizations (Broeders and Engbersen 2007).

The databases will provide the infrastructure that states need for the detection and exclusion of irregular migrants 'at home'. When it comes to irregular resident migrants, they are basically European tools for a domestic problem. That is also clear from the differences in the use of Eurodac in its first years of operation: member states that regard irregular migrants as a serious domestic problem use the system heavily for detection and identification, while member states that that are relatively unconcerned about the presence of irregular migrants on their territory do not actively use the system. For those member states that are serious about the exclusion of irregular migrants, SIS, VIS and Eurodac are instruments to put both of the 'logics of exclusion' set out in this paper into operation. For example, the VIS will also register companies and family members that vouch for the applicant which may have a disciplining effect on their willingness to act as guarantor. Here, registration is aimed at the networks irregular migrants need for travel and residence and follows the logic of exclusion *from* documentation. But the real value of these new systems is for the second logic of exclusion, that of exclusion *through* documentation and registration. The migration databases are massive efforts to identify irregular migrants themselves in their capacity as an irregular migrant, that is, confirming at the same time their irregular status and (re-)affirming their legal identity (that they usually try to hide). As identification and exclusion are two sides of the same coin in modern constitutional states the second logic becomes more dominant, as can be observed from the way (the functions and possibilities of) the databases develop over time – most of them even before they become operational. The inclusion of more information in the system that can link an irregular migrant with formal documentation (visa application, request for asylum) and the overall application of biometric identifiers to make the link as 'watertight' as possible, illustrates the European preoccupation with identification of irregular migrants, especially in some of the northern member states.

However, much will depend on the day-to-day use of these systems in the affairs of police, immigration officers and other authorities that have access to them. Are the already limited points of access to work, welfare and other institutions for irregular migrants being curtailed further on account of these information systems? Does, or will, the number of expulsions of irregular migrants rise because the information in the systems can re-identify and re-document undocumented aliens? These are not unanswerable questions on the basis of the available information. Moreover, all systems are at the beginning of their (new) lifespan: VIS and SIS II are not operational yet and Eurodac has only been in operation for three years. It is still hard to determine what their impact may become. But if Michael Mann's claim (in Torpey 2000, 37) that the 'unusual strength of modern state is infrastructural' is true, then the EU is currently laying the foundations for an impressive digital infrastructure aimed at identification and exclusion.

NOTE

1. Aus (2006, 12) points out that even though the overwhelming majority of the entries in category 2 are from the southern border states Greece, Italy and Spain, the interesting thing is not their high share but the overall low volume of data transmitted to Eurodac. Furthermore, the problem of late transmission of data to Eurodac is also primarily caused by the Greek and Italian authorities, a logical and convenient delay from their national perspective because queries on transit migrants found in other member states do not yield results as long as they are not registered in Eurodac.

REFERENCES

Aus, J. (2003), 'Supranational governance in an "area of freedom, security and justice": Eurodac and the politics of biometric control', DEI working paper 72, Sussex European Institute, accessed at www.sussex.ac.uk/sei/documents/wp72. pdf/.

Aus, J. (2006), 'Eurodac: a solution looking for a problem?', *European Integration Online Papers*, **10** (6), accessed at http://eiop.or.at/eiop/index.php/eiop/article/view/2006_006a/23/.

Balzacq, T., D. Bigo, S. Carrera and E. Guild (2006), 'Security and the two–level game: the treaty of Prüm, the EU and the management of threats', CEPS working document 234.

Bauman, Z. (1998), *Globalization. The Human Consequences*, Cambridge: Polity Press.

Broeders, D. (2007) 'The new digital borders of Europe. EU databases and the surveillance of irregular migrants', *International Sociology*, **22** (1), 71–92.

Broeders, D. (2009), 'Add a little Europe for extra national strength? The Europeanization of justice and home affairs', in W. Schinkel (ed.), *Globalization and the State. Sociological Perspectives on the State of the State*, Houndsmills, Basingstoke: Palgrave, pp. 121–43.

Broeders, D. and G. Engbersen (2007), 'The fight against illegal migration: identification policies and immigrants' counter strategies', *American Behavioral Scientist*, **50** (12) 1592–609.

Brouwer, E. (2002), 'Eurodac: its limitations and temptations', *European Journal of Migration and Law*, 4, 231–47.

Brouwer, E. (2004), 'Persoonsregistraties als grensbewaking: Europese ontwikkelingen inzake het gebruik van informatiesystemen en de toepassing van biometrie', *Privacy & Informatie*, 2.

Bundesminsterium des Inneren (2002), *Schengen Erfahrungsbericht 2001*, Berlin: Bundesminsterium des Inneren.

Bundesminsterium des Inneren (2003), *Schengen Erfahrungsbericht 2002*, Berlin: Bundesminsterium des Inneren.

Bundesminsterium des Inneren (2004), *Schengen Erfahrungsbericht 2003*, Berlin: Bundesminsterium des Inneren.

Bundesminsterium des Inneren (2005), *Schengen Erfahrungsbericht 2004*, Berlin: Bundesminsterium des Inneren.

Cholewinski, R. (2004), 'EU policy on irregular migration: human rights lost.', in B. Bogusz, R. Cholewisnki, A. Cygan and E. Szyszczak (eds), *Irregular Migration and Human Rights: Theoretical, European and International Perspectives*, Leiden, the Netherlands and Boston, MA: Martinus Nijhoff Publishers.

Commission of the European Communities (2003), 'Communication from the Commission to the Council and the European Parliament. Development of the Schengen Information System II and possible synergies with a future Visa Information System (VIS)', COM (2003) 771 final, Brussels, 11.12.2003.

Commission of the European Communities (2004a), 'First annual report to the Council and the European Parliament on the activities of the EURODAC Central Unit', Commission staff working paper, SEC (2004), 557, Brussels, 5.5.2004.

Commission of the European Communities (2004b), 'Proposal for a regulation of the European Parliament and of the Council concerning the Visa Information System (VIS) and the exchange of data between Member States on short stay–visas', COM (2004), 835 final, Brussels, 28.12.2004.

Commission of the European Communities (2005a), 'Second annual report to the Council and the European Parliament on the activities of the EURODAC Central Unit', Commission staff working paper, SEC (2005), 839, Brussels, 20.6.2005.

Commission of the European Communities (2005b), 'Communication from the Commission to the Council and the European Parliament on the improved effectiveness, enhanced interoperability and synergies among European data-bases in the area of justice and home affairs', COM (2005), 597 final, Brussels, 24.11.2005.

Commission of the European Communities (2006), 'Third annual report to the Council and the European Parliament on the activities of the EURODAC Central Unit', Commission staff working document, SEC (2006), 1170, Brussels, 15.9.2006.

Commission of the European Communities (2007), 'Report from the Commission to the European Parliament and the Council on the evaluation of the Dublin system', COM (2007) 299 final, Brussels, 6.6.2007.

Commission of the European Communities (2009), 'Report from the Commission to the Council and the European Parliament on the development of the Second generation of the Schengen Information System (SIS II)', progress report, July 2008 – December 2008, COM (2009) 133 final, 24 March, Brussels.

Cornelius, W., T. Tsuda, P. Martin and J. Hollifield (eds) (2004), *Controlling Immigration: A Global Perspective.* 2nd edn, Stanford, CA: Stanford University Press.

Council of the European Union (2002), 'Presidency Conclusions, Seville European Council', 21–22 June 2002 (SN 200/02).

Council of the European Union (2003), '2514th Council meeting justice and home affairs', Luxembourg, 5–6 June 2003, 9845/03 (Presse 150).

Council of the European Union (2005), 'The Hague Programme: strengthening freedom, security and justice in the European Union', *Official Journal of the European Union*, C53/1, 3 March.

Council of the European Union (2007), 'Interinstitutional file: 2004/0287 (COD), 9753/07', Brussels, 19.6.2007

European Parliament and Council of the European Union (2006), 'Regulation (EC) no 1987/2006 of The European Parliament and of the Council of 20 December 2006 on the establishment, operation and use of the second generation Schengen Information System (SIS II)', *Official Journal of the European Union*, **381** (4).

EDPS (2006), 'Opinion of the European Data Protection Supervisor', Brussels, 20 January 2006.

Engbersen, G. (2001) 'The unanticipated consequences of panopticon Europe: residence strategies of illegal immigrants', in V. Guiraudon and C. Joppke (eds), *Controlling a New Migration World*, London: Routledge, pp. 222–46.

Engbersen, G. (2004), 'The wall around the welfare state in Europe: international migration and social exclusion', *The Indian Journal of Labour Economics*, **46** (3) 479–95.

Foucault, M. (1977), *Discipline and Punish: The Birth of the Prison*, London: Peregrine Books.

Guild, E. (2001), 'Moving the borders of Europe', inaugural lecture, University of Nijmegen.

Guild, E. (2003), 'International terrorism and EU immigration, asylum and borders policy: the unexpected victims of 11 September 2001', *European Foreign Affairs Review*, 8, 331–46

Guiraudon, V. (2001), 'De-nationalizing control: Analysing state responses to restraints on migration control', in V. Guiraudon and C. Joppke (eds), *Controlling a New Migration World*, London: Routledge, pp. 29–64.

Hert, P. de (2004), 'Trends in de Europese politiële en justitiële informatiesamen-werking', *Panopticon*, **25** (1/2).

House of Lords (2007), 'Schengen Information System II (SIS II), Report with evidence, 9th Report of Session 2006–7 of the House of Lords' European Union Committee', London: The Stationery Office Limited.

Jesuit Refugee Service (2005), 'Detention in Europe: administrative detention of asylum–seekers and irregular migrants', Brussels: Jesuit Refugee Service (JRS) – Europe, accessed at www.detention–in–europe.org.

Joint Supervisory Authority of Schengen (2004), 'Activities of the Joint Supervisory Authority. Sixth report January 2002/December 2003', accessed at www.schen-gen–jsa.dataprotection.org/.

Colvin, M. (2000), *The Schengen Information System: A Human Rights Audit*, London: Justice.

Lahav, G. and V. Guiraudon (2000), 'Comparative perspectives on border control: away from the border and outside the state', in P. Andreas and T. Snyder (eds), *The Wall Around the West: State Borders and Immigration Controls in North America and Europe*, Lanham, MD: Rowman and Littlefield, pp. 55–77.

Leun, J. van der (2003), *Looking for Loopholes: Processes of Incorporation of Illegal Immigrants in the Netherlands*, Amsterdam: Amsterdam University Press.

Levinson, A. (2005), *The Regularization of Unauthorized Migrants: Literature Survey and Country Case Studies*, Oxford: Centre on Migration, Policy and Society, University of Oxford.

Lyon, D. (2004), 'Globalizing surveillance: comparative and sociological perspectives', *International Sociology*, **19** (2), 135–49.

Mathiesen, T. (2001), 'On globalization of control: towards an integrated surveillance system in Europe. Social change and crime in the Scandinavian and Baltic region', *Rapport från NSFKS*, 43, accessed at www.nsfk.org/downloads/seminarreports/researchsem_no43.pdf/.

Mitsilegas, V., J. Monar and W. Rees (2003), *The European Union and Internal Security: Guardian of the People?*, Basingstoke: Palgrave.

Samers, M. (2004), 'An emerging geopolitics of "illegal" immigration in the European Union', *European Journal of Migration and Law*, **6** (1), 27–45.

Scott, J. (1998), *Seeing like a State. How Certain Schemes to Improve the Human Condition have Failed*, New Haven, CT: Yale University Press.

Tapinos, G. (2000), 'Irregular migration: economic and political issues', in OECD (ed.), *Combating the Illegal Employment of Foreign Workers*, Paris: OECD.

Torpey, J. (1998), 'Coming and going: on the state monopolization of the legitimate "'means of movement'", *Sociological Theory*, **16** (3), 239–59.

Torpey, J. (2000), 'States and the regulation of migration in the twentieth-century North Atlantic World', in P. Andreas and T. Snyder (eds), *The Wall Around the West: State Borders and Immigration Controls in North America and Europe*, Lanham, MD: Rowman and Littlefield, pp. 31–54.

Welch, M. and L. Schuster (2005), 'Detention of asylum seekers in the US, UK, France, Germany and Italy: a critical view of the globalizing culture of control', *Criminal Justice*, **5** (4), 331–55.

Zolberg, A. (2003), 'Guarding the gates', accessed at www.newschool.edu/icmec/guardingthegates.html/.

15. Recent tendencies in immigration control policies in Europe: undermining legal safeguards and refugee protection?

Bente Puntervold Bø

15.1 INTRODUCTION

The trends in the development of immigration control policies in Europe seem to undermine legal safeguards and the right to seek protection against persecution. Some of the changes and developments referred to have occurred during the past 20 years, others are newly adopted by the EU member states. In particular, the following tendencies in the development of control policies aimed at immigrants and refugees, will be described and discussed in this chapter: Limitation of access; externalization of formerly domestic control procedures; de-professionalization of control regimes; criminalization of asylum seekers; regionalization of protection; and the limitation of the scope of refugee protection due to Europeanization of asylum policies. The chapter takes examples from Norway in the context of European developments.

15.2 THE LIMITATION OF ACCESS

As this chapter will demonstrate, the question of access to states where the application for protection will be examined, is the key issue in present-day asylum policies in western countries. From the late 1980s, western European states have tightened their asylum regimes and tried to limit refugees' possibilities of seeking asylum in their countries. This has been done by introducing visa requirements to all 'refugee producing states': The European Union has made a list of approximately 100 states, including many countries with well-documented human rights abuses, the nationals of which are required to have a visa to enter EU territory (UNHCR 2004, 255): the visa list is mandatory for all EU/Schengen member states. The visa requirement is further supplemented by a rejection policy; applicants whom the authorities assume might be potential asylum seekers get their visa applications turned down (Bø 2002, 358). The Norwegian Ministry of Justice stated bluntly that 'If a visa is applied for reasons of persecution, such grounds fall outside the scope of a visitor's visa. Asylum applicants do not have a right to be granted a visa, since the right to asylum is limited to those applicants who are already situated in the country' (Ot.prp.nr. 46 (1986-87), 116). Similar policies are practised by all western European states: It is stated explicitly in domestic legislation that asylum seekers must be present in the country in question (or at its borders), to have their asylum claims considered, at the same time the authorities (Bø 2002, 358) state, as we have seen in the citation above, that no visa is granted to persons who are assumed to be in need of protection. Legal border crossing is, in other words, not an option for asylum seekers.

To prevent the arrival of asylum seekers without the proper visa stamps in their passports, airlines and shipping companies carry out control of documents in the country of departure and are held responsible for the validity of the passengers' travel documents. The Schengen states have amended their immigration acts with provisions which give the authorities the right to fine the transporters that bring a foreign national without valid travel documents into the country. Police officers from the destination countries also control passports and visa stamps at the international airports most frequently used by asylum seekers to get access to the asylum determination procedures in Europe (UNHCR 2004, 257–8).

Since a visa is demanded for border crossing, but not granted to persons who are assumed to be refugees, border crossing with false documents or by the use of human smugglers, is the only available way for asylum seekers to reach the territory of states where their claims for protection may be examined. That this situation poses a moral dilemma is recognized by the destination countries, but the control of the 'refugee flow' is nevertheless given the highest priority: 'It may be a moral dilemma that the entry of potential asylum seekers is prevented through the use of visa policies. One has, on the other hand, not found that Norway should limit its possibilities to regulate the arrival of foreign nationals who claim to be refugees in order to gain residence in the country' (Ot.prp.nr.46 (1986-87):116). Norway, like the other would-be states of asylum, has introduced laws and regulations to block the access to the asylum determination procedures in their countries; as a result asylum seekers are forced to make unauthorized border crossings to have their protection claims examined.

While barriers between countries and continents are reduced to promote commerce, tourism and labour market exchange, 'Fortress Europe' has proven itself to be a reality for asylum seekers and refugees. It raises serious concerns that these barriers to refugee protection are initiated by the same states which are the signatories of the 1951 Refugee Convention. The former UN High Commissioner for Refugees, Sadako Ogata, said before she left office in 2002 that, 'Many countries are blatantly closing their borders to refugees while others are more insidiously introducing laws and procedures which effectively deny refugees admission to their territory.' She also said that, 'The threat to asylum has taken on a global character' (Cited from Crisp 2003, 4).

The European Commission writes that: 'The question of access to territory is indeed key to any asylum process' (UNHCR 2001, para 8). There is no doubt that the most important topic in refugee policy today concerns access to states where asylum may be claimed. In spite of ever more sophisticated measures of migration control by the European states (see also Chapter 14), many asylum seekers manage to circumvent these barriers and continue to arrive on European shores and territory. A rising number of asylum applications is taken as evidence of too liberal access policies by the public and politicians alike; while asylum advocates point to the fact that the present immigration control regimes are forcing victims of persecution to risk their lives trying to avoid armed guards crossing state borders or oceans, in order to reach the 'safe' countries of Europe. Governments have a tendency to define 'the refugee problem' as a problem of control with 'undocumented' arrivals, ignoring the fact that the refugee protection regime is undermined when asylum seekers are treated as illegal immigrants. This 'criminalization' of asylum seekers serves as a legitimation of further restrictive measures.

Head of the Evaluation and Policy Analysis Unit at the Office of the High Commissioner for Refugees (UNHCR) in Geneva, Jeff Crisp, writes that:

> We should not imagine that there was ever a golden age of asylum. States and other actors have always been prepared to violate the laws and norms of refugee protection when it suited them to do so . . . The past three decades have witnessed a declining willingness on the part of states to admit refugees into their territory, to allow them to remain there, and to provide them with the rights to which they are entitled under international refugee law. (Crisp 2003, 4)

15.3 ENTRY CONTROLS ARE IMPLEMENTED IN THE COUNTRY OF DEPARTURE

As already mentioned, a visa is required but not granted to applicants who are assumed to intend to claim asylum upon arrival in Europe (Ot. prp.nr.46(1986-87), 116). To prevent the arrival of individuals without the proper visa stamps in their passports, control of documents required for border crossing, is now, to a great extent, carried out in the country of departure. Entry controls have in other words been geographically moved from the borders of the destination countries to the countries of departure. This transfer of entry controls to the country of departure is an essential move by the European states to avoid the legal responsibility of processing a great number of refugee claims. Norway has, like most other countries in Europe, explicitly stated in its national legislation that asylum can only be claimed by applicants who are physically present on its territory or at its borders (Article 11 Norwegian Immigration Act of 1988).

The usual international practice for state authorities has been to control travel documents at border crossings and to deny entry to foreigners whose documents are not in order. Formerly, Norwegian laws did not permit any other practice, until legislation was enacted in 1988 to legalize police controls implemented on foreign soil (Fisknes 1994, 235): 'The King may by regulations confer upon the police the authority to demand passports and other travel documents from foreign nationals before entry into the realm and also to order the captain of a ship or aircraft to check that passengers have valid travel documents' (Article 23.3 of the 1988 Norwegian Immigration Act). Since then, police authorities from Norway and most other European countries have extended their practice to include the control of travel documents in a number of foreign countries. According to information to the author from the Norwegian Ministry of Foreign Affairs, Norwegian police officers are at present stationed in 12 different countries in the Middle East, Africa and Asia (year 2007).

These police officers undertake controls of travel documents at foreign airports, in order to make sure that the passengers' passports and visas are valid. Travellers with questionable passports or identities are denied passage and refused entry into the aircraft, whether or not they have valid airline tickets. The denial of passage may also include travellers who intend to claim asylum upon arrival because of persecution in their home country.

Another example of entry controls in the country of departure are 'visa attache' positions which have been created at a number of Norwegian embassies for controlling functions related to processing visa and other entry permits, in order to apply a restrictive visa policy. In this way, entry controls are most effectively moved to countries of departure. The first consulate with these specific control functions was established in Islamabad in Pakistan in 1977. Since then, every Pakistani who wants to enter Norway, either as a tourist, to visit relatives or due to family re-unification, must personally visit the Norwegian embassy in Islamabad for control of documents and identity. For many, this involves great extra costs and several days of travel. On occasion, the visa attache makes control trips to the applicant's village to verify the information. In recent years, visa attaché' positions have been established at Norwegian consulates in 11 different countries in Asia, Africa and the Middle East, countries from where many of the work migrants and refugees originate (information from the Ministry of Foreign Affairs to the author, July 2007). Other European countries have made similar arrangements at their consulates in 'refugee producing countries'.

Why is it Problematic that Entry Control is Undertaken in the Country of Departure?

The right to leave one's country may be undermined when entry control is undertaken in the country of departure. The individual's right to leave his or her country, may easily be undermined. This right is proclaimed in Article 13(2) of the 1948 Universal Declaration of Human Rights of 1948: 'Every person has the right to leave any country including one's own.' This moral right to leave has its legal counterpart in international law: Article 12(2) of the International Covenant on Civil and Political Rights states that 'Everyone shall be free to leave any country, including his own.' Article 2(2), Protocol No. 4 of the European Convention of Human Rights has a similar formulation: 'Everyone has the right to leave any country, including his own.' In order to seek protection from persecution in another state, it follows that asylum seekers must be able to leave their countries.

When immigration control procedures are carried out in the country of departure, persons without the proper visa stamps demanded for entry into another state, or if the identity of the passenger is questioned, will not be let aboard in planes and ships bound for other countries. This will particularly affect asylum seekers trying to escape persecution in their homeland. The blocking of access to international transportation in order to leave one's country, does not seem to comply with states' moral obligations to respect Article 13 of the Universal Declaration of Human Rights nor the legal obligations referred to above. Professor of International Law, Gregor Noll, states explicitly that prevention of immigration is 'violative of international law' (Noll 2003, 2). In the control procedures referred to here, the 'right to leave' is not prevented by the native authorities, which was previously the case when Russian or Chinese citizens were not allowed to leave their countries, but by representatives of the state of (desired) destination operating in the country of departure. Richmond described this control regime in 1994 as one of 'global apartheid': 'Networks of visa restrictions, carrier sanctions and extra-territorial controls have effectively created a system of 'global apartheid' (Richmond 1994). Bauman writes that this new immigration control system protects the 'extraterritoriality of the new global elite and the forced territoriality of the rest' (Bauman 2005).

The right to seek protection against persecution is a recognized human right, articulated in Article 14 of the Universal Declaration of Human Rights: 'Everyone has the right to seek and enjoy protection against persecution'. By denying legal access to the asylum determination procedures for persons seeking protection, the European states violate the norms of Article 14 of the Universal Declaration of Human Rights. The legal right to seek asylum is, as already mentioned, limited by domestic legislation to those already present at the territory of the state where protection is sought. Another question is whether the ratifying states of the Refugee Convention, as argued below, are 'faithful to the intention of the signatory parties,' when they use their lawmaking capacity to block the access to their territories for would-be refugees.

The signatory states of the 1951 UN Refugee Convention have been binding themselves to protect refugees. When individuals who are persecuted in their own countries are denied entry to enter ships and planes, due to lack of valid passports and visas, their escape from persecution is blocked by agents acting on instructions by the same governments which have signed and ratified the Refugee Convention. It is admitted by these governments that visa requirements to 'asylum producing countries' aim at reducing the number of asylum seekers arriving at their territory. It is reasonable to ask whether control measures which are introduced intentionally by the signatory states to prevent the arrival of asylum seekers, are in accordance with the treaty obligations of the Refugee Convention? According to the 1969 Vienna Convention on the Law of Treaties, treaties are binding upon the parties and are to be 'interpreted in good faith in accordance with the ordinary meaning to be given to the terms of the treaty, in their context and in light of its object and purpose' (Article 31(1)). Karin Landgren writes that: 'Good faith implies the requirement to remain faithful to the intention of the parties without defeating it by literal interpretation or destroying the object and purpose of the treaty' (Landgren 1999, 4). When refugees are denied access to an escape route from their homeland by representatives of the countries to which they want to flee, it is difficult to see that the ratifying states are acting in accordance with the 'spirit and purpose' of the Refugee Convention.

When asylum seekers arrive at the Norwegian border, they may not, according to Norwegian law, be dismissed without having their claim for asylum investigated by the immigration authorities (Article 17 of the Norwegian Immigration Act: 'Refugees in the country and at the border have a right to apply for asylum'). It is also a legally binding human right obligation of the state to examine claims for protection against persecution before an asylum seeker is forced to leave the country, in order to protect individuals against exposure to torture and loss of freedom in the country to which they are being returned. This so-called non-refoulement principle is stated explicitly in Article 33 of the Refugee Convention: A refugee shall not be sent back to a country 'where his or her life or freedom would be threatened'. This duty of the states to protect individuals, regardless of citizenship, against torture, mistreatment and loss of freedom, is formulated in a series of binding human rights instruments like the 1950 European Convention of Human Rights (Article 2: Right to life and Article 3: Prohibition of torture), and in the International Covenant on Civil and Political Rights (Article 7: Prohibition against torture: 'No one shall be subjected to torture or to cruel, inhuman or degrading treatment or punishment').

There is also a non-refoulement provision in Article 3 of the 'Convention against Torture and other Cruel, Inhuman or Degrading Treatment or Punishment' (CAT). It is worth noting that in the CAT-treaty, the non-refoulement provision is absolute and operates without qualifications. This means that the protection against non-refoulement is not limited to persons who have been recognized as refugees to be applicable. These human rights instruments demonstrate state authorities' legal obligations to abstain from torture and cruel treatment of citizens and non-citizens alike, and their duty to prevent expulsion of individuals to torture, punishment and loss of freedom carried out by other states. In order to observe these binding human rights laws, states must investigate claims for protection against persecution before the claimant is returned against his/her will to the country of origin or to some other country from where such return may take place.

As mentioned above, Norwegian police officers may carry out control of passports and visas at international airports abroad (Article 23.3 of the Norwegian Immigration Act). Such extra-territorial control procedures are primarily carried out in so-called 'refugee producing countries'. Similar control functions are carried out by the police forces of other EU/Schengen states as well. Passengers without the required documents, or passengers whose identity is being questioned, will not be allowed to board the plane. The rejection of passengers without valid travel documents will include passengers who claim to be asylum seekers.

Norwegian police serving at foreign airports, or aircraft personel acting under Norwegian law, may contact the national police at these airports when a passenger has a falsified visa-permit in his/her passport or uses the passport of another person (a routine procedure according to the airlines, stated in interview with the author). In such cases, individuals who are fleeing persecution from the authorities in their own country risk being handed over to their persecutors by Norwegian authorities (or by airline companies required by law to carry out such controls).

This practice raises the following question: Do Norwegian authorities operating in foreign countries have the same legal duty not to return people to risks of persecution, as they would have had if they were operating on Norwegian territory? The extraterritorial responsibility of the ratifying states under the European Convention of Human Rights had already been recognized in 1965, when the European Commission on Human Rights concluded that Germany was responsible for actions by its consular personel in Morocco (Guild 2007, 18). The right to life proclaimed in Article 2 and the prohibition on torture, inhuman or degrading treatment in Article 3 of the ECHR protects the individual against refoulement and place a corresponding duty on the state: no individual must be sent to a destination or placed at the disposal of another state where there is a serious risk that he or she will suffer torture or inhuman treatment.

It is therefore reasonable to ask whether police officers, who are carrying out immigration control procedures in foreign airports on behalf of Norwegian authorities, may disregard claims for asylum without examination from insufficiently documented passengers, without acting in conflict with this principle of non-refoulement? Asylum claims disregarded without closer examination, may include cases, which the same authorities would have granted refugee status had the case been presented at Norwegian territory. According to the statements referred to above, states are obliged to respect the non-refoulement prohibition when their agents operate on foreign soil as well as in their home countries. Erica Feller, legal adviser at UNHCR, states clearly that: 'The principle of non-refoulement does not imply any geographical limitation, but extends to all states' agents acting in an official capacity whether or not outside the national territory' (Feller 1989).

The prohibition against refoulement applies to airline personnel as well, when they act to meet the requirements of the Norwegian or other European immigration authorities, and deny boarding to passengers without the valid visa stamps in their passports if these passengers claim to be persecuted in their home country. It is not disputed that parties to the human rights conventions referred to above, must respect the principle of non-refoulement within as well as outside their national borders (Fernhout 2006). It takes, on the other hand, a court trial to determine when a rejected and unexamined claim for protection may be defined as a case of refoulement. To my knowledge, the European Court in Strasbourg has not yet considered such a case, which is regrettable and most needed to prevent the evasion of this most important principle of refugee protection.

15.4   IMMIGRATION CONTROL IS DE-PROFESSIONALIZED: CIVIL AGENTS ARE GIVEN IMMIGRATION CONTROL FUNCTIONS

The enforcement of immigration control policies is increasingly subcontracted to private actors. In several of his books, Thomas Mathiesen describes how organizations in civil society are required to undertake police functions. Private guards and watchmen are examples of this phenomenon (Falch and Mathiesen 1981). It appears that de-professionalized control practices are particularly prominent in the policies governing immigration.

In the Norwegian Immigration Act of 1988, civil organizations were for the first time given the right and duty to exercise immigration control tasks. Article 23 of that law requires airline and shipping companies that transport people from foreign soil to Norway, to ensure that passengers have valid passports and visas before entering the airplane or ship: 'The King can issue regulations that require operators of airplanes and ships to undertake controls to ensure that all of their passengers have valid travel documents.' The draft of a new immigration act to replace the 1988 law, has similar formulations (Ot.prp.nr.75(2006-2007): 17.4). Similar legislative provisions on carriers' liability for the validity of travel documents were introduced in a number of countries in the latter half of the 1980s (Feller 1989, 48). Travellers without a valid visa, or when the identity of the passenger is questioned, are not allowed to board the airplane or the ship bound for other countries. If the transporter has failed to identify falsified travel documents, the company will be financially punished by having to cover the costs of the return of the foreigners that are denied entry (UNHCR 2004, 257). The SAS airlines announced in the 1990s, that the cost of returning asylum seekers to their states of departure, easily amounted to as much as 13 000 Euro per person, if police escort was needed (Bø 2004, 146).

The Schengen Agreement, also imposes a fine ('carrier sanctions') for each passenger that has been transported to the country with invalid or insufficient travel documents. The fine the transporter must pay for each passenger without the proper documents, may amount to the equivalent of approximately 3000 Euro (ECRI 1991). Carrier sanctions are now prescribed in supranational law and are thereby binding rules for domestic legislation. The airlines or shipping companies are in other words sanctioned economically, if they fail to discover falsified passports or visa stamps, a task previously carried out by the immigration authorities upon arrival at the border.

A further extension of de-professionalized control of foreigners was announced in Norway in 2004: Customs officials are the new group that will, in all probability, receive police control tasks in the near future. In the draft to the new Norwegian immigration act, scheduled for Parliament in the late autumn of 2008, it is argued that customs officials must aid the police in carrying out immigration control at the border (NOU 2004, 20, pp. 291/292). This is also built into Article 21.2 of the draft law: 'The customs office must assist the police in controlling the entry and exit of foreigners in accordance with the provisions found in the Immigration Act. During the exercise of such control functions, customs officers will have the same rights and duties as police officers when they examine people, baggage and vehicles.'

Customs officials have traditionally only had responsibility for controlling the goods that are brought into the country. The new draft law suggests that customs officials shall also be given a legal right to control the identity of travellers and the validity of documents. People whom they suspect are engaged in illegal immigration may be taken into custody until police authorities arrive. The Police Directorate and the Customs Directorate both support these changes. The head of the Norwegian Customs Officials Union, Paul Gunnar Zindel has stated that 'Customs officials can make an important contribution in the struggles against illegal immigration, human trafficking and terror . . . Finally, we will be able to undertake controls to determine whether or not a traveller has the right to legally enter the state' (*Aftenposten*, morning edition, 10 June 2006). Customs director Marit Wiig, in a statement provided to the public hearings on the new draft law, supports the additional duties to be provided by customs officials. She also underlines the need to clarify the priority customs officials should give to these new duties and the range of force that can be used in undertaking these new controls (op.cit).

A similar development has taken place in the other EU/Schengen states. In Italy, for example, the navy has been given the legal power to board ships they believe are transporting illegal immigrants. These ships may be inspected and required to go to the nearest port for further investigations (Geddes 2003, 52). Formerly these kinds of tasks were defined as police work.

Why is De-professionalized Control Being Questioned?

Civil agents are not trained to respect rule of law principles. When police exercise their control functions, they must do so in accordance with a series of legal rules and principles which must be respected. The police are obliged to report all negative sanctions that are used in the course of their work. The police are further obliged to inform all who are denied entry or who receive negative sanctions, that they have the right to appeal the decision and to have the decision reviewed. Decisions by the police may in other words be reviewed by a higher authority and evaluated to see whether the decisions are in accordance with proper procedures and otherwise justified. A police officer ordinarily has a three year long college education that qualifies that person to engage in professional police work.

Civil agents are not competent to carry out immigration control functions. Persons working in a customs office or at check-in terminals in airports will normally not have the relevant education or competence to undertake entry controls of foreigners. These civil agents have not been educated in the legal rights of refugees and will normally not be acquainted with the Immigration Act. The Norwegian airlines protested when the legal duty of the transporter to perform immigration control tasks was originally introduced. Their protest was lodged during the public hearings held before the Immigration Act was enacted in 1988: 'One cannot expect the representatives of airlines employed at airports to have the necessary competence to be able to determine whether or not travel documents have been falsified. Furthermore, it is principally wrong to require private companies to execute control functions that formally are the responsibility of the Ministry of Justice' (Letter from the Office of Air Travel to the Ministry of Justice, dated 20 December 1989). Neither of these arguments influenced the decisions made by the Ministry of Justice. In the new draft law, the same arguments about transporter's lack of competence in the field of immigration law is discussed again and once more disregarded (Ot. prp. nr. 75 (2006–07)17.4.2.2).

When police control tasks are transferred to civilians, a weakening of legal safeguards easily follows. Civil agents, who carry out former police tasks, will normally not have the necessary knowledge to inform the 'clients' about their rights, nor the routines to handle complaints and give additional information. Organizations in civil society have other priorities beyond the execution of control. The added tasks of control can only result in less extensive reporting and reduced statistics concerning the amount and kinds of controls and sanctions that are performed, compared with controls procedures carried out by the police. De-professionalized control will therefore most likely lead to increased 'invisibility' of the control policies being practised.

The de-professionalization of immigration control leads to a blurring of the distinction between the state and civil society, the unclear lines of responsibility which follow weaken the legal safeguards for the individuals affected.

15.5 'CRIMINALIZATION' OF ASYLUM SEEKERS

Would-be refugees are prevented from gaining legal access to safe countries: this is done by introducing visa requirements followed by a strict rejection policy to all applicants who are assumed to be potential asylum seekers. Severe control procedures are established to prevent the arrival of foreigners who try to cross the border without the required visa stamps in their passports. To reach the asylum determination procedures, unauthorized entry is the only option. When asylum seekers are unable to obtain visas and cross the border in a legal manner, they have no choice but to use the services offered by smugglers, thereby 'confirming' the connection between asylum and criminality. Webber uses the term 'crimes of arrival' (Webber 1996) to describe the situation of the asylum seekers in Europe.

Media and politicians alike are focusing on 'illegal border crossing' and the 'exploitation and smuggling of human beings', in this way the image of the asylum seeker is repeatedly linked to criminality. The 'criminalization' of asylum seekers in the media and public debate functions to legitimize further restrictions and ever more severe control measures among the public and politicians alike, without highlighting the fact that the frequent introduction of new barriers increases the dependency on human smugglers and false documents to reach the asylum determination procedures. By introducing all these restrictive measures, the European governments have firstly created an international market for the smuggling and trafficking of asylum seekers, thereafter the same governments 'define "the refugee problem" as a fight against transnational organised crime' (Morrison 2001, cited in Weber 2002, 13), thereby creating ever greater barriers to the asylum determination procedures in their countries. The need to have legal avenues for individuals seeking protection from persecution, is long overdue, but has been given little attention by European governments (Selm 2005).[1]

Another symbol of criminalization is the detention of asylum seekers – increasing all over Europe, but under varying conditions and to a varying degree (UNHCR 2004, 275). Detention of asylum seekers is most frequently used in the following three kinds of situations: during the processing of asylum claims; before deportation is effectuated; and when the identity of the asylum seeker is questioned. Detention is used to prevent asylum seekers 'going underground' as a result of a negative decision and thereby evading a deportation order.

The power to detain is given to the immigration authorities under administrative law, and is normally not a decision by the police or judges after criminal proceedings (Weber 2002, 14). Detention of asylum seekers is therefore not regarded as punishment in judicial terms, but may nevertheless take place in ordinary prisons, while the tendency during the last years has been to build specialized detention centres or reception units, where the asylum seekers are locked up under prison like conditions.[2]

In the Norwegian Immigration Act it is stated that 'foreign nationals who must leave the country, after their applications for asylum or residence have been turned down, may be arrested and imprisoned to ensure implementation' (section 41.5). It is important to note that the individuals in these situations have not committed any crime or broken the law, detention is applied as a purely preventative matter. According to the Norwegian Immigration Act, it is not a requirement that the assumption that an asylum seeker is likely to evade the deportation order, is based on information about that particular person's previous behaviour. The immigration authorities may base the grounds for imprisonment on their 'general experience' with similar cases (Bø 2002b, 34). This implies group-based grounds for imprisonment; does not imprisonment on such grounds amount to discrimination according to human rights standards?

Norwegian immigration authorities may further imprison or detain asylum seekers as a preventative measure, before the final decision in the case in question has been made. According to the Norwegian Immigration Act, section 41.4, foreign citizens may be imprisoned before the final decision that they must leave the country has been made. As it says in the statute, detention may be used 'when any case which may lead to such a decision is being dealt with'. The statute demonstrates clearly the extent to which immigration control is given priority over generally accepted rule of law principles (NOU 2004, 26).

The European Committee for the Prevention of Torture wrote in 1994 in its report to the British government, that when immigrants and asylum seekers are placed in detention: 'many detained persons will find it hard to accept being in custody when they are not suspected of committing a criminal offence'. Weber writes that 'detainees consistently report being confused and ashamed at being treated like criminals' (Weber 2002, 9).

Are Such Grounds for Imprisonment Acceptable from a Human Rights Perspective?

In the European Convention on Human Rights, Article 5.1, the acceptable grounds for imprisonment are listed. Among those are 'the lawful arrest or detention of a person to prevent his effecting an unauthorized entry into the country or of a person against whom action is being taken to a view to deportation or extradition'(Article 5.1.f). Imprisonment of asylum seekers is, in other words, not unlawful as such, if there is reason to believe that the asylum seeker, if not arrested, will stay illegally in the country when his application for asylum is turned down. The question is whether asylum seekers may be placed in detention while their claim for protection is being examined or after a negative decision has been made, if no information indicates that the person in question will remain in the country in spite of an order to leave (Bø 2002b, 34).

UNHCR, non-governmental organizations (NGOs) and refugee advocates have expressed concern about the more frequent use of detention of asylum seekers during the processing of the asylum claims and when negative decisions have been taken and the asylum seekers must leave the country. UNHCR has particularly criticized detention of asylum seekers when this is done more or less as a routine matter, not limited to those cases where the immigration authorities have reason to believe that the asylum applicant will try to evade a deportation order. The Court in Strasbourg has stated as a general rule that detention may not be used as a preventative measure (*Guzzardi* v *Italy* and *Lawless* v *Ireland*), as this would be inconsistent with the rule of law (Harris *et al.* 1995, 117).

It is usual that a foreigner may be detained for the purpose of identification, in order to make repatriation possible. It is stated in section 37.1 of the Norwegian Immigration Act, that it is a legal duty for foreign nationals to cooperate to clarify their correct identity. It is further said that lack of such cooperation may lead to imprisonment (section 37.6). In Italy, the period of time during which a foreigner may be detained while the authorities try to clarify his identity, has been doubled from 30 to 60 days in the new Italian Immigration Act (Geddes 2003, 51). But is 'unknown identity' a legitimate ground for imprisonment?

Article 5(1)b of the European Convention on Human Rights permits the arrest or imprisonment of a person for 'non-compliance with the lawful order of a court or in order to secure the fulfilment of any obligation prescribed by law'. The issue at stake in the cases we deal with here is the correct identity of the asylum seeker. The legal obligation of the asylum seeker to 'cooperate' to 'clarify' his correct identity, is stated in section 37.1 of the Norwegian Immigration Act. The asylum seekers may, however, insist that they have informed the police about their correct identity, they may therefore claim that they have not 'failed to comply with a legal obligation'. The problem arises because the information given by the asylum seekers is not trusted by the police or the asylum seeker is not able to produce sufficient evidence to support the correctness of the given information. The question is whether this might rightly be defined as situations of 'non-compliance' and 'lack of cooperation' and thereby a legal basis for imprisonment (Bø 2002b)?

According to Harris, O'Boyle and Warbrick's commentary on the European Convention, to justify detention, 'the obligation in question must be a specific and concrete obligation which he has until then failed to satisfy' (1995, 112). The question is whether it might rightly be said, that the asylum seeker in these situations has failed to satisfy the obligation to inform the immigration authorities about his or her identity. It is doubtful whether one may say that it follows from the fact that the police question the veracity of the information given, that the asylum seeker has 'failed to satisfy a specific and concrete obligation'. If no such automatic conclusion might be drawn, imprisonment is not justified in these kinds of cases.

Asylum Seekers are Linked to Terrorism

The terrorist attacks on New York and Washington which took place on 11 September 2001 led to the introduction of a whole new series of security measures both in the USA and in Europe (Guild 2003, 1). In the fight against terrorism, the main concern of states seems to be 'the exclusion from their territory of feared terrorists, rather than their arrest and trial in the interests of international security and solidarity'. The UN's High Commissioner for Human Rights, Mary Robinson, very much regrets this development, and points to the fact that it is a greater danger if terrorists are removed to another country where they may resume terrorist activity, than if they are placed in custody (Guild 2003, 9). The interaction of security issues, terrorism and immigration control has weakened the legal status of immigrants and asylum seekers. New legal measures to fight terrorism, with profound effects on refugee policies, have been introduced all over Europe and the US (Brouwer *et al.* 2003).

Different European states have reacted in different ways: in England, the emphasis has been on expulsion of suspected terrorists. If expulsion is not possible, suspected terrorists may now, according to amended British legislation, be subject to indefinite detention. The British Anti-terrorism, Crime and Security Act of 2001, authorizes the use of detention against asylum seekers who are defined as 'suspected terrorists'. Imprisonment or detention without a fixed time limit, is definitely in conflict with rule of law principles. The new legislation in Great Britain has been highly criticized by UNHCR, NGOs and lawyers in the field of refugee law (Catz 2003, 85).

In Germany, new grounds were introduced for withdrawal of residence permits (Brouwer and Catz 2003, 169). In addition German authorities developed a computer system for identifying (computer profiling) 'suspect' foreigners in their search for 'possible fundamentalist Muslim terrorists' living in Germany (Brouwer 2003, 41). The target group was single Muslim men with a technical education who spoke different languages and frequently had applied for a visa. A German newspaper has reported that in Hamburg alone, this 'search' led to further control of information concerning as many as 30 000 male students, while 140 persons in Hamburg were contacted by the German police for 'security reasons' (Brouwer 2003, 41).

When the distinction between asylum seekers and terrorists has become blurred in the public debate, and the unauthorized entry of would-be refugees is looked upon as a security threat; it follows that stricter border control is regarded as a needed measure of security. That the same control measures block the access to safety for persons in need of protection from persecution, is not given much attention.

15.6 'REGIONALIZATION' OF REFUGEE PROTECTION

If asylum seekers manage to cross the European external borders, they are met with a new set of barriers: the EU/Schengen states have introduced geographical limitations to their general obligation to investigate asylum claims, and they frequently pass over the responsibility to examine claims for protection to other states. Both these measures raise serious problems (Zwaan 2005, 19). The admissibility to the determination procedures is blocked for asylum seekers from certain states and regions, and the legal obligation of states to investigate asylum claims is blurred when the responsibility is transferred to another state.

The term 'regionalization' is used to characterize this limitation of the scope of refugee protection which takes place today, sanctioned by newly adopted EU directives and the Dublin convention. Three examples of such 'regional' refugee policies which are in frequent use in Europe today, will be discussed briefly.

The 'safe third country' policy implies rejection of asylum claims on the grounds that the asylum seekers could have found protection elsewhere, in another 'safe' state. The destination states claim that the asylum seekers should have sought protection in the safe country they have transited through or stayed in on their way to the country where they apply for asylum. In practice, this policy implies that foreign nationals applying for asylum in Norway or any other EU/Schengen state, will not get their applications processed if it can be shown that they have travelled through or resided in a so-called 'secure country' before entering the country of destination. If this can be demonstrated, the applicant will be returned to the aforementioned country. Such a return will take place in cases where no guarantee is given that the authorities in the return country will process the application for asylum or provide the returnee with a residence permit.

As long as the country of return is considered 'safe', the claim for asylum will not be examined by the destination country (Verstad 2006, 177).

The High Commissioner for Refugees is critical of the way that the 'safe third country' policy is applied in Europe: 'Asylum should not be refused solely on the grounds that it could be sought from another State; nor is the mere fact of having resided in an intermediate country alone sufficient to justify refusal of substantive determination of refugee status' (UNHCR 2004, 267). UNHCR: 'The country to which an asylum application is submitted has the primary responsibility for considering it and, as such, remains ultimately responsible for any indirect or 'chain' refoulement. Accordingly, if that country wants to transfer its responsibility to some other country, it must be established that that other country is 'safe' with respect to the refugee claimant in question' (UNHCR in de Sousa *et al.* 2004, 268).

The term 'safe country of origin' addresses situations where asylum seekers are from states that the immigration authorities consider 'safe', and for that reason they will not examine their asylum applications. The 'safe country of origin' policy implies that the nationality of the asylum seekers is the admissibility criteria to the asylum determination procedures. Asylum claims from such 'safe countries' are not given an individual examination, but dismissed on grounds of the nationality of the applicant.

All EU nationals, including citizens of the newly accepted member states from eastern Europe, are considered to come from 'safe' countries, and for that reason excluded from getting their claims for protection considered by other EU states. Article 2(c) of the EU Qualification Directive makes this clear by defining a 'refugee' as 'a third country national', thereby disqualifying EU citizens as eligible for protection.

The Qualification Directive undoubtly limits the scope of refugee protection by restricting the right to asylum to third country nationals. It looks like a case of discrimination if the nationality of the asylum seeker decides whether or not the claim for asylum will be treated or dismissed. Article 14 of the European Convention on Human Rights (ECHR) prohibits measures based on ethnic origin or Article 3 of the Geneva Convention not to discriminate on the grounds of nationality. UNHCR stated that 'protection under the Geneva Convention should be granted to all applicants who fulfil the Convention's refugee definition' (cited from Gil-Bazo 2006, 10).

In recent years, European governments have refused to grant asylum or residency to asylum seekers if 'safe' regions in 'unsafe' countries can be located and the asylum seeker has some connection or previous experience to any such 'safe' regions. The tendency to limit and 'regionalize' the scope of refugee protection is formalized in the newly adopted EU Qualification Directive. In Article 8 of the Directive, the regionalization policy is expressed clearly: 'Refugee status may not arise when an internal flight alternative exists.' This policy implies that asylum seekers are returned by force, not to war zones, but to countries in war, where fighting and persecution takes place in some of its regions, while other districts are considered reasonably 'safe'. The EU/Schengen states do not have a uniform return policy; the immigration authorities rely on information about the 'safety' in the countries in question from their local consulates. UNHCR and the non-governmental organizations draw different conclusions on this issue.

This return policy is highly controversial.[3] Many individuals and humanitarian organizations, well informed about the conditions in, for instance, Afghanistan and Somalia, have challenged the 'safety' judgement of the immigration authorities. There has, for instance, been disagreement about the safety conditions for returned asylum seekers in specific areas like Kabul. There is also disagreement concerning the safety for asylum seekers who are returned to areas where they do not have immediate family who will offer them protection, shelter and food. UNHCR has warned against the forced return of asylum seekers to regions where they are not protected by their families.

15.7 THE EUROPEANIZATION OF ASYLUM POLICIES: STRENGTHENING OR WEAKENING OF REFUGEE PROTECTION?

Since the early 1980s, widespread cooperation has developed between the states of western Europe in their policies and practices concerning entry and border control. By the Treaty of Amsterdam in 1999, the European Community was given the full responsibility for immigration and asylum issues, including visa policy, control of external borders and asylum policies (Zwaan 2005, 3; Verstad 2006, 64). It is now EU laws, and not domestic legislation, which decide which states, shall be met with visa requirements and sanctions towards transporters bringing in insufficiently documented passengers. A 'Europeanization' has in other words taken place implying that these policy areas are moved from the nation-state level to a regional EU-level. This 'Europeanization' has resulted in a series of treaties and directives, legally binding for all the EU/Schengen member states.

The EU Qualification Directive

The EU Qualification Directive (Directive 2004/83 on minimum standards for the qualification and status of third country nationals or stateless persons as refugees or as persons who otherwise need international protection), which was adopted by EU in April 2004, aims to harmonize EU asylum law by defining who qualifies for international protection either as a refugee or a beneficiary of subsidiary protection. This is the first legally binding supranational instrument in Europe that states the qualifications needed to be recognized as a refugee or a person otherwise entitled to international protection by the EU member states. It is most important that the Qualification Directive, Article 13, explicitly recognizes the legal right for refugees to be granted asylum. The Directive further lists the rights refugees, and the reduced rights of those who are granted subsidiary protection, are entitled to in the member states. The fact that the Qualification Directive establishes legal rights for the beneficiaries of international protection implies a strengthening of the refugee regime.

Article 6 of the Directive further clarifies that persecution by non-state agents does not exclude asylum seekers from being recognized as conventional refugees, contrary to the practice by many European governments (including France and Germany). In addition, persecution specific to gender and children are recognized as giving rise to protection.

Other articles in the same directive limit the scope of refugee protection compared with the rights granted by the UN 1951 Refugee Convention (McAdam 2007). The exclusion clauses in the Qualification Directive for persons with subsidiary protection are for instance broader than those contained in the Refugee Convention (cf. McAdam 2007). In Article 14.3 (b) of the Qualification Directive it is stated that 'member states shall evoke, end or refuse to renew, the refugee status of a third country national or a stateless person, if, after he or she has been granted refugee status, it is established by the member state concerned that his or her misrepresentation or omission of facts, including the use of false documents, were decisive for the granting of refugee status.'

As long as asylum seekers are denied legal access to the member states by visa rejections to any would-be refugee, they have no choice but to use false documents to reach the refugee determination procedures in Europe. If the use of false documents is sufficient to refuse to grant protection, the whole refugee protection regime in the member states may easily be undermined. UNHCR is critical of this exclusion clause of the Qualification Directive and has said that 'the mere use of false documents should not render an asylum claim fraudulent'. UNHCR further says that only if the asylum seeker has intentionally misled the immigration authorities by giving false information about his need of protection, would such an exclusion clause be acceptable (McAdam 2007, 14).

According to article 14.4 (a) in the Qualification Directive, a person is excluded from protection 'if there are reasonable grounds for regarding him or her as a danger to the security of the member state, in which she or he is present'. Such grounds for exclusion (national security grounds) were considered in connection with the Refugee Convention as well, but it was concluded that this was inconsistent because it would undermine the non-refoulement principle of the refugee Convention. There is no definition of 'danger' in the Directive. It is up to the discretion of each member state to decide how this term shall be interpreted. There is no discussion in the EU document of the risk of refoulement in this connection. Security concerns as a ground for exclusion was opposed by Belgium, the Netherlands, Finland and Sweden, which regarded them as being contrary to the Geneva Convention (Gil-Bazo 2006, 16)

According to Article 14.4.(b) of the Qualification Directive, member states may revoke, end or refuse to renew the refugee status to a third country national if he or she has been 'convicted by a final judgement of a particularly serious crime', and as such may represent a danger in the member state. For asylum seekers who are granted subsidiary protection, the exclusion clauses are broader than for refugees: Article 17 (3) of the Qualification Directive allows states to exclude third country nationals from subsidiary protection if a person 'prior to arrival, has committed a crime which would be punishable by imprisonment in the member state, and if he or she had left the country of origin to avoid being punished for the crime'. There is no definition of 'crime' in the Directive, nor a discussion of the risk that political opposition and criticism of the government in the home country by a refugee may be considered a 'crime' in the country of origin.

The prohibition against refoulement or forced return of asylum seekers to countries where they risk torture or other inhuman treatment is the key-stone in international protection of refugees. In the first paragraph of Article 21 of the Qualification Directive this principle is respected: 'member states shall respect the principle of non-refoulement in accordance with their international obligations' (Article 21.1). But the prohibition against refoulement may easily be undermined by the next paragraph of the Directive: 'member states may refoule a refugee, whether formally recognized or not [when] there are reasonable grounds for considering him or her as a danger to the security of the member state in which he or she is present' (Article 21.2(a)). What kind of acts constitutes a danger to member states is not defined in the Directive.

The Swedish government was criticized by UNHCR, Amnesty International and by CERD (the Committee on the Elimination of Racial Discrimination) for acting against its international obligations when it expelled two Egyptians suspected of terrorism in Egypt, before the concerned individuals had been given an opportunity to appeal the deportation order. The CERD committee held that the guarantees given by the Egyptian government that the individuals in question would not be tortured or subject to the death penalty, was not sufficient to satisfy its obligations under international human rights law (Løøf and Gorlick 2004, 5). Persons who initiate, plan or finance terrorist acts are excluded from protection by the non-refoulement principle. UNHCR has expressed its concern about the 'insufficiently precise way offenses are qualified as 'terrorist acts' in the Qualification Directive (Brouwer and Catz 2003, 134). Gil-Bazo writes that 'The Directive contains provisions on exclusion, revocation and non-refoulement that arguably fall short of existing and evolving international law and standards [and goes] beyond what is permissible by the Geneva Convention' (Gil-Bazo 2006, 15). As international law stands today, Article 21(2) of the Directive in its current wording allows member states to remove individuals in breach of international law' (Gil-Bazo 2006, 23).

15.8   CONCLUSION

In the Treaty of Europe it is stated that 'the Council shall adopt measures on asylum in accordance with the Geneva Convention' (Article 63(1) of TEC). Gil-Bazo writes that the European Treaty therefore 'establishes an obligation for EC secondary legislation on asylum to comply with the Geneva Convention and its Protocol' (Gil-Bazo 2006, 4). Based on the broader cessation clauses and lack of definitions of key terms demonstrated above, it is reasonable to ask whether the Qualification Directive does comply with the Refugee Convention. Compliance with international human rights obligations has been questioned by UNHCR, human rights and refugee lawyers alike. By not defining either 'terrorism' or 'crime', it is left to the discretion of each member state to interpret these key concepts. Such definitions will reduce the group of persons who are recognized as falling under the protection regime. The Qualification Directive seems to be a document motivated by the EU member states' wish to reduce its legal obligations to refugees by narrowing the scope of protection compared to that of the Geneva Convention.

The new EU asylum documents reflect a compromising of refugee rights – which is an unacceptable development. The main concern of the EU states seems to be to keep 'would-be refugees' away from their borders, while the member states pay lip service to the Refugee Convention. What one can witness today, appears like a 'shrinking process' of refugee rights. It is a matter of serious concern if the legal protection of refugees has materially worsened by the drafting of these EU harmonized asylum documents.

NOTES

1. The general public is not aware of the fact that Article 31 in the Refugee Convention explicitly states that unauthorized border crossing is acceptable as long as the purpose it to seek protection against persecution; asylum seekers shall not be punished for such illegal entries.
2. It is important to note that the European Convention of Human Rights does not distinguish between imprisonment and detention when both include forced isolation and locked doors. Weber writes that the legal distinction between criminal and administrative immigration enforcement practices 'seems inconsequential in Britain' (Weber 2002, 9).
3. Asylum seekers are at present returned by force to regions in Somalia and Afghanistan characterized as 'safe' by the Norwegian immigration authorities. In Somalia, asylum seekers have been returned to the Mogadishu area if the asylum seeker has any network or family connections in that region of the country. A similar return of asylum seekers from Afghanistan to the Kabul area is at present taking place.

REFERENCES

Aftenposten (2006), morning edition, 6 June.

Aftenposten (2006), morning edition, 10 June.

Baumann, Z. (2005), 'Between assimilation and exclusion: refugees in a double bind', lecture at Nottingham Forum, UK, 21 June.

Brouwer, E. and P. Catz (2003), 'The European Union: terrorism and the struggle for competence in community law', in E. Brouwer, P. Catz and E. Guild, *Immigration, Asylum and Terrorism: A Changing Dynamic in European Law*, Nijmegen, the Netherlands: Instituut voor Rechtssociologie, Centrum voor Migratierecht.

Brouwer, E., P. Catz and E. Guild (2003), *Immigration, Asylum and Terrorism – A Changing Dynamic in European Law*, Nijmegen, the Netherlands: Instituut voor Rechtssociologie, Centrum voor Migratierecht.

Brouwer, E. (2003), 'Germany: controlling data', in E. Brouwer, P. Catz and E. Guild, *Immigration, Asylum and Terrorism: A Changing Dynamic in European Law*, Nijmegen, the Netherlands: Instituut voor Rechtssociologie, Centrum voor Migratierecht

Bø, Bente Puntervold (2002a), *Immigration Control, Law and Morality: Visa Policies Towards Visitors and Asylum Seekers: An Evaluation of the Norwegain Visa Policies within a Legal and Moral Frame of Reference*, Oslo: UniPub, Oslo University Press.

Bø, Bente Puntervold (2002b), 'Imprisonment of non-nationals: do recent amendments to the Norwegian Immigration Act comply with human rights and moral standards?', *Current Issues in Criminal Justice*, 14, 16–37.

Bø, Bente Puntervold (2004), *Søkelys på den norske innvandringspolitikken*, Kristiansand, Norway: Fagbokforlaget øgskolen.

Catz, P. (2003), 'United Kingdom: withdrawing from international human rights standards', in E. Brouwer, P. Catz and E. Guild, *Immigration, Asylum and Terrorism: A Changing Dynamic in European Law*, Nijmegen, the Netherlands: Instituut voor Rechtssociologie, Centrum voor Migratierecht.

Crisp, Jeff (2003), 'A new asylum paradigm? Globalization, migration and the uncertain future of the international refugee regime', New Issues in Refugee Research working paper 100, Geneva: UNHCR.

ECRE (1991), *The Effects of Carrier Sanctions on the Asylum System*, Copenhagen: The Danish Refugee Council, The Danish Center of Human Rights.

Falch, Sturla and Thomas Mathiesen (1981), *Vekterstaten*, Oslo: Pax.

Feller, Erica (1989), 'Carrier Sanctions and international law', *International Journal of Refugee Law*, 1 (1) pp. 48–66.

Fernhout, R. (2006), unpublished notes to the author on states' extraterritorial responsibilities.

Fisknes, Eli (1994), *Utlendingsloven med kommentarer*, Oslo: Universitetsforlaget.

Geddes, Andrew (2003), 'Italy: emphasizing exclusion' in E. Brouwer, P. Catz and E. Guild, *Immigration, Asylum and Terrorism – A Changing Dynamic in European Law*, Nijmegen, the Netherlands: Instituut voor Rechtssociologie, Centrum voor Migratierecht.

Gil–Bazo, M.T. (2006), 'Refugee status, subsidiary protection, and the right to be granted asylum under EC law', New Issues in Refugee Research research paper 136, Geneva:UNHCR.

Gorlick, B. and R. Løøf (2004), 'Implementing international human rights law on behalf of asylum seekers and refugees: the record of the Nordic countries, New Issues in Refugee Research working paper 110, Geneva: UNHCR.

Guild, E. (2003), 'Introduction', in E. Brouwer, P. Catz, E. Guild (eds), *Immigration Asylum and Terrorism – A Changing Dynamic in European Law*, Nijmegen, the Netherlands: Instituut voor Rechtssociologie, Centrum voor Migratierecht.

Guild, E. (2007), *Security and European Human Rights: Protecting Individual Rights in Times of Exception and Military Action*, Nijmegen, the Netherlands: Wolf Legal Publishers.

Harris, D., M. O'Boyle and C. Warbrick (1995), *The Law of the European Convention on Human Rights*, London: Butterworths.

Landgren, Karin (1999), 'Deflecting international protection by treaty: bilateral and multilateral accords on extradition, readmission and the inadmissibility of asylum requests', New Issues in Refuge Research working paper 10, Geneva: UNHCR.

Løøf, R. and B. Gorlick (2004), 'Implementing international human rights law on behalf of asylum seekers and refugees: the record of the Nordic countries', New Issues in Refugee Research working paper 110, Geneva: UNHCR.

McAdam, J. (2005), 'Complementary protection and beyound: how states deal with human rights protection, UNHCR: New Issues in Refugee Research working paper 118, Geneva: UNHCR.

McAdam, J. (2007), 'The qualification directive: an overview', in K. Zwaan (eds), *The Qualification Directive: Central Themes, Problem Issues, and Implementation in Selected Member States*, Nijmegen, the Netherlands: Wolf Legal Publishers.

Noll, G. (2003), 'From protected passports to protected entry procedures? The legacy of Raoul Wallenberg in the contemporary asylum debate', New Issues in Refugee Research working paper 99, Geneva: UNHCR.

Richmond, A. (1997), *Global Apartheid: Refugees, Racism and the New World Order*, Toronto, New York and Oxford: Oxford University Press.

Selm, J. van (2005), 'European refugee policy: is there such a thing?' New Issues in Refugee Research working paper 115, Geneva: UNHCR.

de Sousa, C.D.U., P. Bruycker and U. Brandl (2004), *The Emergence of a European Asylum Policy*, Brussels: Bruylant.

UNHCR (2001), *Towards a Common Asylum Procedure*, Geneva: UNHCR.

UNHCR (2004), 'Towards a Common European asylum system', in C.D.U. de Sousa and P. de Bruycker, *The Emergence of a European Asylum Policy*, Brussels: Bruylant.

UNHCR (various years), *European Asylum Law*, Nijmegen, the Netherlands: Wolf Legal Publishers.

Vevstad, V. (2006), *Utviklingen av et felles europeisk asylsystem – jus og politick*, Oslo: Universitetsforlaget.

Webber, L. (1996), 'Crimes of arrival', in K. Zwaan (ed.), *The Qualification Directive: Central Themes, Problem Issues, and Implementation in Selected Member States*, Nijmegen, the Netherlands: Wolf Legal Publishers.

Weber, L. (2002), 'The detention of asylum seekers: 20 reasons why criminologists should care', *Current Issues in Criminal Justice*, **14** (1), 4–25.

Zwaan, Karin (2005), *UNHCR and the European Asylum Law*, Nijmegen, the Netherlands: Center for Migration and Law, Rad bound University.

Laws and Human Rights Conventions:

European Court of Human Rights, ECtHR 16 November 2004, Case 31821/96: *Issa and Others* v *Turkey*.

European Court of Human Rights, HCt HR *Guzzardi* v *Italy* and *Lawless* v *Ireland*.

The European Committee for the Prevention of Torture 1994

The EU Qualification Directive: Council Directive 2004/83 EC on minimum standards for the qualification and status of third country nationals or stateless persons as refugees or as persons who otherwise need international protection.

The Convention against Torture and other Cruel, Inhuman or Degrading Treatment or Punishment (CAT).

The 1950 European Convention of Human Rights (ECHR).

The International Covenant on Civil and Political Rights.

NOU (2004) 20 Ny utlendingslov.

The Norwegian Ministry of Justice, Ot.prp. 46 (1986–87), Om lov om utlendingers adgang til riket og deres opphold her, Utlendingsloven.

The Norwegian Ministry of Justice, Ot.prp. 75 (2006–2007), Om lov om utlendingers adgang til riket og deres opphold her, Utlendingsloven.

The Universal Declaration of Human Rights of 1948.

The 1951 UN Refugee Convention.

The 1969 Vienna Convention on the Law of Treaties.

The Schengen Agreement of 1985.

The Dublin Convention of 1992.

Index

'Administration, Business and
    Management'
    percentage of migrant workers in
        109
admission to EU, conditions
    level of development of country 28
advanced passenger information (API)
    237
Afghanistan, safety problems 289
ageing and dependency 19–22
ageing of demographic structure 140
ageing population increase in Spain
    drop in fertility 162–3, 165
agencies for immigration 158
agency workers, underpaid 109
agricultural employment collapse 22
agricultural work in Poland, fruit
        picking 154
agriculture,
    demand for cheap labour 2
    need for service workers 145
aircraft personnel acting under
        Norwegian law
    extraterritorial responsibility 279
Airline Liaison Officers (ALOs) 239
    pre-screening passengers 237
Algarve, retired migration 124
Antalya, Turkey 125–41
anti-communism
    Polish older generation 113
Armenia, Ngorno-Karabakh 146
Armenian preferred destinations for
        migrants
    Russia, Turkey and Great Britain
        152
assimilation
    of ethnic groups 204–5
    of minorities 196
asylum claims, multiple filed by one
        individual 262
asylum seekers 10

control of documents in country of
        departure 273
    and irregular migrants 260
    link to terrorism 286–7
'asylum shopping', in more than one
        country 260
Austria
    employed foreigners in 1995 to 2006
        43
    employment developments in 1990s
        38
    immigration from Germany 43
    labour migration to 32–40
    low intentions to move 59
Austrian Federal Economic Chamber
    adoption of four freedoms 42
    smaller businesses 41
    worker shortage projections 47
Austrian Institute for Economic
        Research
    worker shortage projections 47
Austrian labour market
    developments 1985–2006 33–6
    effect of eastern enlargement of EU
        40–48
Authorised Economic Operator (AEC)
        process
    simplified customs controls 238

balance of power in employment
        relations
    home countries 111
'Balkanization' of labour market in
        UK
    separation of indigenous and
        migrants 116
Baltic States, high intentions to move
        66
    Lithuania, Latvia, Estonia 59
basic education, return migrants 220
Belarus, male preference for Russia 152